MY STOLEN SON

MY STOLEN SON

THE NICK MARKOWITZ STORY

SUSAN MARKOWITZ

WITH

JENNA GLATZER

BERKLEY BOOKS, NEW YORK

THE BERKLEY PUBLISHING GROUP
Published by the Penguin Group
Penguin Group (USA) Inc.
375 Hudson Street, New York, New York 10014, USA
Penguin Group (Canada), 90 Eglinton Avenue East, Suite 700, Toronto, Ontario M4P 2Y3, Canada
(a division of Pearson Penguin Canada Inc.)
Penguin Books Ltd., 80 Strand, London WC2R 0RL, England
Penguin Group Ireland, 25 St. Stephen's Green, Dublin 2, Ireland (a division of Penguin Books Ltd.)
Penguin Group (Australia), 250 Camberwell Road, Camberwell, Victoria 3124, Australia
(a division of Pearson Australia Group Pty. Ltd.)
Penguin Books India Pvt. Ltd., 11 Community Centre, Panchsheel Park, New Delhi—110 017, India
Penguin Group (NZ), 67 Apollo Drive, Rosedale, North Shore 0632, New Zealand
(a division of Pearson New Zealand Ltd.)
Penguin Books (South Africa) (Pty.) Ltd., 24 Sturdee Avenue, Rosebank, Johannesburg 2196,
South Africa

Penguin Books Ltd., Registered Offices: 80 Strand, London WC2R 0RL, England

The publisher does not have any control over and does not assume any responsibility for authors or
third-party websites or their content.

MY STOLEN SON

A Berkley Book / published by arrangement with the authors

PRINTING HISTORY
Berkley mass-market edition / September 2010

Copyright © 2010 by Susan Markowitz and Jenna Glatzer.
Cover photograph by Wachsman Staley Photography.
Interior text design by Laura K. Corless.

ISBN: 978-0-425-23634-5

BERKLEY®
Berkley Books are published by The Berkley Publishing Group,
a division of Penguin Group (USA) Inc.,
375 Hudson Street, New York, New York 10014.
BERKLEY® is a registered trademark of Penguin Group (USA) Inc.
The "B" design is a trademark of Penguin Group (USA) Inc.

PRINTED IN THE UNITED STATES OF AMERICA

10 9 8 7 6 5 4 3 2 1

Most Berkley Books are available at special quantity discounts for bulk purchases for sales, promotions,
premiums, fund-raising, or educational use. Special books, or book excerpts, can also be created to fit
specific needs.

For details, write: Special Markets, The Berkley Publishing Group, 375 Hudson Street, New York,
New York 10014.

To my son,
I am so sorry.
—Mom

CHAPTER 1

CAUGHT

Well, it wasn't a Mercedes, but it would have to do. He was driving a 1976 Volkswagen Beetle and moving from apartment to apartment near Rio de Janeiro. Gone were the days at the Bellagio in Las Vegas and the model girlfriend who'd tattooed his name on her lower back. He'd met an older woman named Marcia Reis and latched onto her because he saw her as his ticket to freedom.

He'd told Marcia that he was in some kind of trouble in the United States and that's why he had moved to Brazil, but he probably hadn't mentioned that the trouble was that he orchestrated the execution of an innocent fifteen-year-old boy. His documentation said his name was Michael Costa Giroux, and he claimed to have been born in Rio de Janeiro, to Canadian and Brazilian parents. People around him thought that seemed a bit odd, because Giroux certainly didn't look like a native, and his Portuguese was barely passable.

The truth was that Giroux was an American who had been on the run since August of 2000, when he was twenty years old. After a stint in Canada, where he decided it was just too cold, he chose Brazil because he liked the movie *Blame It on Rio.* By now, in 2005, he was living with Marcia in a modest apartment in Saquarema, a little fishing village known for attracting surfers.

Neighbors there didn't like him much. He drank a lot, and when he drank, he picked fights. Aside from that, Giroux didn't speak much to anyone—a quick "Good day" at the bar, maybe. The neighbors did notice that the couple would sometimes host barbeques with out-of-town guests, and that Giroux would often jog along the beach with his two pit bulls. He sometimes taught private English classes or picked up side money as a dog walker, and he worked out with weights that he kept on the front patio.

His domestic squabbles with Marcia were loud enough for people to hear, too. But Giroux wasn't in this for love. He had hooked up with the thirty-five-year-old woman because he had heard about the tale of Ronnie Biggs, a British man who participated in the Great Train Robbery of 1963. After he was convicted, Biggs broke out of prison and hid out in Brazil, where he was able to avoid being extradited back to his country because he fathered a Brazilian child with his girlfriend. Brazil does not extradite criminals who have Brazilian children.

Giroux thought this was the perfect plan, so he set out to find a woman who'd carry his child—and thus, his insurance policy that would keep him from serving any jail time if he were ever found. The child would help him get away with murder.

He found what he wanted at a singles bar.

"He said he was studying; he had come to Brazil to study," Marcia Reis would later say. "When I met him, I thought he was very young. I thought he was a little lost. He had had a lot to drink."

But, she says, he was good to her—kissing her hands and feet, getting her everything she wanted—and that was enough to make her overlook whatever "dark secret" he had.

Meanwhile, Giroux's father stayed back in California,

helping to keep detectives off his son's trail. Having money helped, and his father had plenty of it, thanks to a flourishing drug-dealing business. He was a major marijuana supplier, and possibly dealt in other illegal substances as well. Through the years, he had gained many friends willing to do just about anything for him and his family—and in places where he didn't already have friends, he could always buy some.

It had been a long time since father and son had seen each other, but Giroux's father still helped to take care of him, reportedly managing to get him twelve hundred dollars each month for living expenses even though the boy was on the FBI's "Most Wanted" list and surely they both knew that the family was being closely watched.

Maybe they had just let their guard down a little after almost five years. A long-lost American cousin was flying to Brazil and was going to meet Giroux and his girlfriend at an outdoor mall. Marcia was pregnant now and happily showing off her belly. The two of them had just taken seats at a table on the beach, waiting for their guest to arrive.

As his cousin approached, Giroux walked over to her with his arms outstretched to give her a hug . . . and instead, he found himself fitted with handcuffs.

It wasn't his cousin. Apparently he didn't know her well enough to recognize her, and he simply assumed that the woman walking toward him must be his cousin. Instead, it was plainclothes federal police agent Kelly Bernardo, who had just been given the signal to move in.

Bernardo's team was close behind her. It looked like Giroux might have tried to run, except that he was in flip-flops and was clearly outnumbered. As the agents grabbed him and led him away toward their waiting car, Giroux's girlfriend screamed out, "Kidnapping! Kidnapping!"

Her screams summoned the military police from their kiosk across the street, and they drew their guns at the Interpol agents. The screaming and the violent standoff was enough to send people running, but the Interpol agents managed to stuff Giroux into their car and drive away.

Minutes later, his girlfriend calmly walked down the strip and bought herself a cookie and a soda. She didn't seem concerned; she had almost certainly already been briefed by her boyfriend on what to do when he got caught. A few phone calls and this problem would all go away.

At the police station, it was soon confirmed that Giroux's real name was *not* Michael Costa Giroux. His documentation was fake, though he spent two hours sticking to his story and insisting loudly that there must've been some kind of mistake.

But it was no mistake. Fingerprints confirmed that "Michael Costa Giroux" was actually Jesse James Hollywood, the youngest person ever on the FBI's "Ten Most Wanted Fugitives" list. And yes, "Jesse James Hollywood" was really the name his parents gave him, named after an uncle but with a sense of homage to the outlaw. While he'd been on the run, he'd occasionally also used the pseudonym Sean Michaels, a black porn star of more than six hundred movies who sells "male performance enhancers," creams, sex tips, and a replica of his own genitals online. He was not going to get away with any other false identities here, though. Hollywood was unquestionably caught, putting an end to the five-year international manhunt.

In the Brazilian police precinct, he screamed in Portuguese at the officers about how they were violating his rights and how angry his father would be. Then he demanded a drink of water. They threw it at him, soaking his shirt and hitting him in the nose. No one was amused by this mini-thug's arrogance.

Back in the United States, on the same day of Hollywood's arrest, his fifty-year-old father, Jack Hollywood, was also being arrested, on charges of manufacturing the date-rape drug GHB. It was no random coincidence that the two were arrested on the same day; detectives had carefully timed it to ensure that Jack Hollywood would be unavailable to bribe anyone when he found out his son was arrested in Brazil.

Despite Marcia Reis calling out, "No! This can't be! I

have a son with him!" as agents drove Hollywood away from the outdoor mall, the tactic didn't work in his favor the way it had for the train robber, for one simple reason: the train robber had had a valid passport, while Jesse James Hollywood was in the country illegally. Brazilian authorities didn't worry about whether or not to extradite him; all they had to do was deport him as an illegal immigrant. He had no right to be in the country in the first place.

So Brazilian officials turned the fugitive over to the U.S. FBI, and on March 8, 2005, Hollywood was on an airplane headed to Los Angeles International Airport. Because it was a deportation case instead of an extradition, officers were not allowed to be armed, nor to handcuff him—so they improvised, tying his arms behind his back with rope and covering it with a sweatshirt so as not to scare the other passengers. When he needed to use the bathroom, the officers had to cut the rope off him with nail clippers.

The plane stopped on the tarmac so the officers could stuff Hollywood into the elevator meant for the food cart. Agents were waiting to catch him and arrest him at the bottom of the elevator, and the media—who had been alerted that he was going to be on this flight—was confused when he never stepped off the plane.

In transit to the jail, Hollywood said nothing except, "My dad is going to be mad you guys got me like this."

Because he had not yet been read his rights, detectives couldn't question him—but they could hope for him to talk on his own, so they talked to each other about things they thought might rile him.

The Michael Jackson molestation trial had just begun, and one detective turned to another and said, "Isn't it amazing that Michael Jackson took top newspaper headline over Jesse James?"

That was all it took to get him agitated. For the rest of the ride, Hollywood talked, mostly bragging about how he evaded capture for so long. At no point did he take any responsibility for what he'd done or show any remorse. Instead, he said things like, "This is bullshit. I wouldn't

even be here if my name weren't Jesse James Hollywood."
Then he went on and on about all the ways he had been
wronged in life.

At the Santa Barbara County Jail, Hollywood was
booked and kept in solitary confinement.

———————

I fell to my knees when I heard the news. It had been so
long since I had cried, really cried. It had been a long time
since I had allowed myself to feel much of anything. But
now I cried at the senselessness of it all, at the finality, at the
selfishness and stupidity that had torn apart my family.

Jesse James Hollywood killed my only child.

CHAPTER 2

A DREAM IS BORN

It seemed like I had spent many years searching for a child to call my own. I was twenty-five when I had him—no old spinster, sure, but it had seemed like an unbearable wait to finally find the right man and the right time.

When I did find the right guy, well, it wasn't quite the typical love story. Not only did I meet the man of my dreams in a bar, but we met on Screw Night.

One fine weekend in 1982, a staff member at a local San Fernando Valley bar handed each woman a plastic nut and each man a plastic screw as they walked through the door. The objective was to walk around trying to find your match. As if the excuse to walk around making innuendos toward the opposite sex wasn't enough reward, you could also win a cash prize if you found the first winning match.

"Would you like to see if we match?" I asked one man, walking over to his bar stool. I'd like to tell you we were the perfect fit, but we weren't. "Too tight," I said, and was about to walk away when he asked my name.

"Susan," I told him.

He reached out and shook my hand and told me his

name was Jeff. Little shock waves ran through our hands. His eyes were so gentle.

"May I have your phone number, Susan?" he asked. "I'm good with numbers. If you tell it to me, I won't forget it."

I already had two failed marriages under my belt. The first was a drummer who wanted to live off the land. I married him when I was seventeen, and we were divorced in nine months. Then, when I was nineteen, I fell in love with a much older man who had full custody of his three children. Their ages ran close to my own, but they didn't hold that against me. They were great kids, and he was a great father and husband. There was just one problem: I longed for a baby of my own so much it ached. When we first got together, that's what he said he wanted, too, but when it came down to it, he changed his mind. He was through having kids, he decided.

But I wasn't. All I really wanted in life was to be somebody's mom. The need for a baby of my own was so strong that there was nothing I could do to convince myself otherwise. In four hours, I packed up four years' worth of life and memories and took off—a decision that still leaves me with a lot of guilt. Those kids didn't deserve to have another woman walk out on them. But I just hadn't known what else to do.

And now, as I stood before this man in this bar, something told me that maybe the third time would be the charm, after all.

I gave him my number and went on my way. A few hours later, I was startled awake by the phone. It was 3 a.m. And it was Jeff.

"Jeff? It's late," I said. "Call me another time."

I went back to sleep with a grin. He had felt it, too.

Like me, Jeff was recently separated. He had two children from his first marriage: Leah and Ben. Leah was six and Ben was four at the time of their split, and they were adorable. Unlike my ex, however, Jeff didn't have custody: he saw the kids every other weekend. In between, we shopped for Jeff's new bachelor pad and cruised on the high seas in his thirty-six-foot sailboat at Marina del Rey. He was my knight in a shining red Audi. Courting was wonderful, and time disappeared like cotton candy in my mouth.

Jeff worked in his family's business, an aerospace machine shop. He was a hard worker and usually worked late hours. I admired his work ethic and loved the way he treated me with kindness and affection.

A little more than a year after our first date, my dream came true: we found out I was pregnant. It was unplanned but unconditionally wanted by both of us. Sure, it was a little out of order, but we had both been disillusioned about marriage—the idea of a wedding wasn't high on our priority lists. The idea of a baby, though? Nothing else mattered. I felt like my life, my real life, had just begun.

I ran over to my sister's house to share the news. She already had two children, and both times she gave birth, it filled me with such a sense of longing. Of course I was happy for her, but I was also impatiently waiting for my own happy news. And now it was here. As she opened her door, I exclaimed, "I am pregnant!" We hugged, she and I, with baby in the middle. It was finally my turn.

Jeff and I moved into an apartment together during my pregnancy. I kept a journal with details about every little movement I felt. He had hiccups for the first time on June 21; he kicked me in the ribs for the first time on June 25 . . .

I wrote little love notes to my baby, telling him how I couldn't wait to meet him. Jeff got in on the action, too:

I just got home from the gym. Your mom is writing thank you notes for your baby shower.

First, I just want you to know what a wonderful mommy you are going to have. She is very pretty, warm and thoughtful. The two of you growing together for nine months has made her the happiest woman in

*the world. Your mom and I love each other very much
and when you finally get here, I think we will even be
closer.*

*I will love you,
And care for you,
Forever,
Daddy*

As his due date came near, we waited for the baby to
make his big entrance into the world. And waited. And
waited. He was supposed to show up around August 27,
but on September 18, he was still having a cozy womb rest.
That was the doctor's official deadline—he had told me
that if the baby hadn't arrived naturally by the eighteenth,
we were going in after him.

Labor was induced, and after nineteen and a half hours
of back labor (yes, I would do it again), Nicholas Samuel
Markowitz was born, just an ounce shy of nine pounds, on
September 19, 1984. I wrote to him in his baby book:

*Our world is blessed and honored upon your arrival. We
have waited for such a long time to see your beautiful
face. You have fulfilled my life. I knew you would, but
it is better than I ever imagined. I feel so complete, so
happy. I love you very much.*

*Your Mom,
Susan*

Leah and Ben came to see their new half brother in the
hospital, and six-year-old Ben was worried.

"His head looks like an egg," he told us.

"It won't stay like that forever," Jeff assured him. "He
just got a little squished on his way out into the world."

Squished head or not, he looked perfect to me. The happiness didn't wear off, either. Nick was a wonderful baby,
and being with him made me feel like I had finally figured

out my purpose in life. I was here to love and protect this little boy. His start in life was so promising, too—two parents and two sets of grandparents who loved him and wanted him very much, plenty of toys and attention . . . what more could a baby want?

It was important to me not to show favoritism, though. After all, Jeff's two children spent every other weekend with us, and they had to feel loved and welcomed, too. I went out of my way to show them I loved them and was proud of them. Nick didn't get any special treatment; they all had to live with the same rules, and I tried to be just as affectionate and attentive to all of them.

What we didn't know then was that their mother had begun asking them about their "little bastard brother." It took many years for Leah and Ben to tell us about that. We knew that Jeff's ex was very angry that he'd moved on so fast after they'd separated, but we didn't expect her to sink so low. She apparently grilled the kids about our every move, wanting to know all the details of our relationship and our comings and goings.

We bought a house, and while we waited for construction to be completed, we moved in with Jeff's parents. Almost three months after Nick was born, Jeff's mother ordered us to get married.

"You take a day off of work and you two get married," she told Jeff. So that's just what we did. On Pearl Harbor Day, December 7, 1984, Jeff's parents watched Nick while we headed down to the L.A. Courthouse to say our "I do's." I wore Jeff's mother's blue quarter-length-sleeve wool dress, and Jeff wore a sports jacket with patches on the elbows. Aah, the 1980s. What a fashionable decade.

It felt a little like being in a Baskin Robbins at the Justice of the Peace, going up to the ticket dispenser to take a number and waiting to be called. I don't remember much about the ceremony, though Jeff does—that's my romantic man for you. We used Jeff's father's plain gold wedding band as my ring for the ceremony. Jeff bought me a wedding ring afterward, and said that we were doing everything backward for good luck. Being married didn't feel very different; we were already married in our hearts. This just made it official.

Being a mother was everything I hoped it would be. The physical connection that started in the womb and continued through breast-feeding made me feel such a strong bond with this little person and his kissable peach-fuzzed head and chubby cheeks.

Nick was a terrific baby who turned into a sweet toddler in no time at all. By his first birthday, he said "Thank you" every time someone handed him a present and "Bless you" every time someone sneezed. At seventeen months, he could name the seven dwarfs, even when they were turned backward. He had them memorized by the color of their hats. Sneezy's name, however, was "Achoo."

His sense of humor was apparent right from the start, too. When he was two, after watching cartoons, he posed his Snoopy figurine at the edge of the bathtub.

"You're going to fall down into the water, right after these messages!" he said.

Sometimes he was funny on purpose, and other times he didn't realize he was being funny, like when he ran through the house looking for his grandfather, shouting, "Honey! Honey! Honnnnnney!" because that's what he heard his grandmother call his grandfather. Nick was supposed to call him Papa, but if "Honey" was what Grandma called him, then "Honey" was good enough for him, too.

What I have now are the snapshots and the videos to remind me that Nick was real, and that he was ours, and that I'm not looking back on him with rose-colored glasses. He really was as cute and smart and wonderful as I remember.

There will never be another video of Nick, making the ones I have valuable beyond all measure. On one of them, Jeff had turned the clunky, old-fashioned video camera on two-year-old Nick—with his dirty blond hair with the slightest wave to it, white OshKosh overall shorts, and bare feet—kissing the dog and giggling and riding his blue motorized car across the lawn.

Then came a scene from Christmas: Nick sitting at the top of the stairs, waiting patiently while I finished getting him dressed in his special outfit with the red and green suspenders. His dad was trying to be patient, too, but it was tough for him. He had been waiting by the tree for us to come down and was bursting with eagerness . . . it was the first Christmas that Nick was old enough to appreciate his presents and understand what was going on, and that was definitely occasion to break out the old ten-pound video camera.

"I have one more sock to put on," Nick reassured his dad. "I love you."

A tall box with red wrapping paper was the first to be torn into. His first basketball hoop, just his height.

"Are you good at basketball?" Jeff asked.

"Yeah, I am good!" Nick replied, and proved it by "dribbling," then walking up to the basket and depositing the ball into the basket. "I'm strong," he added. "Very strong."

We didn't have Leah and Ben with us that day, but they came back to us the next day, which we dubbed the "second night of Christmas," and the first night of Hanukkah. The video showed all three kids playing together—Nick waddling around in a diaper and red pajama top giving orders to his apparent teammate Leah: "You go that way." They were sneak attacking Ben.

The next scene skipped ahead to Nick's third birthday—a backyard dinosaur party where Nick steadfastly avoided the mild-mannered dinosaur character for the first half of the party, then assaulted him with balloon swords and poodles the second half. Not just Nick, either—all the kids at the party found great amusement in stepping on the dinosaur's tail and messing with his costume. At one point, the dinosaur actually complained to a group of little girls, "Come on, I can't paint anyone's face if you hit me."

When Jeff asked Ben what kind of face painting he was

going to get, nine-year-old Ben gave the camera a serious look and said, "I'm not going to get painted."

"You're too cool?" Jeff asked. Ben nodded and took a swig from his Dixie cup.

Then it was time for the happy birthday song, and Nick stood there in his dinosaur shirt and blew out the candles on his dinosaur cake, and when Jeff asked, "How old are you?" Nick called out, "THWEE!"

There were all manner of cousins and neighbors and some children whose names we didn't even know (Where had they come from? Do preschoolers normally crash parties?). Their moms were there, too, with decade-appropriate frosted and permed hair.

It was exactly the life I'd always pictured. We made fun out of thin air. It never really mattered what we were doing: if we were together, there would be love and laughter. Some of our best times were on the sailboat, sailing together on the high seas, where the kids would take turns steering the boat and wearing the captain's hat.

Nick started preschool that year at a place called the Farm School, and he would come home with his pockets filled with acorns. Acorns can still make me feel sentimental today. It was an exciting time because he loved his little friends there. I kept every finger painting, every turkey made out of a hand tracing, his phone number written inside a picture of a telephone, the "A Is for Apple" and "C Is for Cat" work sheets . . .

For a time, life really felt perfect.

Interspersed with all this perfection, however, were the court battles. Jeff's ex wanted more money. She had the kids in private school and couldn't afford the tuition. Instead, we asked for—and got—more visitation with the kids. Each time she asked for more money, we asked for more time. Eventually, it was a fifty-fifty split. We had the kids every other week, plus half of all holidays and vacations. That seriously steamed her.

I don't mean to insinuate that the only reason we wanted more time with the kids was out of spite. We really thought, at the time, that we were the more capable parents and the more stable household, so it would be better for the kids to spend as much time with us as possible.

By that point, Ben was nine and Leah was twelve. Beautiful kids, both of them. Ben had a "little-surfer-dude" look about him, with windswept dirty blond hair, and Leah had long, shiny brown locks and an electric smile. They were good to their little brother, and he liked following them around. On the rare occasions when they fought or made fun of each other, I'd make them write sentences in a notebook. ("Leah does not look like a nerd. Leah does not look like a nerd.")

One of our first moves once we had equal custody, and it was a wrong one, was to take the kids out of private school and put them in public school. *Why do we need to spend so much money on private school?* we thought. How could it be so much better than the public school that everyone else's kids went to without complaint?

Plus, we really wanted to keep the sailboat.

If I had to trace our family's tragedy all the way back to its root, that's what I'd point to right there. We couldn't afford to keep the boat and send the kids to that private school. What we should have done right then was sell the boat and give the money to Jeff's ex to keep the kids where they were comfortable. But we were stubborn and just plain wrong. We let our priorities get mixed up.

So we kept the boat, got the kids half the time, and switched them to a new school—uprooting them from their friends and teachers, putting them in a new atmosphere with bigger classes and less monitoring. They weren't happy, and Ben's behavior problems began soon thereafter. Attention deficit disorder (ADD) is what they called it. Who knows if that was the real problem? ADD was very "in vogue" at the time.

I thought part of the problem might be because Ben seemed to be physically uncomfortable all the time. He was always clearing his throat and making weird sounds that seemed to me like he must have allergies or sinus problems, so I took him to a doctor and sat with him while he got poked with way too many needles. Afterward, he kept thanking me. It was sad and cute.

His mom was furious. She was absolutely livid that I had taken him to a doctor without her consent. I hadn't really considered it at that point, but I later understood that I wouldn't have wanted someone to take my son to a doctor without my consent, either. At the time, though, my only concern was trying to figure out what was bothering Ben so much.

Then things really went wrong.

Depending on who was arguing with whom at the time, Ben and Leah bounced back and forth between our two houses. First, Leah came to live with us during the week, while Ben stayed at his mother's house.

Some days, Jeff's ex had to leave for work before Ben had to go to school, so she started dropping him off at our house on those mornings so that I'd take him to school. Luckily, his middle school was just down the block, but she never gave us any warning or asked for permission. She never called to check if I was home or to make sure it was OK for me to take Ben, and there was no consistent schedule—some days he'd just show up on our doorstep and ring the bell, and some days he wouldn't. I told her to stop it and to call ahead if she wanted me to take Ben to school.

That didn't happen. So the next time she showed up with him in tow, I just didn't answer the door. I pretended not to be home—which they both knew was a lie.

"Keep knocking. That bitch is home," she called out to Ben.

It killed me to stand by that door and know Ben was standing on the other side, just a pawn in this game of ex-wife and new wife. Come what may, though, I was going to stand my ground this time. I was not backing down to this woman anymore. Just because she was bitter that I existed didn't mean that I was going to take over any responsibility she felt like shoving my way.

Ben trudged back to his mother's car, and they drove

away. Maybe she took him to school early; maybe she went to work late. But he got to school somehow. It was wrong of me; I had made Ben a pawn just as much as his mother had. I shouldn't have made him feel like I was avoiding him.

The next weekend when she came to pick Ben up, I was outside watering the lawn. I turned to her in the driveway and told her, "Stop putting the kids in the middle of this. If you want special favors from me, you call me first. You don't just drop Ben off unannounced and expect that I'll handle everything."

A tidal wave of profanities flew out of her mouth. And just in case I didn't get the point verbally, she decided to take it a step further.

She tried to run me over with her car.

No, I mean it. *She tried to run me over with her car.*

Jerking the car forward at me in the driveway, she grazed my pant leg with the car bumper, and I did the first thing that came to mind: I turned the hose at her and sprayed it full blast. Her car had the sunroof open, so the water showered down on her and the car seats. In shock, I'm sure, she drove up across the lawn, then backed up into the street, while I got out of striking range.

"Ben! Get over here," she screamed, and she backed up across the front lawn.

Oh, Ben. I turned to see that he had been standing at the door the whole time, seeing and probably hearing everything. He hesitated; what was he supposed to do? His mother was cursing and drenched and practically foaming at the mouth, but she was his mother, and I was the one holding the hose. I was always going to be the Other Woman, even though I had nothing to do with the breakup of their home. Poor Ben, with his eyes open wide, looking at me, then at her. She flung the car door open and screamed again for him to get in. He walked over and got into her car wordlessly. As she peeled out, she tried to rip up the front lawn, squealing her tires all the way down the street.

I filed a police report, but I dropped it before it got to

court because it seemed like the wrong thing to do to the kids. As much as I wanted her to be held accountable for her actions, I didn't want Ben and Leah to see us tearing each other's throats out in another legal battle. They had enough ugliness between our two households as it was. In those early years, we were all immature and wrong about the way we spoke about each other. We name-called. We let the kids hear things they shouldn't have. And it hurt them—they had no idea who to believe or who really wanted them, and they took sides depending on whose house they were in at the moment.

You could see trouble coming with Ben even from very early on. He didn't seem to be able to control his impulses. For one thing, he was extremely fidgety, always moving and poking people and trying to get attention. There were also aggressive tendencies that came and went. He was a loving son and brother but very easily got off-track and would knock things down or throw things across the room. It seemed like there was no censor inside of him telling him to relax and get a grip until it was too late. Then, when he was calm again, he could be a sweet kid and a lot of fun.

When Nick was in the second grade, he completed a fill-in-the-blank book. It had entries like "My favorite book is *The Big Book of Why*" and "My favorite food is cheese omelets." One of the sentences to fill out was "I worry about _____," and he wrote "my brother."

Even then, we all saw danger signs, and it didn't take a genius to figure out where they were coming from. We just didn't know how bad it would get.

At age eleven, Ben and a friend got caught using a screwdriver to puncture tires. There was no animosity behind it; the other boy just told him to do it, so Ben did. He wanted acceptance from this boy. Unluckily for them, however, an off-duty police officer happened to be jogging in the neighborhood just as Ben was doing the deed. He got caught, and my instinct was to pull Nick closer to me. It worried me that Ben had gotten involved in something illegal, and my intuition was that this was just the beginning.

Ben's teachers frequently complained about his misbe-
havior. His friends were a rough, older crowd who liked to
live dangerously, and he didn't trust either one of his parents. At one point, Ben was being uncooperative with his
mother and tried to walk out the door. A friend of Leah's
boyfriend was standing in his way, so Ben pushed him
away—and the sixteen-year-old boy beat Ben up. He did it
in front of Ben's mother, and she didn't intervene.

Then Ben and a friend went to visit another friend of
theirs. No one answered the door, but they decided to walk
in anyway—the door was unlocked, but no one was home.
The boys spotted car keys on their friend's table, and they
thought it sounded like a cool idea to go for a ride. Ben
took his friend out for a joyride in that family's car, crashed
it, and damaged three other cars in the process. How he
learned to drive at all at eleven years old was beyond me.
We were lucky that no one was hurt, and at the time, we
were glad that the police didn't get involved. Jeff paid for
the damages to the cars, and we decided it was time to do
something about Ben.

We took him to a psychiatrist, who prescribed the
"wonder drug" Ritalin. Well, it did help him focus more in
school—but the problem was that it also made him more
focused on getting the things he wanted.

One night, what eleven-year-old Ben wanted was to
see the R-rated movie *Boyz n the Hood*, and his mother
said no.

"You're not going to see that," she said.

"Yes, I am," he told her, and headed toward the front
door.

She blocked the door, and they got into a knock-down,
drag-out fight. She hit him with the telephone, then began
swinging at him, windmill fashion. He blocked her punches
and restrained her arms. She bit him on the arm to get him
off of her, leaving teeth marks, and he ran out the door. She
called Jeff to tell him what happened and that Ben was out
in the streets somewhere.

Jeff went out and picked Ben up and brought him back to

our house. I took photos of the bite marks in case we were about to get into another custody battle, but that wasn't to be. She gladly turned him over to us at that point. He lived with us full time and didn't visit with his mother at all for the rest of the year. Her choice. I don't think they ever even spoke on the telephone for months.

"All that bad stuff he did, he did under *her* watch," we thought. We were sure that we were the better parents and would have a much better handle on him. He had certainly never stolen a car while he was at our house, for goodness' sake, or had any physical confrontations with us, either. So we assumed that her mothering skills were probably to blame, and we'd get Ben straightened out in no time.

We tried counseling, figuring he was still having a hard time with his parents' divorce and the bickering between the families. At the time, though, we considered counseling something you could do every now and again when problems cropped up. We went maybe once a month and tried to talk about our expectations and fears about his behaviors.

A few months later, Ben came to me with a broken arm; he told me he fell off of his bike, and I was naive enough to believe him. I took him to the hospital to have a cast put on.

Meanwhile, Nick had just been named "Citizen of the Month" in his second-grade class. He was a sensitive kid who once became nearly inconsolable over Mexican jumping beans—he worried about the plight of the little jumpers inside the beans.

"Whatever is in there, cut the bean open and let it out!"

He loved to read and had already accumulated quite a collection of books. At night, he would fall asleep to the sounds of audiobooks. I'm not sure exactly what he was picking up from those books, though, because this is a note he wrote to his second-grade girlfriend, Gina:

It has been too long since we have kissed. About three days. So why don't you kiss me fool? I did not mean that, love dove. I think it's time we got married. Sorry your cousin died. I will save this note forever. Dear Gina, our relationship has been long as well as love. XOXO. I love you. Your lover Nick.

Around this time, he also began learning the piano. Maybe this was to impress Gina. Elementary school ladies do love musicians.

In front of Nick, I was talking to a friend about a diet I was on—the latest in many I had tried—and he said something that left me with my head cocked.

"Mom, you're the perfect size for your weight."

One afternoon, Jeff was taking Leah to a football game, and twelve-year-old Ben asked for a ride to the movies. He said he was meeting a friend there and would get a ride home with the boy's mother later. After he dropped Ben off, Jeff went home and called the friend's mother. "You're picking the kids up, right?" he asked.

"I don't know what you're talking about," she said.

With a sinking feeling, Jeff drove right back to the theater. The movie was still playing, and the theater was dark, but he walked the aisles and didn't see Ben. As the show let out, Jeff stood outside the theater, and—just as he feared—no Ben. The kid had just disappeared, and we didn't have the first clue where to find him or what might have happened.

Jeff called his ex-wife—we were on speaking terms at that point—had she heard from Ben? She hadn't but wanted to be kept informed about what was happening.

A flurry of phone calls began. Jeff tracked down every friend of Ben's he could locate and pressed them about where he was. No one wanted to talk, but as other parents got involved and details slowly leaked out, a few of them caved, and we pieced together the whole story.

It started with the broken arm, which had been no bike accident. It turned out that Ben had been jumped as part of his initiation into a gang called Down to Serve (DTS). We had seen their graffiti tags all over the San Fernando Valley, though we never knew what "DTS" stood for before. The gang was known mostly for vandalism, such as taking baseball bats to mailboxes. But lately, they had taken to stealing cars.

One of the members called Ben and pretended to be a police officer wanting to question him about the car thefts. Ben bought it and decided he needed to escape rather than face police questioning in front of us. That's why he had asked for a ride to the movies—he had no intention of actually going to the movies, just using that as an excuse to get out of the house and meet up with a friend.

Once he was out . . . he stole a car.

Then he headed to a party in Palm Springs, about a three-hour drive away. By the time we learned that, though, he had already gone there and was on his way back to a friend's house in the San Fernando Valley in the stolen vehicle.

Jeff rounded up his brothers and his father and decided that, because they knew the address where Ben was heading, they'd beat him there and block off the street so that he couldn't escape. They went to the friend's house and explained what was happening, and the boy's older brother, who was in training to be a police officer, joined in the effort to get Ben back home.

It turned out that Ben was with a fifteen-year-old boy who was also new to the gang. They had used a dent puller to rip out the ignition, then used a screwdriver to start the car. The fifteen-year-old said he didn't know how to drive, so it was Ben—the twelve-year-old kid with his right arm in a cast—who drove the car. Even more unbelievable, the car was a stick shift. Yet somehow, they made it almost three hundred miles without incident.

But as he approached the friend's block, Ben saw his grandfather hiding behind a tree, and he got spooked—

gunning the gas pedal and taking off. Ben's friend's older brother jumped into a car and took off after him, getting into a high-speed chase in the middle of a suburban street. Finally, Ben's ride came to an end when he ran a red light doing fifty miles per hour and broadsided another car.

No! Jeff screamed. Then there was silence and that moment where the world seems to stop all at once, frozen in time. Was Ben dead? Had he killed a carful of people?

It was a miracle: although both cars were totaled, no one was even injured. Relief washed over Jeff, coupled with total bewilderment about the bizarreness of the situation.

"What were you thinking?" Jeff yelled, approaching Ben in tears. "Haven't I said 'I love you' enough? Where does this come from out of the blue? Why, Ben?"

There wouldn't be any good answers, though. Ben just stood there looking shaken and caught. The tools the boys had used to break into the stolen car were still in the backseat when the police arrived. They arrested Ben and the other boy—then they opened the trunk and found a .22 caliber rifle.

Jeff called me, sobbing, and I drove over to meet him at the scene. Ben's mother arrived around the same time I did. She didn't say a word to anyone, just watched what was going on, a weighty sadness hanging over all of us. She hadn't laid eyes on Ben in maybe six months, and as he was taken to jail, she got back into her car and drove home.

Jeff and I had been so cocky, thinking that Ben's previous problems had all been her fault and that we would do a better job keeping him in line. But look what happened on our watch; the whole thing stunk of failure. Was it a cry for help, for attention? When Ben was with his mother, we thought he was crying out for our attention. Maybe now that he was with us, he was crying out for hers.

Car theft and illegal gun possession bought Ben a ticket to a juvenile detention center for about three weeks. That left the question of what would happen when he got out. His mother didn't want him in her house, and I sure didn't want him in mine anymore, either. We talked about putting him into a private military school, but the tuition was about sixty thousand dollars per year, and Jeff still really wanted to keep that sailboat.

Maybe this would be the wake-up call that Ben needed, though, we hoped. Maybe a few weeks in a detention center would be enough to make him straighten up. From the sounds of it, he was truly sorry.

He didn't have much of an explanation for what he did; it didn't seem like there was much thought process behind it at all. But he promised to drop the gang and clean up his act. Very hesitantly, I agreed that we'd give him one last chance.

For some time after his arrest, things were relatively quiet. Perhaps grateful that we hadn't shipped him off anywhere, he did his best to behave. With enough love and attention, I thought we could still get through to him. There was so much good in Ben, in between the bad patches. He lived with a devil on one shoulder and an angel on the other; unfortunately, the devil kept kicking the crap out of the angel.

Getting him involved with sports seemed a positive way to channel his energy, so we let him enroll in baseball and tae kwon do. His sister, Leah, also joined tae kwon do, on top of her cheerleading schedule, and Nick soon followed in their footsteps and joined, too.

When Ben was thirteen, I bought a journal for us to write notes to each other. On the first page, I wrote, "Ben, you make me so proud. Your efforts are shining through! Keep up the good work. If I can help let me know." He happily took to this form of communication and kicked off his first entry, discussing his plans and his then-girlfriend:

Susan, I really like staying home. And you have been really helpful with Tae kwon do and everything. Lara and I are not really close any more, like we used to be. Do you think its cause she is out of town, most of the time? She used to want me to go out there, but now she

says the house is embarrassing because there is noth-
ing in it. What do you think? . . . Tomorrow, I'm prob-
ably going to wash my Uncle Monte's R.V. Make some
money, and have something to do.
    Gotta run,
    You're kinda great yourself!

Love, Ben ☺ hi

Some of our entries were funny and loving, covering the
usual topics a thirteen-year-old thinks about most. Considering how tough he was trying to act, it was sometimes
easy to forget what a sweet and sensitive kid he was, but
then I look back and see his words:

I appreciate every little thing you do for me. Even
though at the time I might not act like it. I won't let you
or dad down this time. So don't you worry about it.

or

I just want to thank you for letting me do tae
kwon do.

or

Thank you for giving me some extra rope this little
vacation. I really enjoyed it.

or

I love you.

Ben signed his name and a peace sign under some of his
entries, noting that the peace sign was his "official mark."
Sometimes he wrote about his friendships, sometimes
about vacations or places he wanted to go, but some of the

most poignant entries were more indicative of our troubles and power struggles about the rules in our house.

For some reason, Ben was more respectful of me than he was of his father—maybe because I demanded respect. In his journal, he often asked me to intervene and get his father to ease up on him. Unfortunately, every time we did ease up, we ended up regretting it. When I went through his drawers (which I did pretty often), I found a set of markers. He had been graffiti tagging, I figured. Why else did he need markers?

In March 1992, he wrote to me:

Dear Susan

I feel that both you and dad are wrong when you go looking through my stuff without telling me. I don't care if you think it's necessary or not. You should tell me, or ask me if you can and do it in front of me. So then, I don't feel like I have to hide love letters and stuff, because that's the only thing that I worry about.

Dad says that I can't wear the new shoes you got me. That sucks! And I should be able to wear them. Nobody has come up to me and asked where are you from, or are you in a gang for a real long time. In fact, I think the last time was in September. It's like, what is "gang" related? People dress the way they want to dress. Hell, dad wears some stuff that a few gang members I know wear. Who cares? Dad's work pants are considered gang. His tennis shoes are considered gang to some extent, but nobody bugs him about it.

I know what I did was wrong, but it doesn't mean I should pay for it for a while. Stop thinking and hanging onto the bad, think about the good. Oh, and give me back my candy I had in my drawers.

Love, Ben

I wrote back to him:

Ben,

I asked you to be honest with me about the tennis shoes. We know there are certain items that if mixed with other certain items, makes them gang related. Some certain items we do not want to put money toward, nor may you wear them. If you are in the wrong place at the wrong time, "bad things happen." You know it, and they know it. Why would we take that chance?

It is not just your safety we have to be concerned for.

I know you will say, "They wouldn't do anything." But we're the adults, and we have to handle it the way we feel best.

We are not asking you for your opinion on this subject, because along with the markers, pretending to have a gun? With the gang affiliation in your past, we will not take chances.

We love you, and that is the way it is. Be thankful you are not wearing K-Mart clothes, and appreciate what you do have and can wear.

Love ya, "honest,"
Susan

We also tried to give Ben a lot of positive reinforcement for the things he did well. He was a natural athlete and competitor, and he progressed quickly to his yellow belt in his tae kwon do school. It seemed to help focus him and give him something positive to be proud of. That translated to better grades, too; he got three positive report cards in a row. It looked like things were finally improving, and even his big sister noticed the change. She wrote this note in his journal:

Ben

I know that I'm not supposed to be in here, but I just wanted to tell you that I'm proud of you for staying out

*of trouble. I'm also proud of you about your school-
work. Keep it up.*

*Love you,
Your Sister, Leah*

P.S. I didn't read anything.

In April of 1992, we traveled to Florida for a tae kwon
do tournament, where Ben won gold and silver medals for
his division. When we got back, he went straight to his
journal:

Susan

*See I knew I could do it. I won! It was real nice too,
because right after I won I saw dad, and he gave me
a kiss for like the first time this year. So, I got a lot out
of this trip.*

For a little while, things almost felt . . . calm. I compli-
mented Ben on his mannerism and said that he was going
to make some girl a great catch someday—he'd be a fun
husband like his dad.

"*What does mannerism mean?*" Ben wrote back. "*Oh
well, I think it was a compliment. Thank you!*"

But it wasn't enough to sustain him on a long-term basis.
Despite the discipline that sports provided, there were too
many temptations and too many opportunities to get into
trouble. When he was in our sight, he was fine. But with his
peers, things were unpredictable.

One afternoon when Ben was thirteen, he was standing
in front of our house with a group of kids. I looked out and
saw that they were passing a gun around between them,
like it was just a baseball or a cool new video game. As if
they did it every day.

It turned out that a girl had taken the pistol from her
father and brought it to Ben because he thought he needed

protection. Why would a thirteen-year-old think he needed a lethal weapon to protect himself?

"Why didn't you talk to me? If you feel like you're in danger, why didn't you come to me and tell me?" Jeff asked Ben later.

Ben didn't have an answer. Some kids at school were threatening him, so he just figured he'd keep this gun around "just in case." And that's the way it would be thereafter; Ben's life would become about being the biggest, the baddest, the one nobody wanted to tangle with.

Everyone has a breaking point. That one was mine.

I was in charge of Nick. That was my son, my adorable seven-year-old son who loved to read Shel Silverstein and play with his dog, and he deserved to have a seven-year-old's life. He shouldn't have to even know about this underbelly of a world that Ben was exposing us to. And having Ben in the house was starting to become a danger to Nick, not to mention the rest of us. What was going to happen if some gang member came charging into our house looking for Ben?

I felt not only disappointed, but deceived. All the effort that had gone into building up our relationship and trying to guide Ben so he could earn our trust felt like it had been for nothing.

When Jeff came home that night, I had a pile of clothing on the bed.

"Are you cleaning out the closet?" he asked.

"No. I'm packing," I told him. "I'm leaving with Nick. Something is going to go wrong."

How right I was.

CHAPTER 3

BROTHERLY BOND

Ultimately, however, Nick and I didn't leave. I don't remember exactly how Jeff talked me into staying, but he did. I really didn't want to leave my husband, and I didn't want Nick to be without his dad, so I pushed my fears about Ben as far back in my mind as I could. What was going on with him made me profoundly uncomfortable, and I didn't yet know if I was going to stay for good—I wanted to see if Ben was going to get his act straight before I decided.

The clothes went back into the closet, I started drinking on weeknights, and Ben went to more counseling. He continued on an erratic path of bouts of good behavior, then bouts of bad. That September, he began high school, and I was nervous about how he would make the transition.

"Be aware," I told him. "Big school can be big trouble."

We kept an even closer eye on him and researched the signs of gang involvement. Although Ben had sworn to us that he was no longer part of the gang and never would be again, we were jaded enough to keep our guard up.

Before long, we knew what clothing to watch out for, what hand signals, what colors, what haircuts. Ben wasn't allowed to wear his hair slicked back, which made him upset. No black jackets or hats unless he was with us. And he wasn't allowed to have markers.

He resented every moment of it. When he saw that we had been in his room or looked through his drawers, he would always complain. "The worst feeling in the world is the feeling of being invaded," he told me.

As well as I could, I kept explaining to him that we were doing this because we loved him and cared about his safety and our own. We weren't going to stop. And we weren't born yesterday.

On Nick's eighth birthday, I got him his own journal for us to write back and forth, just like I had done with Ben.

Mom

Thanks for the letter. By the way my day was pretty good and bad. But I will get better. I am really glad you got me this book. I think this will be fun. And I realy realy like my new desk.
   Please write back

Love Nick

And underneath his name was a peace sign. The same little peace sign that Ben used under his name.

I told him I thought it would be a good idea if we always wrote in the journal in ink. "That way it won't fade in later years, OK?" He agreed, and so it was.

When you write back, tell me what you think I should be for Hollaween pleeeese becase I don't know what to be. What a delima huh?
   I love you too

XOXOXOXOXOXOXO
Nicholas

When I told him once that I'd had a long day because I had to get up early to get my car serviced, he wrote back, "I am lucky compared to you."

But our lighthearted entries were interrupted by a serious one in October.

Dear Mom,

I had a terrible day I ~~whish~~ wish I was dead. Sometimes I forgot my math books and my teacher said if I and a few other kids didn't have our math done by Mon. we are in big trouble. Right now I'm crying bad. I messed up my leggo ship. I'm really sad. I think I want you to talk about it in the morning with me.

Love, Nick
☮
I ♥ U.

Luckily, I spotted that entry right away, and wrote back immediately.

Nick,

How about if we don't sleep on this . . .
First of all, I don't ever want you to wish you were dead. I don't think any of us really understands death, except for it to equal gone, "forever." And I don't want that ever for you, as I'm sure you feel the same way for me.
About the math books, you need to try to be more responsible for your homework. I'm not in class to hear or remind you of things. That's your place to be a "big boy," OK?
In the morning, I'll help you with Legos.
Just remember I love you so much.

Xoxo Mommy

Nick often looked to me for counsel, and he was sensitive to being teased. He took it to heart when a group of kids told him his bike "sucked," and he once told me that I was the only person he could really talk to. That wasn't true, of course; Nick always had plenty of friends. But he cared a lot about what kids thought of him, and he was self-conscious about whether or not he fit in.

———

The honeymoon period where Ben was quiet and repentant after the gun incident slowly faded away, and soon he was skipping school and mouthing off to his dad. Not to me—he knew I wouldn't stand for it—but Jeff still felt some guilt about getting divorced and breaking up his kids' home. I think it was that guilt that made him go easy on his kids when they disrespected him, which in turn only misguided them.

Leah and her dad got into arguments about dating; she wanted to start dating at fourteen, and we didn't think she was ready for that. One day, she just brought home this older guy who thought he was going to drive her out around town, and Jeff said no, so she called her mom and said she wanted to move back in with her. Then she was gone, simple as that.

And now it was Jeff's turn to be petty. Instead of working things out with Leah, he stopped contacting her for a few months.

That meant it was just the two boys again, plus Jeff and me, but before long, it felt like Ben was the one who demanded all our attention, all our care, all our worry. When he didn't get his way about something, Ben would lose control of his temper. It was like watching a Jumping Jacks firework ignite and zip all over the street, changing directions and randomly hitting whatever was in its path.

I often ran interference when Ben talked back to his dad.

"I hate it when you do this!" Ben said. "You don't think he can handle himself against me? I'm sure he'll be just fine. He's a big boy."

I told Ben that just because his dad was willing to over-look things out of a sense of guilt didn't mean I was. I had no guilt about his parents' divorce. And I sure wasn't going to let Nick grow up in a household where it was OK to disre-spect his parents. If Nick was going to learn the values I held dear, I couldn't be hypocritical in how I demonstrated those values. Ben was going to show his father respect, period.

Except that wasn't Ben's plan. He thought we should all develop instant amnesia every time he did something bad, and he got very angry whenever Jeff tried to set rules or enforce discipline. I couldn't be the one to do it; I was not his mother, which was held very clearly over my head. It was not my place to ground Ben or Leah or to give them a good "talking to" when the situation called for it. Every time I had tried, it just complicated things worse—they'd go running to Dad to tell him what mean ol' Susan had done, and I ended up having to explain everything twice. So I learned to just go straight to Jeff when something was wrong and let him handle it.

Whenever Jeff tried to set stricter boundaries, Ben threatened to run away, but I never believed him. Where was this fourteen-year-old going to go?

But that became the big question in November of 1992. During one of my checks through Ben's drawers, I found a gun clip. I stood there in disbelief for a minute. I had certainly never held a gun clip before, though I had seen one of Jeff's. And here it was in an unlocked drawer, just a room away from where seven-year-old Nick slept.

Jeff made a beeline for the high school to track Ben down and find out what was going on.

"It's from Kevin's dad's gun," Ben said. Kevin was a friend of his from tae kwon do class. "Kevin brought it over and put it in my drawer, but I took a second thought and brought the gun back."

Ben had taken the clip out and smuggled the gun into his high school under his T-shirt. They'd exchanged it in the school parking lot, and no one had spotted it.

While we debated what to do, we told Ben he wasn't to

see a single one of his friends or his girlfriend until further notice. As usual, Ben balked. He wrote to me in our
journal:

> *Dad is talking about putting me into another school,*
> *or taking me to work. I don't think that's right. Before,*
> *I would have carried it. I might have even used it. But*
> *I think I did right by second thinking it, and giving it*
> *back as soon as possible.*
>
> *You say the next place I'm going to is a home, or a*
> *school, but I see myself going someplace else not so*
> *radical. If you don't understand, I'm not gonna live like*
> *a criminal again, and living on the streets is better than*
> *that. You would feel the same if you experienced it. You*
> *guys (dad and you) are so ignorant. You can't even see*
> *past your own little family life, into the real world.*
>
> *I really did like this little family thing going, but I*
> *don't think I can handle it. At least like this.*

> *Love, Ben*

Ben briefly stayed with Jeff's parents while we talked
about what to do. All I knew was that he wasn't coming
back in the house again. An unusual solution presented
itself soon afterward.

"Let me take him for a while," Ben's tae kwon do
instructor told us. "I can help him."

We thought it was very generous—and a little crazy—
for the sensei to want to do this for Ben. Nevertheless, we
agreed to it. Jeff would pay the instructor rent money and
give him money for all of Ben's expenses, and the instructor would provide discipline and a strict environment for
Ben to get his act together. Every morning, Ben would rise
at 5 a.m. and go to the gym before school. After school,
he'd go back to the gym, then help train the younger tae
kwon do students at the studio, then train one-on-one with
the sensei until 9 p.m.

It just might work, I thought. Ben respected this guy, and

tae kwon do had been one of the few things to have a positive impact on his life. We envisioned a "teenage drill camp" scenario; the instructor was tough and serious. At the very least, Ben wasn't going to mouth off to him anytime soon.

On the day he left, I wrote in our journal:

Benjamin,

You poor baby. I wish I could keep you, but it's out of my hands now. This is the second time you have put our family in unnecessary danger. You like living on the edge. Personally, I don't want to fall off with you. Last week's warnings, sadly, were not taken seriously.

We love you, always will. That's why we must remove you from this environment until you're old enough, mature enough to understand where you'll be headed if we didn't stop you.

I'll always be here to talk.

Love, Susan

Now it was just the three of us. What a tremendous sense of relief it was to wake up and not think about gang colors and weapons and calls from the principal. Maybe now that sitcom family life I had always envisioned would actually begin.

But Nick missed living with Ben and Leah. Leah's stay at her mother's house didn't last long; they fought, and Leah then moved in with Jeff's parents, and later, with her boyfriend and his parents. As much as Nick understood that his sister had made the decision to leave and his brother had been disrespectful and dangerous, he still loved them and liked being around them.

They did see each other often at the tae kwon do school, though. Because Ben was the sensei's assistant instructor with younger kids, we were able to keep close tabs on him. We were there with Nick almost every night.

Nick was never into sports like his older brother was, but he enjoyed going to tae kwon do classes anyway—maybe more to see his brother than anything else. He was a fourth-grader then and had come in fifth place in the school spelling bee. He cherished his books more than anything, always making sure that they looked pristine, no dog-ears or marks in them. He once cried over a torn page. Among his favorite pastimes was playing with bugs, ants, and, in particular, snails.

Before Thanksgiving, Nick took to our journal again.

I am thankful to my mom and dad for giving me food and clothes, without them I wouldn't live. I am also thankful that this is a free country, because if it wasn't I wouldn't have choices.

Giving thanks means appreciate something and telling people you care about them. It also means to thank someone for something they've given or done for you. Because if we're not than that's usually what starts gangs, and people get killed like that. We should also be nice to each other.

His next entry was decidedly less deep.

I don't like roller bladeing because it bores me. I have better things to do that I am widely known for, like reading and making traps for my brother. And playing Nintendo.

I don't think we will find Wilber. Someone will probably step on him and he will scatter across the room. Then everyone can say they found a piece of him.

Wilber was the class pet hamster that had disappeared from his cage.

After about six months with the sensei, we agreed that it looked like Ben was doing well. He never really told us whether or not he was happy, but we didn't hear a peep about Ben getting into any trouble for all that time. He seemed to recognize that he had really screwed up this time and had to fix it.

Considering we were giving the sensei about a thousand dollars a month, Jeff decided that was an expense we no longer needed once it seemed Ben was back on the right path.

After Ben moved back home, we found out that the sensei's influence had not been solely positive. Soon after Ben moved in, some teenagers vandalized the sensei's car. That night, the sensei heard a noise outside. He grabbed a gun and awoke Ben from a sound sleep, telling him to come outside with him. "I think someone's messing with my car again," he said.

When they got outside, they found a man attacking a woman in the backseat of a car parked on the street. The sensei pointed the gun at the attacker and said, "Get out of the car or I'll blow your head off."

While the sensei held the man at gunpoint, Ben went back into the house and told the sensei's wife to call the police. Police showed up and took the man away. So, on one hand, the guy was a hero that night, saving a woman from harm. On the other, this was exactly the kind of influence we were trying to get Ben away from—we didn't want him around guns or violence.

———

After he moved back in with us, Ben wanted to go out one night, and Jeff told him he couldn't go anywhere until he helped to finish painting his room—we were converting the garage into a new bedroom for him. Jeff had already put in a lot of time designing and furnishing it, and he wanted help with the finishing touches. But Ben wanted to go out *now*, and as usual, he flew into a rage when he didn't get his way.

He lunged forward and slammed Jeff, and the two of them got into a physical fight. No warning. Jeff was caught so off guard because he hadn't even yelled at Ben or said anything that he thought could provoke such a violent response; essentially, all he had said was "No."

Jeff managed to wrestle Ben to the ground and hold him there.

"This sucks! Who the hell cares if I paint my room today? I'm not doing it!" Ben yelled.

"You're going to spend a couple of hours painting this room with me, and then you can go," Jeff said. Giving in at all at that point was probably crazy, but at that moment, he just wanted to cool Ben's temper. The violent response was so stunning that Jeff later figured Ben must have been on something. Cocaine? Speed?

The next day, Jeff, Leah, and Ben had a scheduled meeting with a therapist. At that meeting, Jeff said, "I'm tired of putting up with all this. I'm not going to have a physical confrontation with my kid!" He looked at Ben and said, "You follow the rules or you get out."

On the ride home, Jeff reiterated that there weren't going to be any more excuses or any more allowances. As they pulled up to the house, he said, "Now, we're going to finish painting the goddamned bedroom!" Jeff walked off to collect the paintbrushes, then turned back and saw only Leah.

"Where did he go?"

Leah said she saw him walking down the street and around the corner. Jeff and I assumed he would go to his mother's house.

Fine, Jeff thought. *I'm not following him.*

About a week went by before we heard from Ben again. Perhaps he expected us to cry and beg him to come home, but that isn't what we did.

"You're not coming home until you've made the decision to follow the household rules," Jeff told him.

Months went by. Ben would call and let us know he was fine from time to time, and he checked in with his mother sometimes, too, but he held out on his decision. He never told us where he was, only that he was with friends and he was fine.

We didn't know then that a few weeks prior to his running away, he had been out walking with friends at CityWalk, the strip of stores and restaurants at Universal Studios in Hollywood. They met some guy named Eric, who invited all of the kids into his limousine. That night, Eric gave Ben his contact information and an open invitation to stay with him anytime. So Ben had just been biding his time; he knew he'd have somewhere to go if he decided to run away. Some random guy he'd met at CityWalk would take him in. It turned out that this Eric was a bounty hunter who also owned a tattoo parlor, where Ben was now a happy apprentice. On one of his calls, he told Jeff, "I'm learning how to cartoon, Dad."

He failed to mention that he was "cartooning" in permanent ink, on himself. We were naive enough to think he meant he was learning how to be a cartoon artist . . . maybe a useful trade. During each conversation, he would assure Jeff that he was fine. We were more or less playing a game of chicken, wondering whether Ben or we would crack first.

"Had enough of this yet? Are you thinking of coming home?" Jeff would ask.

"No, I'm cool."

He was telling people he was eighteen, though he was still really only fifteen. We had no idea if he was on drugs, stealing cars, or even worse. For now, we were just hoping he would come back home. He couldn't possibly live on his own forever, we thought; something was going to have to wake this kid up and make him realize that the home life he had wasn't so bad after all.

And we were very hopeful on the day that a call finally came that sounded different. It had been six months since he ran away. He had been kicked out of the tattoo parlor owner's place because a friend of his had brought some kind of drugs into the house. Even though the tattoo owner was a tough guy, he was firm on his stance against drugs. He was also full of contradictions: he was Jewish, with a Star of David tattooed on his stomach and, inside it, a gun pointing straight outward. In the Jewish religion, it is forbidden to tattoo your body.

Now Ben had been out in the streets. He stayed here and there with people he met. This life was getting harder, though, and he was probably testing the waters when he called his dad and said he'd like to meet. Jeff went to meet him at an In-N-Out Burger, relieved that maybe his son was through with this rough living and ready to come home. But as Jeff pulled into the parking lot, he noticed what looked like a skinhead in a wifebeater shirt, covered in tattoos.

Oh my God. It was Ben.

The sight made Jeff break down in tears on the spot. His handsome blond son was gone. There was no trace of that boy anymore. In his place was this tattooed street kid. It was a nightmare; Jeff couldn't even speak.

This wasn't the reunion he had hoped for, but he wouldn't give up on Ben, and the problem was that Ben knew it.

Even when Ben claimed that he was ready to follow our rules, Jeff knew he couldn't bring Ben home to us. Instead, his sister, Leah, picked him up and took him to Jeff's parents' house while we figured out our next move. After some talking, we agreed that Jeff would rent an apartment with Ben to try to work with him one-on-one. It was a small one-bedroom apartment, and across the street was a park with tennis courts. Despite all that was happening, Ben and Jeff still enjoyed playing tennis together, even though Ben didn't look like a typical tennis player.

By this time, Ben had been kicked out of El Camino Real High School—the same high school his father had attended—because he got into a fight with one of Leah's friends. The girl threw a milk carton at him, and he slapped her and got expelled. Jeff had to do some hard selling to get Ben enrolled in another school. He told one local school that Ben needed special-education classes, which is why they should accept him—and they briefly did, though it was soon apparent that he was not in need of special education, aside from special lessons in how to stay out of trouble.

For a few months, Jeff balanced a crazy schedule. He drove Ben to and from school every day, then brought him back to work with him. Most days, he put Ben to work running manufacturing equipment. Ben's mother was now starting a new life with a man who had sons of his own. Ben felt totally unwanted. Worrying about Ben and trying to keep him in line was a full-time job, but Jeff's life was split in two; he traveled back and forth to spend time with Nick and me.

Then a friend and his wife invited Jeff and me to Palm Springs for the weekend. It sounded like a welcome break from the chaos. Jeff and his friend were both avid tennis players, so it would be a couple of days of tennis, sun, and friendly conversation.

"I need to be able to trust you," Jeff told sixteen-year-old Ben before leaving. "Just chill. Don't have anyone over. I'll be back in two days."

Two days later, before Jeff could even walk into his apartment, the building manager came charging at him, screaming and flailing his arms.

"Your son!" he yelled. "You can't stay here with him! You have to get out! Your son had a big drug party while you were away!"

The manager said there had been fistfights, destruction, and definitely drugs. And now Ben was gone.

He disappeared for about a week. Jeff came home and talked to Ben's friends' parents. Did anyone know where Ben was?

One parent, Rose, was a wonderfully caring woman. She was very open to "troubled kids" and had taken a liking to Ben. When he finally resurfaced, she and her husband offered to take him in. There were a lot of kids in and out of that house; it seemed like sort of a halfway house for kids in trouble. We weren't sure if that was a good idea or a bad idea, but at that point, she had a roof and a heart, and that's all that mattered.

Rose and Jeff got Ben back into continuation school— basically a neutral term for a school for kids who couldn't get along anywhere else. No matter how many people tried to help him, though, nothing worked. After Ben had been at the new school for a month or so, Jeff got a call from the principal.

"Mr. Markowitz, you have to get down here!"

"What's happening?"

"Your son has incited a gang war."

The previous day, Ben had an argument with a black student. The boy told him that another student said Ben didn't like black guys. It was a setup. The other student had said that just to cause a fight between the two of them. Ben walked into the classroom to find the boy who had set him up, and he knocked the boy out cold. That would have been bad enough, but now, Ben's new gang members had arrived in their lowrider cars and confronted the black student. The day before, Ben had been initiated—or "jumped into"—a gang called the Black Hearts Pariah. He had met the gang members during the six months he had spent on the streets and with the tattoo parlor owner.

At the moment the principal called Jeff, there was a standoff outside the school, and it looked like there was going to be a fight.

"Get over here and talk to him!" the principal demanded.

Jeff drove down there in terrible fear, imagining what exactly he, a white-collar Jewish dad, was supposed to do in the middle of a gang war.

Luckily, by the time he got there, the police had arrived, and the crowd had dispersed without any bloodshed. But that was the end of Ben's days in high school. He had run out of chances.

If you can't make it in continuation school, you're pretty much stamped as a lost cause.

Rose didn't think so, though. She let Ben stay at her place despite all the trouble. Because he wasn't going to school anymore, he and his buddies decided to take a trip. His friend showed up in an Acura Legend, and they planned to go to San Francisco. A marijuana run, most likely. They stopped in Chinatown, where Ben bought brass knuckles.

They stayed overnight; then, the following day, they took the Acura to a local beach with Rose's teenage daughter. When they arrived at the beach, she noticed someone down the beach and exclaimed to the guys, "That's the guy who was calling me six months ago and threatening to rape me!"

The guy was there with his friends.

Ben walked over to the young man, hands in his pockets.

"Do you know this girl?" he asked. His right hand already fitted with the brass knuckles, Ben swung and clipped the guy on the top of his head. His head split open.

What Ben didn't know was that the guys had driven around the toll booth and lifted a chain to enter the beach parking lot without paying, so the person at the ticket booth had called police. At the same time that Ben was hitting the guy, police were walking toward the group and saw the fight. They took Ben to Lost Hills Police Station, and this time his mom went to pick him up. She got him a public defender and had him released on bail.

A few days later, Ben was driving around in the Acura Legend, the same car he had taken to San Francisco. He found out the hard way the car was stolen. Red lights flashed in his rearview mirror, and the chase was on. Ben pulled up to a warehouse and ran to the back to hide from police.

"Come out, or we're sending the dogs in after you," the police called into a bullhorn.

Ben surrendered.

Now he had two charges against him: grand theft auto and assault with a deadly weapon.

He might have seen himself as a crime-fighting hero that day on the beach, but it didn't matter this time. Ben pled guilty to the charges against him. Sixteen years old, and he was off to a juvenile detention facility. Frankly, it was a relief for me.

Strange thing, that. I don't think you're supposed to feel happy when a family member gets sent off to jail, but by that point, it's what I had been hoping for. It gave me a break from worrying about what Ben was going to do next, and how we were going to protect ourselves and everyone else around him. And it gave me the hope that maybe *now* he'd get it.

Maybe.

CHAPTER 4

PUSH AND PULL

The detention center was called Challenger Memorial Youth Center, and it housed several "camps" of kids who had committed different categories of crimes. These were no playful summer camps. Although the kids weren't handcuffed, they had no privacy whatsoever in bathrooms and showers, they were monitored everywhere they went, and the concrete walls were surrounded with barbed wire.

Ten-year-old Nick was so sad that his brother was gone. December 6, 1994, he got his first letter from Ben.

Nick,

Hey, what's going on with you lately? Not much here, except for kicking back in the day room of the camp I'm staying at. It's called Challenger, but the dorm I'm staying in is called Smith. It's all right in here except for the fact I'm the only white guy in here and we just sit around and talk.

Well anyway, I'm writing to tell you a few things. First of all if you think me going to camp is something

I want to do, you're wrong, cause if I could do what I wanted I would be home with you, your mom, and dad. Another thing, for the longest time I haven't hung out with you like a big brother should with his little brother. I want you to know I've always wanted to, but for some reason (and believe me it's always been a good one); your mom and our dad have always wanted to supervise me being with you. From now on, I want to hang out, and I want to be your big brother, not only on paper, but also in life too!

I love you,
Your big brother,
Ben

Ben's letters came frequently—every few days, sometimes even more. He wrote to tell his dad that he was working on his fractions in math and that he was reading *Treasure Island* in his free time. He also told his dad that "some fool" had punched him, but he didn't fight back because he didn't want to earn himself any more time at the detention center. The staff applauded him for coming to them instead of "handling it" on his own, even when he knew he would now get labeled as a rat.

"P.S. Tell Susan and Nick I love them also," he wrote.

On December 15, Ben wrote to Jeff.

Dad

Other than being away from my family and having to worry about being shanked, it's all right. Anyway, what have you been up to? Same old thing here.

I saw a minister while I was in Sylmar, and we had talked for a while. I told him how you and my mom had been divorced since I was four, and all that junk. He told me that I was your treasure, and even though you had another son, I was your first, and that because you were wrapped up in your divorce, you didn't take time

*away, and pull me aside to tell me I was your treasure.
Is that true, or is it bullshit? He said a whole bunch
of stuff, and it really made me think, but that's good
for me.*

*Anyway, I'm just writing you to tell you I'm OK, and
I love you, so write back when you get a chance.*

Love Ben

He wrote to each of us individually and collectively, and
he didn't hold it against us that we didn't write back nearly
as often. He said he understood.

Proudly, he mentioned that he was on the honor roll and
that his teachers were encouraging him to take the GED,
a high school equivalency exam that would enable him to
get a high school diploma. Aside from studying and lift-
ing weights, there wasn't much else to do there. Sometimes
he played dominoes, he said. And he was even reading a
mushy romance novel that wasn't half bad.

December 21, 1994

Nick

*Hey how are you doing? I'm OK, except for the fact
that I'm going to be missing Christmas this year. I don't
know—but it hurts when I think about it.*

*I moved camps on Monday, and now I'm at camp
Scobee. It's at the same facility, meaning Challenger.
But it's for people who are 707B's. I don't know if you
know what I did, but I hit someone with brass knuckles.
And that is an assault with a deadly weapon.*

*The supervisor of the camp that I'm at said if I do
good, I could get out in two to three months from now.
The thing is, is that I have to stay here for eight weeks,
and if they see that my behavior is good, I go to an open
camp. If they see my behavior is bad, then I go to a lock
down camp. An open camp is more like kickback, and*

I will be able to leave at certain times. A lock down camp is a prison. Now if I do excellent while I'm here I could do the eight weeks and come home. But when I say excellent, I mean I have to be on good terms with all of the staff and I have to do excellent schoolwork.

You know I'll try my best.

Now about you, if your mom and dad are coming down on you pretty hard, I hate to say it, but I am to blame. They see me, and how they treated me while I grew up and then they think they went wrong somewhere.

So don't go haywire, and get all-rebellious while I'm away. Deal with it until I get home. And I promise when I do come home I will help you, and talk to them. If there's anything you want me to tell them now, just write me, and let me know.

I love you
Ben

On the bottom of the page was a marking that said "OK to send out," followed by a staff member's initials.

Ben knew he had a problem keeping his temper under control, and in his letters, he talked about how he sometimes felt like he was about to explode on someone but that he was doing his best to keep his composure so he could come home sooner and get a "fresh start."

From what we could tell, Ben was not just doing well there, but actually feeling some pride when the staff recognized his good behavior. He had a coveted "board leader" job, and said that the other guys were very jealous about it. He also took to informing the staff when guys needed to be kept in line, although that gave him "snitch" status and resulted in a fight.

The fight happened in the janitor's room, where Ben had gone to get sponges to clean a bathroom. Even though someone else attacked him, Ben was sent to the "box" (solitary confinement) for forty-eight hours, and his board leader job was taken away.

One thing that got him through, however, was that his

girlfriend stood by him. "She writes to me almost every day and every letter I get from her fills me with love and joy," he wrote. It was nice to hear, even though we had very mixed feelings about the girlfriend—she was twenty years old and had a son. What was she doing with a boy who was just sixteen years old? We thought it was ridiculous, but it was hard to argue with something that filled him with "love and joy."

He also wanted to set a good example for Nick. Jeff must have mentioned to Ben that Nick's grades had slipped and Nick was gaining a bit of a "class clown" reputation, so Ben offered to talk to him—if we'd let him. He wrote Nick a letter.

I heard you have been having a little trouble at school. Well, I can only say this. If you're going to be a class clown, you're not going to ever get into any college, and if you have to be a class clown, you might as well be a screw-up all around.

If I were you, I would just do my work when I'm supposed to, but when I was your age, I wouldn't listen to anyone. But look where I am now! I guess you're going to do what you want, but think about tomorrow, not only today. Just think, I want to take you and your friends to Disneyland when I get out. But do you think Mom and Dad will let you go if your grades are bad? I don't.

Well, enough about that. How is baseball? I heard Dad beamed you with a pitch. Don't sweat it. I can't even tell you how many times he's hit me. The main thing is not to be afraid of the ball. Yeah, it hurts when it hits you, but it isn't going to kill you. Who knows? Maybe you can be as good as me one day. I really doubt it, though. (Ha-ha.)

Write back and tell me how you are.

Be good,
Love, your Big Brother,
Ben

From Challenger, Ben was moved to Camp Miller, a low-security facility where he got to play on a traveling baseball team. When Ben's release date neared, Jeff and Ben began preparing a plan for when he'd come home. He would work in the shop with Jeff from 7 a.m. to 3 p.m., and his curfew at night would be 10:00 p.m. Beyond that, Ben looked to me for guidance.

I really want it to work this time when I come home, so please work with me and I will do more than enough to make you happy with me. As of now, I am just waiting for you to write me back and let me know my boundaries at home, and what you can and can't live with. I really want them in writing as soon as possible, so I can get them in my head, and get used to the idea, and learn to live with them.

On February 25, 1995, Ben came home from Camp Miller. We gave him a "welcome home" card and got him enrolled in a baseball league again. A few weeks later, Nick wrote in our journal:

Dear Mom,

We haven't written in so long! I am really excited Ben came home. I want to do a lot of stuff with him.

For so long I have been so lonely with no one to look up to. Dad's never home so I barely get to see him.

I hope Ben changes from what he used to do because sometimes he hung out with the wrong crowd.

Love Nick

Then Nick told me that he'd like to start keeping a journal with Ben, just like the one we kept with each other. I told him it was a great idea and that he'd never regret it. A few months later, though, Nick noticed that Ben hadn't changed much. As far as we knew, he had avoided gangs and violence, but we suspected he and his girlfriend were both still using drugs.

"What's her problem? Doesn't she care about herself or Ben?" Nick asked me.

I didn't have a good answer for him. Why do kids decide to screw up their lives? I have no idea, but some of them just seem determined to do so no matter how many chances they get to do the right thing. Ben was still an enigma to me. I wondered if he'd ever really get his act straight, if that angel on his shoulder would ever knock out the devil for good.

"We'll see," Nick said.

I worried about Ben being home again, and whether or not I'd find another gun in the house, or a gang on my front lawn. Some days I wished he were still in the detention center, where I could care about him from a distance and know that my son was safe from his influence and the dangers that seemed to follow him.

In October, I wrote to Nick:

I am very proud of you . . . who you are . . . how you act.

The past 11 years of your life, my life has never been so complete. You are why I am who I am. And why I act the way I act. Our mutual respect and communication will take us through another 11 years.

Let's see—you'll be 22. That would be either 3 or 4 years into college. I'm sure 11 years seems like forever. But I can honestly tell you, you'll be looking back at this comment and thinking, "1995! That was like yesterday! And here it is, 2006."

It would be nice if we could slow down life, especially during the fun times, but we can't. That's why it's so important to be as good as you can be. Make each day your best . . . be honest . . . be respectful . . .

Just as you are!

I love you, Nick.

P.S. Ben is wearing me down mentally . . . as you said, "We'll see."

In 1997, my father moved in with us following colon surgery. It was a very uncomfortable experience at first, bathing my own father and dealing with his pain. Nick had a very hectic after-school schedule that included tae kwon do lessons, three-times-a-week Hebrew and Judaism classes, and three-times-a-week drama club rehearsals. I was so stretched to the limit that I became frazzled at the stupidest things. When my father told me he didn't want the chocolate ice cream I bought for him, I actually cried.

Then our on-again, off-again living arrangements with Ben turned off-again when he came home with a pair of pit bull puppies.

"You can't have those dogs here," Jeff said.

"They're my dogs!" Ben said. "If I can't have them here, then I'm leaving."

And he did. Ben never stayed put very long at that time. He lived with a girlfriend, then with a couple of friends, then with Leah and her boyfriend, with occasional stops at our house, too, from time to time. Jeff made it clear to Ben that he was welcome at our house anytime, so long as he agreed to follow the rules. If he couldn't follow the rules, we were through putting up with it.

What made it worse was that Nick, now nearly thirteen, was going through what felt like a rough patch, too, where he was very concerned about fitting in. It was hard for me to understand—he was handsome, girls had crushes on him, and he was well-spoken and funny. Yet he felt like he didn't know where he belonged socially. On one hand, he really loved the friends in his drama group. On the other, were drama kids cool enough?

He began wearing safety pins on his clothes in a punk style to match with a tougher group of kids. I took the safety pins away, which upset him. Nick liked this new group of friends, and he didn't like that his mom was standing in his way of "expressing himself." I told him that I didn't like that he was being influenced, rather than being a leader.

He also wanted us to quit calling him Nicholas.

"My name is *Nick*," he would say. That only incited Leah, who loved to tease him.

"OK, Nicole," she'd say, which drove him up a wall. There were enough years between them that she didn't see Nick as a pain-in-the-butt little brother; she and her friends enjoyed teasing him and hanging out with him. Even they noticed a difference in him around this time, though. You could just see the turmoil spinning around inside him.

Nick's friends described him as a good listener and well liked. One of the positive traits he shared with Ben was that he also thought it was important to stand up for underdogs and not let other kids get bullied. By no means was Nick a tough guy, but he was big enough to be imposing, and smart enough to intimidate even many of his teachers. He took advantage of that point sometimes when he was reprimanded in school. It was hard for teachers to argue with him when he could verbally outsmart them.

That was partly due to his love for reading, which never let up. He treasured his books, and learning, though not necessarily the subjects that were taught in school. He wanted to learn about the things he felt like learning about, on his own schedule. So he would read history and science books for fun and still get only mediocre grades in his classes because he didn't do the required homework—strange for a boy who had been placed in a gifted program in elementary school.

I didn't want to be one of those moms who lost her handle on her child because she wasn't paying attention, so I boosted my already-impressive roster of spying techniques. I regularly went through Nick's pockets and drawers and read his notes. Do you have any idea how hard it was to refold a letter into one of those crazy origami configurations kids used? Before long, I had to master stars and triangles just so that Nick wouldn't realize that I'd read his love letters . . . which were very, very sweet. He made his mom proud. *My romantic son!*

Of course, my overprotective instincts did not go unnoticed. It bothered Nick that I didn't want him walking down the street to McDonald's alone or that I wouldn't let him go to a friend's house if I didn't know that friend's parents—or their phone number. It bothered him that I was so "in his business." But, I told myself, one day he would be glad that he had a mother who cared enough to keep him on track.

In the midst of this struggle, he was making great strides in his drama club. Watching him perform, I thought, "Now, I may be biased because I'm his mom, but this kid is good!"

Turned out my mom-bias was shared by lots of others. That month, he competed in his first drama festival. His group performed Shakespeare's *Twelfth Night* and took second place out of twenty-three schools. Nick competed in the "B Division"—a level usually reserved for older students. Friends said they had never even heard of a seventh-grader like Nick in the B Division.

His drama teacher was so impressed with him that she called us at 10 p.m. one night to ask if Nick could audition for a Disney commercial. That was exciting for all of us. I told Nick that I would gladly be his chauffeur if he wanted to become an actor.

That summer, we also began preparing in earnest for Nick's bar mitzvah. The bar mitzvah is a ceremony marking the age of maturity (usually thirteen), when a person is expected to be ready to accept Jewish responsibilities and participate as an adult in the synagogue. Every single day of August was filled with planning. The celebration after the ceremony had to be at a big, beautiful hall (we planned to invite a lot of guests, after all). We needed to arrange dresses and suits, balloons, limos, flowers, challah, prayer books, yarmulkes, funny table decorations with a fast-food theme . . .

At the ceremony, Nick spoke about how meaningful his bar mitzvah was to him, which I knew was true because he'd been talking to me about how important it felt to him. His father had not had a bar mitzvah ceremony, so Nick felt that made it doubly important—he wanted to honor his dad. During the ceremony, he called his dad to the Torah to recite a blessing, to make up for the one he'd never gotten to say when he was thirteen.

Nick surprised even himself when he decided to continue his Jewish education by enrolling in the Los Angeles Hebrew High School program.

The party afterward was a great celebration. Nick wrote beautiful little speeches to honor his guests, inviting each of them up with him to light candles. I embarrassed Nick by hugging and kissing him in front of his friends.

There was a DJ and dancing and drinking . . . for Ben, a little too much drinking. Jeff hadn't been paying attention, but I'd been watching how many drinks Ben had. At the end of the night, I overheard Ben asking his dad if he could drive Nick and his girlfriend home, and Jeff said, "OK."

"No," I interrupted. "You've been drinking, and we're responsible for these kids." I knew he wanted to share a few minutes alone with his brother on this special day, but I obviously couldn't allow him to drive them home. Ben looked to Jeff to override me, but Jeff doesn't do that.

"Sorry, Ben. I didn't know you were drinking. You can't take them," Jeff said.

Angrily, Ben left the party, jumped into his friend's car, and screeched the tires down the street.

Instead, as planned, Nick and his friends took two limousines back to our house, where we continued the celebration. Ben showed up and Nick followed him to his room. After a while, I walked in and said to Ben, "I'm glad you could pull yourself together and come to the house. This is a very special day and celebrating without you wouldn't have felt right."

He stared me in the eyes and said, "I don't believe you. I have never believed anything you've said to me."

I cried, which got Nick upset. Then came the anger. This was Nick's day. This was a day I wanted to remember—how well Nick had done reading the Torah, how he'd handled the squeak in his voice, how handsome he'd looked. And yet somehow it was going to be about Ben again.

Someone summoned Jeff from outside and told him I

was upset. He came in and witnessed Ben and I yelling at each other.

"You're going to have to leave," Jeff said.

On the front lawn, Ben called out, "You're a bitch. You do whatever she says. I'll never talk to you guys again."

At some point that night, Ben gave Nick his father's ring. It wasn't really what Jeff had in mind. Because Jeff had received it as a gift for his sixteenth birthday, and gave it to Ben for his sixteenth, the idea was that Ben would one day give it to his own son on his sixteenth birthday, too. But maybe as a way of making up for the scene he had caused, Ben gave Nick the ring instead—and it never left Nick's finger afterward.

Soon after the bar mitzvah, we also threw Nick a thirteenth birthday party at our house. His friends played Ping-Pong, darts, and billiards. We gave them all disposable cameras, and they took pictures of the kinds of things thirteen-year-olds take pictures of. I have pictures of my toilet. Aah, kids.

To compensate for my overprotectiveness, I also tried to be a fun mom. I let the kids and their friends listen to loud music even if it irritated my ears. I made fruit and ice cream smoothies for Nick's friends, and I let Nick decorate his room however he wanted, as I had done with the other two kids, too.

In March of 1998, Nick wrote in our journal:

To whom it may concern, Of course you realize that in a few years NASA is going to send this very book into space, trying to frighten alien life forms. What could be scarier than our problems!?

Just in case they read it 300 years from now, Ms. Young rocks! I'm in 8th grade. Now that I'm through being sweet, did you know that Geoff Capes threw a brick 146 ft 7 inches?!! Now you know.

Love Rabbi Nick Markowitz

That gave me a smile. Rabbi Nick. He would go on to sign a few of his journal entries this way, and it made me wonder sometimes . . . was my son really going to be a rabbi? He'd be the funniest rabbi in town, surely.

We spent that summer going camping and on a cruise. Nick also convinced his dad to buy Rollerblades so the two of them could go in-line skating together. Nick was already pretty good at it when Jeff joined him for the first time. On their way down a hill, Jeff realized he didn't know how to stop. He tried to roll into a patch of grass and instead tumbled into someone's driveway.

"Dad! Are you OK?" Nick said, racing over. With nothing hurt but his pride, Jeff got back up and kept going. The two of them would skate for miles together that summer and the next.

We also let Nick take a trip to Colorado with Leah, and when he came home, he was glowing with energy and happiness. He told us a story about the trip—as they drove through the mountains in complete blackness listening to *Sgt. Pepper's Lonely Hearts Club Band*, a lightning storm began. With each enormous flash of light came some of the most awe-inspiring sights either of them had ever seen. Out of pitch blackness, silver-lined purple mountains remained lit for at least fifteen seconds at a time. Both of them felt it was breathtaking and otherworldly.

The two of them were a good team. Leah acted as Nick's confidante and tutor, and Nick taught her how to play video games and kept her laughing. They loved playing with people's heads . . . they'd challenge each other to make up crazy "facts" and get people to believe them. There may still be adults out there who believe that the first tampons were made of bread, thanks to the convincing lessons by Nick and Leah.

In September 1998, Nick started high school. My son, in high school? Wasn't it just yesterday that he was finger painting and making macaroni necklaces? I tried to be a mature and reasonable mother, but I really just wanted to drag him back home and make cupcakes and try to get him to quit this whole growing-up thing.

High school was an easy transition for him, though . . . easier than it was for me. He got smarter and smarter, and his vocabulary was increasing beyond mine. It embarrassed me sometimes that my son could out-argue me. He loved to argue about anything and everything, in particular psychoanalyzing us to try to weasel his way out of the household rules—he wanted to stay up later, use the phone later, go out with his friends whenever he wanted, postpone his homework.

There was a fight brewing in his mind between being Mama's Boy and Independent Cool Guy, but he was still my loving son. On my fortieth birthday, Jeff rented a limo for me to go out with some friends, and Nick made me a tape to play on our ride so we'd have continuous music. Songs like "Brown Eyed Girl" and "We Are the Champions" along with some purely silly songs and even some rave music.

———

Leah had been in college in Colorado Springs, then lived with us again while she worked at Disney Studios, where she met Ian, the man who would become her husband. Ian was loving and easygoing, willing to do anything for Leah. I wanted to help her plan a big fairy-tale wedding, but in the midst of the plans, she realized she was pregnant—and going through horrible morning sickness—and wanted to scrap the big ol' catering-hall idea.

In July 1999, they married in Las Vegas. Nick and Ben were both in the wedding party, but Ben was late for the ceremony. Ben's new girlfriend was in Las Vegas, too, but I don't think she even showed up for the ceremony. They were drunk or on drugs, or both.

The reception was at the Bellagio overlooking the beautiful fountains, and Ben wanted his dad to give him money to gamble. He had just turned twenty-one a couple of weeks prior, and somehow had gotten it into his head that we'd given Leah a lot of money for *her* twenty-first birthday. We hadn't; I don't know where he got that idea. But he argued with Leah about it right there in the casino after her wedding.

"They gave you thousands of dollars for your birthday!"

"What in the world are you talking about? They did not!"

"Yes they did, and now it's supposed to be my turn. I should have money to gamble. Or are we just going to forget that it was my birthday, too?"

Jeff and Ben ended up in a screaming match that nearly came to blows. Another big event for someone else that somehow wound up with Ben as the center of attention. Leah kicked him out.

She and Ian moved into an apartment with a tennis court close to our house. Nick, now almost fifteen years old, was Jeff's doubles partner. They would challenge Ian and his friend Roberto about once a week, then come home crowing about their victories.

One thing was bothering Nick, though: he was tired of us keeping him from Ben. More and more, he seemed to look up to Ben for reasons that were hard for me to figure out. He would sneak off and go to parties with Ben and his friends—including at least one at Ben's friend Jesse James Hollywood's house. I didn't know that until years later.

Hollywood was a drug dealer who mostly dealt "high-end" marijuana and other recreational drugs. His father, Jack Hollywood, was a major drug dealer dealing more in low-grade marijuana. Of course, I didn't know anything about the Hollywoods or their lives then . . . but they would one day take a place of monumental importance in my life.

Nick's best friend, Ryan Orenstein, had been at a party at Jesse James Hollywood's home with his older brother, too. Both Nick and Ryan had older brothers who were into the party scene, so the younger boys were invited along from an early age. Nick sometimes came home smelling of cigarettes. I chalked it up to normal teenage rebellion and didn't make too much of it. I didn't know he was with Ben at those parties, or that the parties were full of drugs, and guns. Actually, I didn't realize that he ever went to parties other than the drama club parties that I took him to.

Jesse Hollywood liked to pull out his guns to show off to people. Maybe he liked the idea of keeping people in line by reminding them that there was always a threat of death in the air. Jesse had many underlings, including Ben, who sold drugs for him, and he operated on a "consignment" basis—the other guys would take the drugs and try to sell them, then pay fees back to Hollywood. Several of them ran tabs, including Ben. They called the system "fronting."

When Hollywood took out his new TEC-9 semiautomatic pistol to show around the room, Ryan and his older brother left. But Ben, who noticed that the gun was loaded, decided to stick around with Nick. Hollywood also had a shotgun and an HK 40 semiautomatic handgun from his godfather that he kept on his nightstand and took with him in his waistband when he went out on drug runs and other trips.

Hollywood also had a full-sized gym in his house, where he and Ben worked out together. One day, Hollywood went with Ben when Nick skipped school and called his brother for a ride. Nick failed a class that year and had to go to summer school; for a boy as smart as Nick, it obviously wasn't because he didn't understand the material, but aside from his drama classes and his social circle, he just didn't care about school anymore by then.

I didn't like what I saw. Nick was taking steps closer and closer to Ben, while I wanted them to have as little contact as possible. But the more I tried to pull him back, the more Nick pushed away from me.

Then came a day that July 1999 when Nick disappeared after an argument. I went out of my mind with worry. *Where could he be? What could have happened?*

A little while later, we got a call from Ben saying that

Nick was with him and that he and his girlfriend were talking to him to get him cooled down. Nick had "run away" by calling Ben on the house phone, then walking around the corner and waiting for him. Later, Ben suggested that he'd like to keep Nick for the night and would get him to summer school on Monday morning. Ben brought Nick home to us after school, but Nick was still angry. "I don't want you keeping me from Ben," he said. "He's my brother and I love him."

How do you explain to a fourteen-year-old that you're only trying to protect him? How can he see into the future and know that when he's twenty-four, or thirty-four, he'll understand why we did the things we did?

We couldn't, so we called in a mediator. We also attended family counseling with Nick to try to help us get him to understand that we weren't trying to punish him by keeping him away from Ben—we were just trying to get him on the right path and away from trouble.

Ben was a strange paradox when it came to Nick. On the one hand, as we'd later learn, he punched a cousin when he found out that the cousin had smoked pot with Nick and Ryan—their first time getting high. The last thing he wanted, he said, was for Nick to follow in his footsteps. And yet before long, he was getting high with Nick, too, and introducing him to friends of his who dealt drugs. Mostly, Nick "just" smoked pot, but he apparently occasionally tried harder drugs. And for a couple of weeks, Nick was a "self-proclaimed pot dealer," selling dime bags to his friends, Ryan later said. I had no idea.

Everyone in school who knew Nick also knew Ryan, and vice versa. They shared most of the same friends, but Nick had some groups he hung around with separately, too. He loved to play board games, while Ryan didn't get that at all—he was more of an outdoors type. So Nick found some "board-game friends" to play with, too.

Ryan's family had a tradition that they would all graduate from Bryn Athens school in Pennsylvania, so that's where he went for school his sophomore year. It was a big adjustment for the two best friends to be apart. They'd been inseparable since kindergarten, and after just a month, Nick flew with Ryan's aunt and mother to visit Ryan just before his own sophomore year started.

We continued seeing the counselor, where we tried to work on our problems—primarily, that Nick was still angry with us. When Leah's daughter was born, and everyone was celebrating, Nick was oddly sad. He watched Ben hold the baby, but he couldn't seem to bring himself to hold her.

"She's not really my niece," Nick told Ben.

"Of course she is. What do you mean?" Ben asked.

"I feel like we're not really related. You're her uncle, but who am I?"

Nick always felt the strains of the separation—the "half" part of "half siblings." Ben and Leah were the only siblings he had, and he didn't want there to be anything distancing them. In part because I hated seeing him so torn, and in part because Ben was now responsibly working with his dad, and—to my knowledge—no longer involved with drugs, I let Ben and his girlfriend move into our house. *Maybe Nick will stop being so angry with us*, I thought.

Not only did Ben's return go peacefully, but something unbelievable happened . . . I started talking to his mother. After all those hateful years, the two of us came to a sort of understanding and said we would try to put the past behind us for the kids' sake.

As we got closer to New Year's Eve, I felt more and more that it was an important occasion—it was a new millennium, after all! I didn't want to ring in the year 2000 by phone with my loved ones; I wanted them all to be together so I could hug them. So I planned a party at our house and told Nick to invite his friends, too.

We covered the tables with black and gold lamé fabric and had black and gold balloons covering the ceiling. A Ping-Pong table, pool table, and darts stayed in use the whole night, and loud music blared from the stereo. The neighbors didn't complain, because they were all there!

Ben and Leah's mom came too, and we toasted to the New Year together. It felt like a night of peace and new beginnings—we even shared a cigar and let the kids paint our faces with an "invisible-ink" marker that showed up only under black light. Boy, were they lousy artists.

It was one of those nights I never wanted to end. And I was oblivious to the fact that, in the next room, Ben had just slapped Nick across the face in front of all his friends because Nick had taken some kind of a pill and was stoned out of his mind. All I knew was that it looked like everyone was having fun.

Leah tried to tell us what was going on, but Jeff and I weren't listening. She liked to tell us how blind we were to what he was doing. Maybe I *was* blind, but Nick's behavior just looked like normal teenage rebellion to me. I suspected he might have tried smoking pot, but things were already so touchy with him that I didn't want to come down too hard. I wanted him to know he could always talk to us.

Ben and his girlfriend didn't stay with us for long. He found out that she was doing hard drugs, and he was trying to clean up his life. I think he told us he was going to take on a new construction job. We didn't leave off on bad terms, though, and Nick didn't seem so mad at us anymore.

The rest of the school year was pleasantly uneventful. On our drive each morning, Nick would point out the falcon or two perched up on the light posts along our route. He said falcons were some of his favorite birds.

"They always seem to be there," he said.

"Maybe they're watching us," I said.

Nick was an outdoors person, like his dad. In Jeff's youth, he had a motorcycle to get around, and now that Nick was fifteen, Jeff thought it would be fun for the two of them to graduate from Rollerblades; he bought two Yamaha 225 motorcycles, and they puttered around the neighborhood and to the beach, and they'd ride to the park to play tennis and then to the movies together once a week. Early in Nick's "training," they went into a canyon that normally didn't have much traffic, but a car passed and it startled

Nick; he rode to the shoulder of the road and braked, and the bike slid out from under him. He was pretty badly bruised and cut up, and the bike was damaged. Jeff felt guilty and responsible.

I took Nick to the emergency room the next morning to get his wounds cleaned properly, and Jeff said, "I hope this is the worst thing that ever happens to him."

With Nick in high school and the other kids out of the house, I thought it would be good for me to take on a part-time job and make a little spending money, so I started folding clothes at Nordstrom's Rack—a local outlet where you could pick up a dress worth $150 for $19 on a lucky day. The only problem was that I didn't make any money there; I "reinvested" it all in the business. I actually paid to work there!

Nick's friend Ryan came back home for the summer, and it seemed like we were whole again. We went camping, like we did just about every summer. Sometimes it was just us, but in recent years, Nick had usually brought a friend. We'd go for anywhere from two days to a week, usually to somewhere within about an hour from home. On some of the trips, I'd take the kids, and Jeff would join us only at night after work—that was his idea of a vacation.

Nick absolutely loved camping. We'd fish for trout and catfish using Velveeta cheese for bait, play board games, toss around Frisbees and baseballs, and eat sandwiches . . . which usually fell on the ground at some point and became literal *sand*wiches.

Soon after we came home from one of these camping trips, Nick was in such a good mood that a miracle occurred: he washed my car, without my even asking. Now, it's possible that he was just being a terrific son, or maybe it had something to do with that new learner's driving permit that was now hung on the refrigerator. It was getting close to his sixteenth birthday and the start of his junior year. He had just passed his written test and was going to learn how to drive. Maybe he was looking at the car and thinking, "This baby is going to be mine someday soon."

On the days when I was working, either my mom or Jeff would supervise Nick. My mom was in charge of the house one day in August, and Nick loved her dearly. He still called her Grandma Pooh, which had been her dog's name when he was a little boy. He was listening to music with his friends when he stopped in to check on her.

"Is the music too loud for you?" he asked.

"No, I'm just reading. If it gets too loud, I'll take out my hearing aids."

He laughed, gave her a thumbs-up, went back to his room, and turned down the music anyway.

Three days later, the world ended. At least, mine did.

CHAPTER 5

THE OPENING ACT

Ben and Jesse James Hollywood had known of each other since their Little League baseball days, though they weren't close friends. Hollywood had played on the Pirates team, which his father coached. He was a good shortstop, though some of the parents noted that he could get bratty and throw tantrums on the field. Some of his friends were also on the team: Jesse Rugge, William Skidmore, and Ryan Hoyt.

Ben was two years older, so he wasn't on the same team, but he was an All-Star player and knew all of the boys by sight, and he and William Skidmore's older brother had played together. It was, by all accounts, a tight-knit group—both the kids and the parents. The parents ran the Snack Shack, where they took turns flipping burgers, serving hot dogs, and pouring sodas. I often went to the games, sometimes sitting next to Ben's mother. After their games, the Pirates would sometimes go back to the Hollywoods' house to swim in their pool. I wonder how many parents knew what Jack's real occupation was.

It wasn't until Ben was about twenty years old that he began to socialize with Jesse James Hollywood's group.

One of the first times Ben went out with them was at a party in an upscale gated community. Ben was standing nearby when Ryan Hoyt got into a fight with another young man at the party. Before long, the man had Hoyt down on the ground with his head pinned against a stucco wall and was about to kick his head like a soccer ball.

Ben and one of his friends intervened, sending the man fleeing to his car. Afterward, Ben took Hoyt home with him and helped him get his wounds cleaned up, because he was in pretty bad shape. It was a show of mercy he would come to regret deeply. Shortly thereafter, Ben approached Hollywood to ask if he was interested in dealing drugs to him. Ben had burned his bridges with most of the other local dealers by that point, running up bad debts with each of them, so he needed a new supplier. He liked the quick money that selling drugs provided.

Hollywood agreed, and was soon fronting Ben between ten thousand and forty thousand dollars' worth of marijuana per week. Ben would pay Hollywood back the next week for his debts. At times, Hollywood himself could collect more than one hundred thousand dollars in a single drug transaction. In addition to the drug dealing, though, they became friends. Ben was an everyday member of this little clan.

Hollywood had a pit bull named Chump, but Ryan Hoyt was the real chump of the group. Of all the kids, Ryan was probably the one closest to the Hollywood family, starting in early childhood.

Ryan's parents divorced when he was five years old, and his grandmother would later say that his mother was "unstable" and that his stepmother seemed to hate him. His father was no Mike Brady, either. He reportedly beat Ryan's mother while she was pregnant, and he beat up his sons as their stepmother yelled at them. His sister was a heroin addict, and his younger brother would become a convicted felon, serving twelve years for armed robbery.

With all the trouble in both his homes, Ryan went look-ing for a new family and latched onto the Hollywoods, regarding Jack Hollywood as a father figure. He became very ingrained in their everyday lives, taking family vaca-tions with them and even babysitting for Jesse Hollywood's younger brother, J. P.

For one of Ryan's birthdays, Jesse James Hollywood had bought him an inexpensive car, plus some money for new tires and registration—but Ryan didn't get around to switching over the registration and racked up almost one thousand dollars' worth of parking tickets in Hollywood's name. To bail him out of that one, Hollywood fronted him half a pound of marijuana to sell, but Ryan didn't come through on that, either.

Now he owed Hollywood money, which was exactly the position Hollywood liked to be in. Having people owe him money gave him power . . . and having people like *Ryan* owe him money was the sweetest of all. Ryan had no sense of self-worth. He would do whatever Hollywood told him to do, and that now included cleaning his house, painting his fence, getting his little brother from school, and picking up after his pit bulls. In effect, Ryan Hoyt became Jesse James Hollywood's personal servant. Everyone in the group saw it, and most of them thought it was pretty funny.

"I think Hoyt got a lot more crap than everyone else did," said Hollywood's friend Casey Sheehan.

Even Ryan Hoyt's grandmother could see that her grandson was inappropriately kowtowing to Hollywood.

"This young man has been a friend of yours for a long time, but he does not run your life," she once told her grand-son, according to a *Santa Barbara News-Press* article. "It's time you get a decent job and figure out what you're going to do with your life."

Aside from drug dealing, Ryan also had a job working at a local market, but it seemed he was working there only to pay off Hollywood—and when he didn't have enough for his weekly payment, Hollywood would tack on high "interest."

One time in February 2000, as they videotaped themselves smoking from a bong, drinking, and playing cards, Hollywood turned the camera on Hoyt and asked, "How much money you got in the bank?"

"Uh . . . I got four . . ."

"Tomorrow, I want the money you got in the bank."

"All right."

On the same tape, Hollywood bugged Hoyt about the money a second time. Hoyt stood with his backward blue baseball cap pulled nearly down to his eyes, looking like a dog that's getting kicked.

"What's gonna be there tomorrow, Hoyt? I'm serious, man."

"Stop recording."

"What's gonna be in the bank?"

"Five hundred. At least five hundred. Now stop fucking recording."

Hollywood was accustomed to having people do whatever he said, whenever he said. That was the direct opposite of Ben's personality. Ben was one of the main underlings in Hollywood's orbit, but he didn't act much like an underling . . . which is where the trouble started. Ben called himself "Bugsy" after volatile Mob leader Benjamin "Bugsy" Siegel.

Hollywood's position was strange for a man of his small stature: five feet four inches and 140 pounds. About average size, for a teenage girl. He took muscle supplements and lifted weights daily to try to look more imposing, but it was of little use. But Hollywood's power didn't come from his physique. It came from his mouth, his father, his army of sycophants who owed him money, and his gun collection.

At El Camino Real High School, he played second base on the junior varsity baseball team, where his coach remembered him as a serious player and an emotional kid. Toward the end of his sophomore year, he was expelled for a violent fight with an administrator, reportedly stemming from concerns over the tank top he'd been wearing, and was transferred to a different school. The principal never fully explained that one to the media when they asked about it, except to say that it was a pretty bad fight. Likewise, Hollywood was suspended a week before his graduation at his second high school, though the principal there wouldn't explain why either.

But for Hollywood, it didn't matter much. One hardly needs an outstanding academic record to make a living selling drugs. Despite being self-described as obsessive-compulsive about cleanliness, Hollywood liked to throw parties and be the center of social attention. Looking like a mini thug with his backward baseball caps and tank tops, he barked out orders, and people jumped. His position as the leader of his clan of miscreants had gone unchallenged—until Ben decided he wasn't backing down anymore.

It started with a drug deal gone bad. Hollywood was talking about going to San Diego to collect on a drug debt of about two thousand dollars, and not in a polite way. Ben was friendly with the debtor, so he said, "Wait a minute, I know the guy. Let me go down there with you and handle it."

They hopped into Hollywood's black Mercedes and drove. In Hollywood's trunk was a duffel bag with duct tape in it, and a bat. But once they got there, they could see that there was no chance of collection no matter what kind of violence they dished out—the guy had no money at all. So Ben helped the guy cook up a scheme to save himself.

The guy was friendly with an Ecstasy dealer, which got Ben's wheels turning.

"It would be a good idea if you have your friend come over here with the Ecstasy, and we'll make it look like we just jacked you." When the debtor hesitated, Ben told him, "It's probably better that you don't owe Hollywood the money. Owe it to some other dude instead."

The guy called his friend and asked for two hundred pills, saying that someone who wanted to buy them was out in the car. When the first guy came to the window, pretending to show them the drugs for inspection, Ben and

Hollywood grabbed the bag and drove off, making it look like a robbery.

Now Ben told Hollywood that he'd take on the debt himself, and pay it off by selling the pills for twenty dollars apiece—keeping the two-thousand-dollar profit after he repaid Hollywood his two thousand dollars. But after Ben handed off the drugs to someone to sell at a party, he got a complaint from a customer who said that the pills weren't doing anything. So Ben took one himself—sure enough, it had no effect. Later, he went to Hollywood's house.

"These things are bunk. I don't know what you want me to do," Ben said. He told Hollywood that he wasn't going to sell them anymore, which meant he wasn't going to pay back the rest of the money. He gave Hollywood about six hundred dollars from what he had sold at that point, plus another two hundred dollars that he borrowed from his dad. He told Jeff he needed it toward rent because he was staying with Hollywood part-time.

"No, I gotta get paid. You're short," Hollywood said. "You took it upon yourself."

"That's all I got. I'm not selling them."

"You're kidding me, right?"

Ben wasn't kidding. The amount still owed was twelve hundred dollars. Ben tried to give Hollywood the remainder of the fake pills.

"Go fuck yourself. Pay me the money," Hollywood said.

Ben waved him off and walked out.

———————

Hollywood's expenses were not that of a normal nineteen-year-old. He owned his own three-bedroom stucco home in West Hills, drove a black Mercedes and a blue sports car with two-thousand-dollar speakers, and was about to pay for his girlfriend Michelle's boob job. She already had a tattoo just above her backside that said "Jesse James."

To explain why his son could afford a forty-five-thousand-dollar cash down payment on his own home before he was

even out of his teens, Jack Hollywood would later say it
came from insurance money from an accident where his
son had hurt his shoulder. And OK, fine, maybe his son
sold "a little weed."

It was no great secret that the Hollywoods—both Jack
and Jesse James—were drug dealers. For a couple of years
in the early 1990s, it seemed that Jack Hollywood tried
to go legit; he moved his family out to Colorado Springs
and started a sports bar and restaurant, saying he wanted
to get his kids away from gangs and drugs. Ironically,
though, Jesse James would later say that it was in Colorado
that he began selling drugs, during his early teen years.
When the sports bar failed, the Hollywoods moved back
to California.

Now, Jesse James Hollywood's neighbors noticed all the
kids who stopped by for just a few minutes, then sped off.
They saw Hollywood smoking with his friends out front,
all of them in tank tops and jeans, many with tattoos. They
saw the two pit bulls kept tied to a tree in the backyard
and the expensive tricked-out cars—one of which actually
landed in *Lowrider Euro* magazine because Hollywood
had mailed photos of it to an editor there. He used to carry
the magazine around to show it off to people. And Hollywood had no real job aside from sporadic work as a carpenter. So, how did this teenager afford this lifestyle? It
added up to a pretty clear portrait of a young drug dealer,
but no one ever reported suspicious activity to the police.
Nobody wanted to mess with the Hollywoods.

Nobody but Ben.

At that point, even though they were arguing about
the money, Ben still considered Hollywood a friend. The
tough-guy talk was just his way, Ben figured. They'd
get over it. Several months went by, with him not seeing
much of Hollywood because Ben had decided to straighten
out and work with his dad. That meant, however, that he
was making less money than he had as a drug dealer. He
accepted that he still owed the twelve hundred dollars, but
he wasn't making any more payments yet, and Hollywood

wasn't bothering him about it. The two still acted fine with one another when they did see each other.

During this time, Ben proposed to his girlfriend using an emerald and diamond ring I gave him to use.

Then came the fire starter. Hollywood and his girlfriend, Michelle Lasher, ate and drank at a brewery where Ben's fiancée worked as a waitress. At the end of their meal, they skipped out on the fifty-dollar tab, writing a note on a napkin, "Take this off Ben's debt."

His fiancée had to cover the tab, which Ben repaid to her—but he was furious. Where had that come from? After months, why had Hollywood chosen that way to get his debt repaid? Was it to humiliate Ben's fiancée? Was it because he was upset that Ben was "going straight" and not hanging around anymore?

It didn't matter—Ben had been disrespected, and that was never OK. Ben wasn't the kind who could ever let things slide.

"You're a little fucking punk and you're not going to get a dime from me," Ben yelled into Hollywood's voice mail. "The next time we see each other, we're going to handle business."

Ben kicked things up a notch the following day by alerting an insurance company to a scam that Jesse James Hollywood was running. Hollywood had reported his customized Honda stolen, in an attempt to collect thirty-five thousand dollars. Meanwhile, he had chopped it up and sold the parts and then had his cousin smash the car. Ben had gone with Hollywood when he first had the car insured, so he knew which company to call. Because of that call, Hollywood wasn't able to collect the insurance money.

That's when Hollywood vowed revenge, and he let everyone in his little gang know it. They were going to find Ben, and they were going to—well, they didn't know exactly what they were going to do, but they were going to make him pay. The two exchanged more threatening voice mails, and one day Ben drove up to his apartment and saw Hollywood and Ryan Hoyt standing outside. He hadn't told

Hollywood where he was living, but the night before, he had been at a bar with their mutual friend Casey Sheehan, and he had given him the address. Ben knew Hollywood was there to intimidate him. Rather than get into a fight that night, he just kept driving. When he came back a few hours later, they were gone.

"Yeah, you know where I live . . . but I know where you live, too, motherfucker. And I know where your family lives, too," Ben said on Hollywood's voice mail.

Ben moved out of the apartment the next day, and he bought a .25 caliber pistol from one of Jeff's employees. The timing coincided with breaking up with his fiancée; he ended up living with roommates in his next apartment. And he had decided to do construction work with his uncle instead of continuing with Jeff at the aerospace machine shop, work he considered mind-numbingly boring. It was a lot of button-pushing and computer-automated processes, because they manufactured components for commercial and military equipment.

On the other hand, fifteen-year-old Nick had just started working with his dad. It was his first summer job. Every day, he rode to work with Jeff, then took the bus home while Jeff stayed later.

As usual, Ben became nomadic. There was no shortage of people who were angry with him, that's for sure. At the end of July, Ben and a friend walked into a T. G. I. Friday restaurant and straight into the sights of a different local marijuana dealer whom Ben had stiffed—this one, to the tune of thirty thousand dollars. The dealer and his friends weren't happy with Ben and his friend, and a fight ensued. It was five against two, and it ended only because Ben's friend managed to slip out and pull the car around so they could escape.

Around that same time, Hollywood and his girlfriend came back to his house to find one of his two pit bulls dead. Neighbors said they hadn't seen anything, but Hollywood decided that Ben must have poisoned his dog. That was about when Hollywood started talking about leaving

West Hills. What seemed to have sealed the deal was when Ben and a friend broke Hollywood's front windows using aluminum tubing. Hollywood told people that right afterward, he'd gotten a phone call from someone impersonating a Mexican accent.

"This is Little Shooter. How do you like the window job? This is just the beginning, you little midget."

Hollywood rented a storage unit and began boxing up his possessions, moving them into the unit while he decided where to go next. He didn't tell anyone where he was going to move, but he borrowed his father's friend's cargo van the first week of August. When a girl he'd slept with asked what he was up to, Hollywood told her he was moving.

"Too many people know where I live," he said.

On a Sunday morning, three of his friends were at his house: Jesse Rugge, William Skidmore, and Ryan Hoyt. Jesse Rugge was one of Hollywood's pot dealers, and William was a prison-tattooed Spanish guy whose nickname was "Vato Loco" (crazy dude). As Ben later put it, William was the kind of guy who would sell your stuff and then tell you he got "jacked." Even Hollywood didn't trust him enough to deal drugs with him, but he kept him around for entertainment and muscle anyway. William was tall and lean, solid as a brick and intimidating.

I knew William's mother, Florinda. A close girlfriend of mine lived up the street from her, and Florinda was her housecleaner and friend. Many times, William's little brother would go swimming in my friend's pool, along with Nick. I'd see Florinda in Costco, and she'd ask how Ben and Nick were, and I'd ask how her kids were. She always seemed nice.

Around 1995, she'd tried to avert disaster by moving her family to a different subdivision to get away from William's West Hills friends, who she knew were no good. She even resorted to padlocking the pantry because the boys were always taking her food. But unfortunately, William stayed tight with his friends and stayed in trouble. When he was arrested and kept in a Simi Valley holding cell in early

2000, he etched the name of a Filipino gang onto the door and told officers his gang name was "Capone."

While Ben and Hollywood were fighting, William left long, rambling messages for Ben in the middle of the night, sometimes pretending to be Hollywood and wanting to "work it out," or asking why he wasn't "kickin' it" anymore. Maybe he was trying to lure Ben over to Hollywood's house unsuspectingly, so that they could beat him up. But Ben knew Hollywood needed others to do his dirty work for him, and the rest of them were just a big group of loud-mouthed potheads, anyway. They could talk a big game, but when it came down to it, they had never delivered.

Ben ignored the messages, but he ended up speaking to William on the phone on several occasions. It escalated to threats, where William would say things like, "Don't make me have my boys come down there and handle it another way."

William's "boys" were the Long Beach gang Satanas, and he had the gang name tattooed across his chest. Actually, he was so tattooed that the entire rest of his chest was inked, with "Satanas" left in the negative space.

Ben would yell and threaten right back, but nothing came of those threats until Sunday morning, August 6, 2000.

At about 10:00 a.m., Hollywood called another friend and told him to be ready—they were going to pick him up that afternoon and go out partying in Santa Barbara, one hundred miles up the California coast from Los Angeles.

Which they did, of course. It's just what happened in between that complicated matters a bit.

CHAPTER 6

LATE FOR BREAKFAST

We had him cornered—or so I thought. My fifteen-year-old son, Nick, had just come home a full hour before his curfew. That happened roughly once in every . . . never. I was impressed for a few seconds; then I saw that he brushed past his beloved niece. That also never happened. Normally, he'd be overjoyed to see Leah, Ian, and their baby daughter. But tonight he was distracted and clearly trying to sneak past unnoticed as I snapped one more picture of the happy family.

"Nick, look who's here," I said. "It's your favorite niece. I mean, your only niece."

And that's when I caught on: Nick had the unmistakable glaze of drugs in his eyes and a strange bulge in his jeans pocket.

"He's stoned!" said Leah. She was exasperated; for the past couple of months, she had been ratting him out to us every time she saw her brother's bloodshot eyes. Nick was angry with her for doing it, but it wasn't like she was playing high-and-mighty—Leah had done more than her share of drugs in high school. But she had also done some growing up, and she wanted Nick to do the same.

He shot her a dirty look and tried to keep walking. I motioned for his father to get up and stop Nick from continuing to walk past us.

"What's in your pocket?" I asked, as Jeff and I both advanced on him.

"Nothing," he said.

"Let us see what's in your pocket, now!"

"Leave me alone!" He bolted past us, straight out the door.

Although I ran after him, by the time I got to the door, he was already across the street. I lost sight of him in the darkness almost immediately and knew it was pointless to try to chase him.

My beautiful son. He was pushing his teenage boundaries, that's for sure. A few months earlier, he had been caught smoking a cigarette off school grounds, and the vice principal searched his pockets before letting him back into the school. The vice principal found a small bag that had the residue of a marijuana joint in it and called the police. Nick was arrested and fingerprinted.

It was probably best that he chose to call his dad from the police station that day instead of me. He knew I'd be devastated. Jeff let him stew at the station for a while, then went to pick him up.

"We can't go through this again," Jeff told Nick. What we'd been through with Ben was too much for any parent to deal with. The drugs, the fights, the guns. But Nick wasn't like that. Loving and funny and loyal and sensitive, he was my boy. My sweet son.

He looked remorsefully at the ground and accepted his lecture and his grounded weekends without complaint. I hoped and believed it would be the last time he'd ever need that kind of punishment.

All teenagers need a little room to grow, to learn who they are and test their freedom. I had given him just a little of that room, but I hadn't expected him to get caught with drugs. What I really expected was more like the last little surprise he'd given me: he shaved off his widow's peak. I always thought it was cute, but he was self-conscious about the way his hairline looked. He didn't want me to see what he'd done, so he began wearing a hat every day. One of my hats, actually—a plaid Scottish one that he liked to wear backward. Finally, I asked him, "How come you're wearing that hat all the time now?"

"Because I did something stupid," he said, slowly taking it off to show me. It was in a funny state of stubble. He told me how he had to shave it every day now or it looked ridiculous, so he wanted to grow it back in—but he didn't know how, without looking awkward for weeks.

I suggested that I'd shave the rest of his hair shorter so it would blend in better when it was growing back in. Heck, I'd shaved the dog before . . . how different could it be? Very, it turned out. My haircutting skills left his hair uneven and patchy, and a friend of his had to buzz it even shorter to get it to look reasonable. It made him look like a tough guy. Too bad. I loved his longer hair, always nicely combed back.

Couldn't we just stick to those sorts of acts of teenage independence? I could handle weird hair experiments. I could even handle the fact that the condoms I'd bought for Nick "just in case" were disappearing so fast that I thought he must have been handing them out to his friends in school, or maybe making balloon-art sculptures with them. Not drugs. Anything but drugs. Nick had always been upset by the path his half brother was on, and he told me he wished that Ben would make better choices. It was hard for me to accept that my son had taken a step on that same path he had always reviled.

Yet here we were. My husband was blissfully innocent when it came to recognizing that his kids were high. I was more aware of the signs: the half-closed eyes, the delayed reactions. So it was up to me to be the watchdog—a role I hated but took seriously. Nick was my only child, and I sure wasn't going to let him lose himself to drugs.

It seemed that was becoming a literal reality, however: now that he'd run off down the street, where had he disappeared to? That one time, Nick had run away and gone to Ben's house. He had sworn to me he'd never do that again, just as Ben swore he wouldn't take him in again. But as the minutes ticked by, I grew more frantic that Nick had slipped off to his brother's again. A life without curfews, without supervision, without boundaries could sure look tempting to an adolescent—but Ben's house was about the last place I'd want any child to be, particularly my own. Wherever Ben went, serious trouble followed.

"Don't worry. He'll be back," Jeff assured me.

Soon after, Leah and her family took off and left me to my vigil. I stared out that front window, waiting to catch a glimpse of Nick.

A few blocks away, Leah spotted her half brother walking along the road.

"Let me come back to your house tonight?" he asked her.

"Hell, no. You get back in there and face the music," she told him.

After twenty minutes, just before I lost my mind with worry, Nick walked back in. I didn't know whether to be angry or thrilled, so I was both at the same time.

"Don't you ever run off on me again!" I said. "You promise me. I can't take that again."

"I promise, Mom. I'm sorry," he said.

"I love you, and I need a hug."

He hugged me tight and told me he loved me, too. Had I known then what I know now, I would never have let him go.

"Why did you run off like that?" I asked.

"I just don't like it when you bug me about having cigarettes."

Yeah, right. I knew he smoked cigarettes. I knew what they looked like in his pockets, too, considering I went through his pockets daily. Whatever had been in his pocket this time wasn't a cigarette. It was a bag of something—but this was going to have to be a conversation for later.

This isn't marijuana, I thought. Nick seemed sped up

instead of slowed down, edgy and jumpy rather than mel-
low. I wondered what he could have taken, and where he
got it, but it wasn't the time to grill him just yet.

"We can't talk when he's high," I said to Jeff. "We'll
talk to him about it in the morning."

I made Nick a bowl of cereal, and he sat on the couch
watching *South Park* with his dad until he got tired enough
to sleep. As disappointed as I was, I was also relieved he
was safe in our home again. I'd get through to him. This
rebellious patch was bound to end its course soon.

Early the next morning, my mother-in-law called;
Nick's friend's father had painted their house, and she
had misplaced his phone number. I woke Nick to ask him
for the number, but he told me his friend had moved and
hadn't given him the new number yet. Jeff was about to
leave for morning tennis, so he went to Nick's room and
kissed him good morning—and, without knowing, good-
bye.

"We'll talk later," he said. "See you when I come home."

Then Nick rolled over and went back to sleep. While he
was sleeping I made breakfast, a little more elaborate than
usual. It was an open omelet, topped with cheese, browned
under the broiler. Nick wouldn't have liked the fresh hash
browns, but he would have loved the bacon and drowned
the biscuits in butter. But when Jeff got home from tennis and I went to tell our son that breakfast was ready, he
wasn't there.

What I didn't know then was that he was never going to
be there again.

If you knew it was going to be the last kiss, or the last
smile, or the last words you'd say, what would you say?

Somewhere between 9:30 and about 11:00 that morning,
he'd disappeared from his bedroom. At first I thought he
was hiding, so I went into every room of the house, calling
his name, peeking behind the shower curtain. No Nick. He
really had crept out of the house without our noticing.

"Shit!" I called out to Jeff. "He left."

I left his plate in the microwave and waited in annoyance for Nick to come home and explain where he'd gone without telling me.

Maybe he'd gone out to his friend's house. They liked to swap games and music, and sometimes he came back smelling of cigarettes. I'd look him over, and he'd say, "What?"

"What?" I'd respond back. I wasn't ready to confront him about the smoking, but I wanted to keep him on edge, let him wonder whether or not I noticed the smell. I don't know why I thought that would work. It sounds asinine now, but I just thought I'd let him go through his phase. It couldn't have been a serious habit—not long ago, he had bought his uncle nicotine patches to help him quit smoking. Nick knew better, but maybe it was just something he wanted to try out, to fit in.

Ten or fifteen minutes were all it would take to go smoke a cigarette, though. Maybe he'd gone to retrieve whatever had been in that bag in his pocket. He must have stashed it somewhere when he ran out the previous night. For now, all I could think about was my annoyance that his breakfast was getting cold.

I had just bought him a pager as an early sixteenth-birthday present, with a stipulation attached: he had to always return my pages within ten minutes. If he didn't, I would take the pager away for one week per minute he was late. I tested my rule twice: once, I paged him in the house. "Yes, Mom, I got your page!" he called back. The next time was when he was at a friend's house, and he returned the page in two minutes.

Now it had been eleven minutes. Yep, I was going to take away his pager for a week. Twelve minutes. Two weeks. But as minutes turned into hours, my anger grew.

He had done it after all, I thought. He ran away to Ben's house again. How could he? He *promised* he wouldn't.

Jeff wasn't too worried. Nick probably just wasn't ready to face us about having been high, he figured.

We called Ben, but got no answer. It wasn't easy to track Ben down—he was always on the go. So Jeff left a message.

"Be expecting a call from your brother," he said. "We had a little argument last night and he took off this morning, so he's probably heading your way today. Please give us a call as soon as you get this to let us know if you've heard from him."

Then we waited and tried to go on with our day. By nightfall, however, there had still been no call back from Nick or Ben. The anger gave way to fear. It was a desperate sort of feeling. Where was my Nick? Even when he'd run away that one time, he still called every day to say he was OK. This wasn't like him at all.

Not knowing what else to do with myself, I cleaned his bedroom in anticipation of his return. His room was filled with neon posters that glow under black light, and glow-in-the-dark stars covered the ceiling. All the names of the constellations were written out overhead, a testament to his lifelong interest in astronomy. Jeff's parents bought Nick a professional telescope for Hanukkah when he was about seven years old, and he loved to peer into the night sky. Just recently, he had excitedly asked me if I wanted to see the dark side of the moon. "Sure," I said, and followed him outside—where he proceeded to pull down his pants and moon me. That was my son.

The word *Karma* was written on his dry-erase board. I erased it without giving it much thought. I pulled the sheets tight on his waterbed and dusted off the black leather headboard. I straightened out the drawers, put the books back on the shelves; my nervous energy kept me going until his was surely the cleanest room on the block. Wouldn't he be surprised? I wasn't even going to give him a hard time about how messy he'd let it get. Boy, as soon as he got home, was I going to breathe a lot easier. And then I'd tether him to the doorknob so he could never get out of my reach again.

With nothing left to clean, I had no idea what to do with

myself. I paced around his room, looking at everything. Twin Dragon tae kwon do certificates hung on the wall, like the "Most Supportive Student" award he'd won as a beginner. One license plate that said "Run, Forrest, Run" and another that said "Stop, Forrest, Stop." Two giant laser discs signed by some musician I'd never heard of. It was as if I was looking for clues, as if I thought I might find some deeper meaning in the neon alien poster hanging on his wall. I considered messing everything up again just so I'd have something else to clean. At least it kept my hands busy.

The worrying was exhausting. I grabbed his pillow on my way back to the living room, where I took a nap on the couch under the open window, so I could be the first to embrace him when he walked back through the door.

But he didn't walk back through the door.

When I opened my eyes and knew without even checking that Nick had not come back, I was gut-punched with a single thought: *My son needs me.*

CHAPTER 7

KIDNAPPED

A woman named Pauline Mahoney was driving back from church with her three boys a little before 1:00 p.m. on August 6, 2000, when she saw a van pull over to the side of the road. Out of the van came a bunch of young men, and she saw them grab a younger boy who was walking down the street, pummel him over and over, then throw him into the van.

Mahoney sped up to get close enough to the van to get the license plate number, then passed them and watched in her rearview mirror to see where they were heading.

"All right, boys, this is the number," she said to her sons. The boys repeated the license plate number out loud the rest of the way home—they didn't have a cell phone, so they had to wait until they got home to call 911. As soon as she got in the door, Mahoney dialed 911 and told the operator what she had just witnessed:

"They [were] beating the crap out of this kid. They were kicking and punching him [with] three or four against one. The boy [was] on the sidewalk in a fetal position trying to protect himself against a wall. Then they picked him up and threw him into the van. They started to drive off and then realized they had left one of their own behind. He got in and they are now going east on Ingomar."

Right afterward Mahoney's call, a UCLA student named Rosalia de la Cruz Gitau, whose parents lived in West Hills, also called the police with the same story. A white van. A brutal beating. A kidnapping. At first, Gitau said, she thought it looked like a gang initiation. But when she saw them throw the boy into the van, she decided that it was time to call the police.

But devastatingly, the calls might as well have been made to the local McDonald's rather than the emergency help line. Two different emergency dispatchers both coded the incident incorrectly. The one responding to Mahoney's call coded it as an assault rather than a kidnapping in progress, and the officers who responded didn't take the report seriously. They drove around the area looking for a victim wandering the streets, and when they didn't see one, they gave up. In fact, they didn't even bother taking written statements.

One of the officers called Mahoney back, but just listened to her account and then hung up. Although the officer looked up the registrant of the van—John Roberts—he misread the address, decided it wasn't very important anyway because they couldn't find the victim, and never took it any further.

That officer was the first person who could have saved my son's life, yet failed to.

While the officer was on the phone with Mahoney, the second emergency call came through to the Los Angeles Police Department. This time, the second dispatcher simply sent it out as a "for information only" radio broadcast, which was sent out only once, while the officer was on the phone—he never heard it. Again, it wasn't coded as a kidnapping, or even specifically as an emergency. Although Rosalia de la Cruz Gitau left her name and number, no officer ever called her to follow up. The dispatcher didn't connect the incident reported in the second call with the first one. No one tracked down the van.

No one knew Nick was inside it.

———

That morning I had paged Nick over and over, growing more frustrated with him as his breakfast got cold. He had to be at one of his friends' houses, I figured. Off telling them what a drag it was to have parents.

Just after noon that day, his uncle and cousin had been driving home from the gym and had seen Nick walking along the road from a nearby park and offered to give him a ride back.

"Thanks anyway, but I'd rather walk," he'd told them, waving them on. If he had taken that ride, dozens of lives would be very different today.

———

Just around the corner, Jesse Hollywood, Jesse Rugge, and William Skidmore had been cruising around, plotting revenge on Nick's brother, Ben. They had looked for him before, but Ben was hard to track down. No one knew where he was anymore. This time, Hollywood had decided, they were going to send a clear message. Maybe they would break the windows in our house as a warning to Ben. Instead, in the midst of their plotting, Nick walked straight into their view—like a rabbit wandering right into a hunter's lair. Hollywood stared incredulously from the driver's seat.

"That's Ben's kid brother!"

Jesse Rugge knew that. He had hung out with Nick before, because he was good friends with Nick's best friend Ryan's older brother. They had even wrestled under a Christmas tree at Ryan's house the previous December.

The van screeched over to the side of the road. Rugge called out, "Don't run, man," and Hollywood jumped out and pinned Nick to a tree and screamed at him, "Where's your brother? Where's your brother?"

"I don't know!" Nick said.

They didn't believe him, so they decided to beat the answer out of him. Jesse Rugge and William Skidmore joined Hollywood in the ferocious attack, while Nick just tried to block their punches, in the middle of daylight in front of witnesses—at least two of whom called the police. Nick was backed up against a block wall. It was a residential street, but the houses didn't face the direction of the attack.

"Get him in the van!" Hollywood commanded. The two others tossed him into the van and slammed the sliding door, quickly driving off . . . without Hollywood. A few feet later, Rugge realized his error, stopped, and let Hollywood catch up and get back in.

"Your asshole brother owes me money. We're going to find him, and he's going to pay me what he owes me. Now tell us where he is," Hollywood demanded.

"I don't know."

"Bullshit."

"No, he moved out. I don't know where he is now."

"He busted out the windows in my house, you know that? He's going to pay for that. Now tell me where he lives."

"I'm telling you, I don't . . ."

Beep-beep. Beep-beep.

It was Nick's pager, going off incessantly.

"Who the fuck is paging you? Is that your brother? Give me that thing."

Hollywood grabbed Nick and went through his pockets, yanking out the pager first. He recited the phone number and asked whose it was.

"That's my mom."

"Oh, great. She's already looking for the kid!" Hollywood said to his friends.

"What do you want to do?" Jesse Rugge said.

"I don't know." He tossed the pager onto the dashboard and turned back to Nick. "Give me everything else you got."

In Nick's pockets were a small bag of marijuana, a wallet that included a little phone book, and a baggie of Valium. That's what had been in his pocket the night before. One of Ben's friends had sold Nick about a dozen Valium pills, and Nick was going to use them with his friends when they went to CityWalk, the strip by Universal Studios. Instead, now his captors passed them around in the van, and they gave one to Nick to take, too. Within minutes, they were also all passing around a marijuana joint.

"You say anything, I'll break your face," Hollywood said. "Let me see your hand." He'd just spotted the ring on Nick's finger—the one that had belonged to his dad, and then to Ben. Over Nick's protests, Hollywood grabbed it and yanked it off.

"Give me back my ring," Nick said.

"You shut your mouth!"

"Come on, that's my dad's ring."

Nick reached out and tried to grab his ring back, but Hollywood slammed him back down. In a quiet moment, Jesse Rugge said, "Man, just give him his ring back." After a few minutes of ranting, Hollywood threw the ring at Nick, who put it back on his finger.

"This is your brother's fault, you know. Your brother's a shithead."

"Whatever money he owes, my parents will pay it to you," Nick said.

"No, fuck that. They're not going to pay. Ben's going to pay me, or I'm going to kick his ass."

Then there was a side excursion: William Skidmore needed his insulin, so the van went to his house so that he could get it. While they were stopped, Rugge asked Hollywood, "Where are we going now?"

"Go get Brian, like I said."

Brian Affronti, nicknamed "Little B," was another of Hollywood's underlings, and William Skidmore's best friend. He was supposed to go out partying with them. They were headed into Santa Barbara for Fiesta, a five-day festival celebrating Spanish culture and history. The tradition had held strong for seventy-six years, but Brian had never been to one of these festivals, and he was looking forward to the trip. When he got into the van, however, he couldn't help but notice the fifteen-year-old kid in the back. He'd never met Nick before, but he quickly realized this wasn't just a friend along for the ride.

The trip lasted almost an hour. Every few minutes, Hollywood would bark another threat at Nick.

"Try to run and I'll break your teeth," he said.

It made Brian uncomfortable, but he didn't dare speak up. He didn't even question why the kid was there. Or why a pager kept going off from the front seat.

Once they had stopped the car for a break, Jesse Rugge again asked Hollywood what the plan was. What were they supposed to do with Nick? Hollywood was agitated; he hadn't thought it through very far. What he really wanted was Ben, not Nick, but now that he had one brother, he wasn't about to just let him go.

"Take him back to your house," Hollywood ordered Rugge.

"I can't! My dad's there."

"Well, we have to take him somewhere."

Rugge thought for a minute. "OK, I know a place."

They drove to one of Rugge's friend's apartments on Modoc Road in Santa Barbara, where a small group of young men and women were smoking pot and drinking. Hollywood told Rugge to go ask them if they had a closet big enough to put someone in. Rugge walked up to the door first and appealed to his longtime friend Richard Hoeflinger.

"I'm in trouble, man," he said. "I need a place to stay. Can I crash here?"

His friend agreed without asking for an explanation. Rugge went back out to the car and summoned the rest of the group. Once inside, they brought Nick into a back bedroom, pushed him onto the end of the bed, duct taped his wrists and legs, taped a sock over his eyes, and stuffed one of his own socks in his mouth.

The guys in the apartment saw Nick in this state, but Hollywood told them, "Keep your fucking mouth shut. You don't say shit."

They noticed something protruding from Hollywood's waistband and figured it was a gun. The threat was enough to keep them quiet.

Richard Hoeflinger had met Hollywood six months earlier, when he visited Hollywood's house with Jesse Rugge, possibly to talk about becoming a drug dealer. Ryan Hoyt met them at the door and pointed a gun at him before letting him in. Now Hollywood was talking on Hoeflinger's phone in his living room without asking, and Hoeflinger decided not to get involved.

One of the women in the house went to the back bedroom to put on her makeup, without knowing what she was walking into. There, she also saw Nick tied up. Despite her shock, she went ahead and put on her makeup anyway, without saying a word, then left the room.

Rugge explained to the guys who lived in the apartment that they were keeping Nick until they could track down Ben and make him pay back his debt.

"Just give us a couple of hours, and we'll be out of here," he told the guys.

Hoeflinger and the others summoned the women, and they all left the house together, trying to forget what they had seen, even though they knew they were leaving behind an explosive bunch of strangers and a young hostage. The only person one of them really knew was Jesse Rugge.

Rugge was a twenty-year-old high school dropout covered in tough-guy tattoos—two scorpions, a skull, and a ripped-open muscle. His parents were divorced, and he split his time between their homes. For the most part, Rugge was a happy-go-lucky type, but he had little supervision. His dad was the greenhouse manager for the University of California, Santa Barbara, whose main claim to fame was growing a rare plant with a five-foot phallus. Rugge had just served a short stint in jail in Santa Barbara for a DUI charge rather than pay a fine, and he was staying at his dad's house, doing electrical work with his uncle and looking for a steady job.

Brian Affronti and William Skidmore both decided they wanted to go home at that point—this whole hostage thing was getting pretty intense, and they weren't so sure they wanted to be a part of it, so they made up excuses. Affronti told Hollywood that he had a date back home.

"You just remembered that now?" Hollywood asked.

"Yeah," Affronti said.

"Wait until I come back. I'm going to take a shower."

With that, Hollywood and Rugge left to go to Rugge's house. While they were gone, Affronti or Skidmore could have just let Nick go, but they didn't. They left him tied up and just waited for Hollywood's next order. Occasionally, one of them would wander into the bedroom and tell Nick not to worry, that things would be OK. Considering his circumstances, Nick was apparently extremely calm. It seemed that he had accepted that this was the way things were going to be for a while; he would just sit there until Ben came around and straightened this mess out.

When Hollywood got back, he relinquished the van keys and let Affronti and Skidmore leave. A short while later, they realized Affronti had left his cell phone behind, so they came back to the apartment. When they got back, they saw that not only was Nick untied, but he was now smoking pot and sitting on the couch playing video games with his captors.

"Be cool," Hollywood told Nick.

Affronti and Skidmore got the cell phone and went back to their houses. They didn't alert anyone to the fact that Nick had been kidnapped. They thought it would "blow over."

Hollywood then said that he had to get home to take care of some repairs so that his real estate agent could get his house on the market, so he left an unhappy Jesse Rugge in charge of Nick that night. The word *babysitter* was bandied about. With few options open to him at that point, Rugge decided to take Nick to his father's house after all. They walked there—it was a few miles away—and Rugge asked his father if they could spend the night. His father, Barron Rugge, didn't seem to notice that anything was amiss; he just figured that his son had a new—albeit younger—friend coming to visit. Even though his son was twenty and Nick was fifteen, Barron didn't ask questions. He just said a quick hello and told Nick, "You can stay here if you want." So he did.

Rugge assured Nick that this would be over soon, and he'd make sure Nick got home safely. Hollywood was just freaking out, is all. They'd get it straightened out.

———

I wonder how Nick slept that night. I wonder if he lay his head on that strange pillow and thought that tomorrow this would all be over. His brother would show up, they'd clear things up—maybe his parents would have to pay Ben's debt and get Hollywood's windows fixed. Nick was so good at acting cool, no matter what was happening. I wonder if he had any clue that things really weren't going to be OK, as Rugge was telling him. I wonder if he was scared.

CHAPTER 8

THE SEARCH BEGINS

Did I sleep that night? I'm not sure. After cleaning Nick's room and taking my nap under the window, I had fought off conflicting feelings that ranged from fear to anger to doom.

Anger was the easy one, the one that I would have preferred to settle on. I was getting very angry with Ben, who I was sure was harboring Nick . . . at least, almost sure. If only Ben would call us back, then I could just be sure and be angry and get some sleep.

We had briefly wondered if Nick was at a new friend's house. The day before he disappeared, he had brought a few friends over to play pool at our house, and Jeff had made his famous toasted peanut-butter-and-jelly sandwiches for them while I was at work. One of the kids was new—Jeff had never seen him before.

It was when he left the house with those friends, only to return that night high and with the bulge in his pocket, that the trouble began. We thought it might have come from the new friend Jeff had seen with Nick earlier.

He shouldn't have even been at our house, I thought of the unknown boy. *If I were that mother, I would have made sure I knew where my son was. I would have had the phone number and called to make sure the kid's parents were home. Who is this kid, anyway?*

So I started calling around. I spoke to Nick's best friend, Ryan, and several other of his close friends, but all of them told me they hadn't heard from Nick and that he wasn't with this new friend. We always left off saying that they needed to call me the minute they heard anything, no matter what, even if they thought it was going to get Nick grounded.

So it had to be Ben. It had to be—right?

But what if he was hurt? What if Nick had fallen into a ditch somewhere, and his leg was trapped, or he was unconscious, or . . .

No, he's fine, I thought.

But what if he wasn't fine?

Somehow, Sunday turned into Monday when I wasn't paying attention. The sun was up, and Nick still wasn't home. Thoughts of him being hurt and unable to call us kept crawling under my skin, but I pushed them back. Had to. I couldn't allow myself to get stuck on thoughts like that or I'd be paralyzed with worry. I had to find Nick.

At one point, I'd had all of Nick's friends' parents' phone numbers in my Palm program, but he'd erased them—by accident, he said. Now I had to search through his room to get the numbers back. I went through every notebook, every drawer and pocket, every little slip of paper. One by one, I made the calls, and I programmed the numbers back into my Palm as I went along.

Hello. This is Susan Markowitz. By any chance, have you seen my son Nick?

No.

I documented all of the calls, keeping notes on what everyone had said and who they suggested I try next. And in the midst of that, Ben showed up.

He hadn't seen Nick.

And that's when the room started spinning.

———————

There Ben was, sitting in our family room, telling us he had been away in Arizona working a construction job with his uncle. He swore that he honestly hadn't heard from Nick. He would tell us if he had. Did he have any idea where . . . ? No.

I didn't hear much of the conversation after that. My mind was far, far away. I briefly tuned in to hear Ben mentioning how he'd hated me all the years he was growing up until he had a girlfriend who had a child. He said it was only then that he understood what it took to be a stepparent.

My mind drifted again. *I don't care. Where is Nick? Something is wrong. Nick is hurt. He needs me.* Visions of him lying bloody on the side of a road came back, and I tried to push them away.

Jeff asked Ben if anyone was angry with him. *Well, of course,* I thought. *Pick a name.* Then I heard Ben mention something about money.

"Ben, you owe someone money?"

"No, Susan, it's not like that."

"I'll write you a check right now."

"I don't owe him anything."

Ben joined us in making phone calls, too, and one of the first people he called was Jesse James Hollywood. He left Hollywood a message. "Listen, I know we're not on good terms, but I really need your help. My brother has been missing since yesterday morning, and if you hear anything, please let me know."

It turned out that Ben did suspect Hollywood was involved, but not the way it was actually happening. One of the people Ben called that night mentioned that Nick might have been hanging out with Hollywood at a party or rave in Santa Barbara—the person made it sound like they were out having fun together.

So what Ben thought was that maybe Hollywood was purposely hanging out with Nick just to piss him off. Acting like a cool guy, befriending Nick so that he'd come home and tell stories that would drive Ben up a wall. What a jerk.

After a while, Ben got up to leave to see one of his friends, and I repeated my offer to write him a check. I didn't connect the two events in my mind. I wasn't thinking that the fact that Ben owed money to someone could have anything to do with Nick's disappearance. I just couldn't stand any more tension that day. Nick was missing, and I wanted everything else to be smooth so we could concentrate on what mattered.

When Ben left, I focused on making "Missing Person" posters and flyers. A few phone calls later, I had a roomful of volunteers ready to go pass them out around town. People headed to the mall, to the local schools, to the park—my goal was to get Nick's face in front of everyone. Someone *had* to have seen him.

Jeff went out to comb the area on his bike. He knew some of the trails Nick might have taken. Every time someone left the house, they took a piece of my hope with them. And every time they returned without Nick, that hope swirled down the drain.

It was August, and one of the hottest summers in decades, yet I found myself singing Christmas songs. There was comfort in Christmas songs. *Silent night, holy night, all is calm . . .*

Again and again, I told myself to stay calm and stay positive. We just hadn't looked in the right place yet. We hadn't turned over the right rock, or looked behind the right hill. He had probably fallen somewhere and was waiting for us to find him. I knew he was coming back, but it was horrible to wait and worry.

That night was worse than the one before. At least the night earlier, I had been able to reassure myself that Nick was probably with Ben. Now I had absolutely nothing. No hints, no clues.

Ben was confident that Nick had just run away to a friend's house, probably due to the fight we'd had the night before—Nick had likely felt that he needed some space and had run off somewhere to stay with a friend for a few days. He'd turn up.

I didn't believe it. The only time Nick had ever taken off before, he had gone straight to Ben, and he'd sworn to me he wouldn't do it again. Nick didn't break his promises.

Something is wrong. We have to find him.

———

The day after the kidnapping, the first person Hollywood went to confess his sins to was his lawyer. Not many twenty-year-olds have their own lawyers, and even visit them at home, but again, the Hollywood family wasn't exactly typical. Stephen Hogg (pronounced "Hoag"), a heavy-set man with glasses and a gray ponytail, was not only the Hollywoods' longtime lawyer, he was a family friend who had even come to Jesse's Little League games. He had represented Hollywood on two previous criminal charges, and his wife, also a lawyer, represented him on civil matters.

Pacing and chain-smoking in the Hoggs' backyard, Hollywood told him that his "friends" had beaten up and kidnapped the younger brother of a tough guy who had busted out his windows. He made it sound like his friends had done this without his consent.

"You know where he is?" Hogg asked.

"I can't tell you that."

"What are they doing with him? Have they got him tied up?"

"No, no, they're all sitting around smoking grass, taking Valium, drinking beer, and playing video games."

"You mean the brother, too?"

"Yeah, I think they're all sitting around doing that."

Hollywood wanted to know what could happen next.

"Look, if it is kidnapping, you can get up to eight years. If they asked for ransom, they could get a life sentence," the lawyer told him.

Hollywood didn't react, but he looked irritated. Stephen Hogg thought about it some more and decided that maybe the situation could be considered just "false imprisonment" rather than kidnapping. But in any case, it was still illegal.

"You have to get the boy back home. Call the police. If you're the first one there, they'll go easy on you."

"I can't. You don't know these people. They'll go off on my family."

"Jesse, you've got to."

Hollywood angrily refused, and when Hogg pressed the issue, he stormed out. At least, that was the lawyer's version. One of Hollywood's friends has a different take on it—according to him, Hollywood said that Hogg told him he was in so much trouble that he should "dig a deep hole."

As Jesse James Hollywood was leaving, Hogg told him not to go home.

"Go somewhere where no one knows where you are, and call me."

Hogg waited, but got no phone call, so he started paging Hollywood once an hour from 4:00 until 8:00 that night. He never called the police. He said later that he "didn't have enough information." A few hours later, by coincidence, Jack Hollywood called Stephen Hogg about a DUI case in Ventura. Jack and his wife, Laurie, were in Big Sur spending a few days at the gorgeous mountainside resort Ventana Inn and Spa. The couple had been separated, but the two were apparently trying to patch things up. Hogg put a damper on their romantic getaway when he told Jack that there was a problem with Jesse.

"What's wrong? Is he OK?"

"Yeah, he's OK, but this is serious. He is very much afraid," Hogg said.

"Well, what's it about?"

"It's not something that we should discuss on the phone."

"OK, well then, I'm going to be down tonight. Get ahold of Jesse and sit on him for me."

Then Jack made a bunch of phone calls trying to track his son down—calling his pager, his cell phone, his girl-friend—to no avail. Jack called the lawyer back and asked him to get in touch with Jack's good friend John Roberts, an alcoholic ex-gangster who had loaned Jesse the van to help him move out of his old house. Maybe John would know how to find his son. After all, Jesse thought of him as an uncle. They were close.

So Hogg called Roberts and asked him to come over, and he filled him in on what was going on. The two of them talked about what to do and mused about going to Santa Barbara together and bribing Nick to keep him quiet. They thought it would be a good idea to scare Nick a little and tell him they'd take him home if he promised to keep his mouth shut. But they decided against it.

John had more important things on his mind—now that he had his van back, he wanted to take it straight to the car wash and tell workers to clean it inside and out with solvent to hide any fingerprints. John could have called the police, but he "didn't want to be involved."

Jack and Laurie Hollywood got back to town about 2 a.m. At some point that day, the Hollywoods met up with Jesse Hollywood at his girlfriend Michelle Lasher's house. But Jesse was not forthcoming; *evasive* was the word Jack Hollywood used. His son was angry that Stephen Hogg had told his dad what was going on. Jesse claimed that he had been trying to track Nick down all night, but that they must have moved to another house or something. Or maybe they had just let Nick go and then took off them-selves. He wouldn't tell his dad where Nick was or who was involved.

Next, Jack dropped his wife at home, then went on to John Roberts's house. Roberts reiterated every-thing that Stephen Hogg had told him—that his son was involved in a kidnapping, that they were all at some friend's house drinking and partying, and that Jesse was worried that when he let the kid go, they would all get arrested.

Roberts volunteered to find out where Nick was and to go get him.

———————

Back at Jesse Rugge's house, Nick and Jesse had spent the morning on the couch watching television together. Barron Rugge and his wife, Jesse's stepmother, were in and out of the house, never paying much attention to what was going on. Barron noticed the boys watching television that day, but he didn't say anything to them and left again.

Jesse Rugge invited friends over for—what else?—partying. Seventeen-year-old Natasha Adams, sixteen-year-old Kelly Carpenter, and seventeen-year-old Graham Pressley all showed up while Nick was playing a James Bond video game on Rugge's shabby couch. Rugge told them that Nick was his "friend from Los Angeles" who would be staying with him for a while. Graham Pressley sat and played video games with him while Nick enthusiastically talked about gaming.

They went out to the back patio and sat on some old lawn chairs, where Nick seemed comfortable around the new guests. There was even a moment when he laughed so hard at something Kelly Carpenter said that he almost fell over sideways in the rickety chair and landed in a large barrel cactus.

It took them a little while to question the whole "friend from Los Angeles" thing; what tipped them off was the way Rugge was ordering Nick around. For one thing, he told Nick to vacuum the carpet before they went out, which was an odd thing to ask of a visiting friend. For another thing, Rugge told the three teens not to let Nick use the phone.

Eventually, when Rugge wasn't listening, Nick himself told Graham Pressley what had happened. He explained that he'd been beat up and thrown into a van and that he had been kidnapped because of his brother Ben's drug debt to Jesse James Hollywood. Graham told the girls, who were incredulous. Was Nick OK? Why didn't he try to escape?

"I'm all right," Nick told them. "I'm going to stick it out for my brother. As long as he's OK, I'm OK."

The stoned quintet went to Natasha Adams's house. She noticed that Nick had some cuts and bruises from the beating he had received the previous day, and she helped him clean his wounds. Even so, she convinced herself that it didn't seem like a "big deal." And like all the others, "I was trying not to get involved," she later said.

The girls nicknamed Nick "Stolen Boy." They liked him, and so did Graham Pressley. Nick was only a year or so younger than they were, and they had easy conversations. He told them about a girl he liked and how he wanted to call her as soon as he got home. This was all the girls needed to hear—they launched into a barrage of advice about how to attract girls. Nick was amused and overwhelmed and gave Pressley a "What did I get myself into?" kind of look.

At one point, Adams went upstairs to use the bathroom, and when she got back, Rugge was unexpectedly gone. It turned out that he went to lunch with Hollywood and his girlfriend, Michelle Lasher, ostensibly to figure out what to do with Nick. Rugge had been trying to get in touch with Hollywood for a while by paging Ryan Hoyt. Each time he connected with Hollywood, Hollywood would just say things like, "Don't worry; don't worry. Make Nick your best friend." But Rugge tired of this and wanted to see Hollywood in person to find out what his next orders were. What was going to happen to Nick? What was actually discussed at this lunch remained their secret.

It was the first time that Nick would be left without any of his original captors. Now he was just with the other teenagers: Natasha Adams, Kelly Carpenter, and Graham Pressley, who had been told not to mess with Hollywood's plans. They knew what a loose cannon Hollywood was, and they all feared angering him. After all, look what he did when he was angry—he had already kidnapped and beaten up someone. No one wanted to stick his or her neck out and become Hollywood's next target.

"Why don't you just go?" one of the girls asked Nick.

"It's OK," Nick said. "I don't want to make any trouble for my brother."

So they stayed. Adams liked to fiddle with her electric guitar, so she brought it out and tried to show Nick some chords. Pressley and Nick put their feet up on the deck railing and listened to "Natasha's bad renditions of some really good songs," Graham Pressley later said.

Rugge called and asked them to bring Nick back to his house. There, they saw Hollywood and his girlfriend. The girls noted her new boob job, courtesy of Hollywood's lucrative drug-dealing business. Nick went upstairs to avoid Hollywood, who stayed downstairs talking to Rugge about what to do with him.

"Tie him up and put him in a trunk so we can go out to Fiesta," Hollywood suggested.

No one put Nick in a trunk, but Hollywood and Michelle left, and Rugge was once again the babysitter. That night, Nick slept over again in Rugge's bedroom.

Sometime during that night, Natasha Adams's conscience kicked into gear. What she knew was that Hollywood was not a good person, and that if he wanted to kill someone, he could have that person killed. She liked Nick and didn't want anything bad to happen to him, even though she was afraid of interfering with Hollywood's plans.

Adams spoke to her mother, an attorney, and asked for some advice. Without giving many specifics, she explained that she'd met a boy who had been kidnapped by some people she knew, and she asked what she should do about it. Her mother advised her to go to the police, but Adams hesitated. It could mean big trouble for her if Hollywood discovered that she'd "ratted" him out, plus she wasn't sure whether or not the situation would just blow over on its own. That would make things a lot easier, so she wouldn't have to worry about whether or not she needed to call police.

The group reconvened the next day at Rugge's house, and this time, Natasha Adams wanted some answers. She, Kelly Carpenter, and Graham Pressley took a walk to a park to talk about "the situation."

"Nick isn't supposed to be here," she said to the others.

"What's going to happen to him? Graham, tell me . . . are they going to kill him?"

"Oh, no, of course not." He paused a second. "But Jesse was offered money."

He told her that Hollywood had offered Rugge two thousand dollars to kill Nick, but that Rugge had turned it down, telling Hollywood he was crazy. Pressley said that the guys didn't know what they were going to do with Nick, but they weren't going to hurt him. Everyone just had to keep their mouths shut because Hollywood could go to jail if word reached the police that he had kidnapped Nick, Pressley explained.

Graham Pressley had his own reasons for not wanting to call the police. He liked smoking pot every day, and calling the cops could mean an end to his carefree lifestyle. Who knew what the police would do if they opened the door into his stoner's haven?

Natasha Adams was in tears. She had no idea what she was supposed to do—this situation seemed much more serious than any other she'd ever been in. Something just didn't feel right about Pressley's answer. Hollywood had offered to pay Rugge to kill Nick, for crying out loud. Her instincts were right. This was insane.

Pressley and Carpenter went back to Rugge's house, but Adams said she needed a few minutes to compose herself. When Nick asked why she was still outside, they told him she was upset. "Is it because of me?" he wanted to know.

They said that it was.

"Tell her not to worry. I'm OK. It'll be a story I'll tell my grandkids someday."

Adams calmed herself down at the park, and when she got back to the house, Rugge said, "You look like you've been crying."

"Yeah, I have been," she said.

"Why?"

"Because Nick isn't supposed to be here, and I don't know what you're going to do with him. You have to promise me you're going to take him home."

Rugge looked her in the eye and swore he was going to take Nick home—a promise he reiterated several times that afternoon, both to his friends and to Nick himself.

"I'm going to take you home. I'll put you on a Greyhound. I'll get you home," he would say.

That was good enough for Adams. She decided not to call the police after all, thus making her yet another in the growing list of people who could have saved Nick's life . . . but didn't.

———————

I had switched sides of the bed with Jeff the previous night because I wanted to be closer to the window so that I could be the first to see Nick when he came home. But when I woke up, he still wasn't there. Every minute felt like torture. I had to stay busy to keep my mind from dreaming up horrible scenarios, but of course, the images came anyway. I began losing touch with reality and floating around in a haze where time didn't seem to function the way time is supposed to function. It was slowed down . . . or sped up . . . I just knew that Nick was in trouble somewhere and that every minute that passed was another minute we had not saved him from whatever trouble he was in.

While Jeff went out searching, I stayed home assigning tasks to everyone who walked through the door—and by now, there were lots of people coming through our doors, family and friends, plus friends of friends. We had officially reported Nick a "Missing Person" and enlisted all the help we could find to comb the area. We tried the hospitals again. We tried stopping strangers and showing them his picture.

Today, we will find him, I told myself. *We have to.*

———————

Across town, Jack Hollywood and John Roberts were back at Jesse Hollywood's girlfriend Michelle Lasher's house meeting with Jesse again. Jesse handed his father a pager number.

"This is Ryan Hoyt's number. He'll know where the guy is, and you guys can go get him."

Jack Hollywood walked to Gelson's Market down the street at about noon and paged Ryan Hoyt from a pay phone. Hoyt called back immediately. Jack didn't want to discuss anything over the phone, so he asked Hoyt to meet him at Serrania Park in Woodland Hills.

According to Jack Hollywood, the conversation went something like this: he said, "What the hell is going on with this thing? And where is this kid? Show me where he is and John and I will go and get him."

"I don't know how to get in touch with him," Hoyt replied.

"Let's find out. Call whoever you need to call, and you can just leave, and John and I will get the kid and take him home."

Hoyt seemed very agitated and rattled, and just said, "I can't. I don't have any control."

He wouldn't give up any names of the other people involved. Then Jack gave Hoyt his phone number and told him to find out where Nick was and call back. "Whatever the consequences are, that's part of the deal, but that's what needs to happen," Jack allegedly said.

"OK, I'll do that," Hoyt said.

But no one ever called him back. Jack Hollywood knew who Ben was, and he knew that Nick was Ben's brother . . . yet he never tried to contact the family or to call police. He just waited for his son to decide to tell him where he was keeping "the kid."

———

I hated the clock. At least August meant that daylight lasted longer than usual, but that's little consolation when you know nighttime is coming and people will go home and stop searching.

Jeff didn't tell me about the phone call he had made to the morgue to ask if they had any John Does. They didn't. Yet.

CHAPTER 9

GET RID OF THE EVIDENCE

He paced in the living room.

"I don't want to be in a *situation*," Jesse Rugge said. "I don't think I should be a part of this, and I'm going to get you home. I'm going to give you fifty dollars, and you're taking a train tonight, and then you'll have some money left over to get a cab home. And all I can say is there better not be policemen coming to my door the next day."

He repeated this sentiment several times, sometimes adding in things like, "How do I know you're not going to tell?"

"Don't worry," Nick told him. "I won't."

Inexplicably, though, instead of handing Nick the money and sending him on his way, Rugge changed course and decided that they should all go to a hotel and have a party that night. He didn't want to be at his father's house anymore, so Graham Pressley's mother, Christina Pressley, picked them up on her way to her 5:30 yoga class and took them to the Lemon Tree Inn. Nick rode in the back of the car, and Christina didn't notice anything out of the ordinary. Her son introduced Nick as Jesse Rugge's friend.

"Nice to meet you," she said.

"Nice to meet you, too. Thanks for the ride," Nick replied.

Rugge booked room 341 at the Lemon Tree Inn in Santa Barbara while his friends sat in the lobby. Once in the room, they drank and smoked some more. It was the same group—Jesse Rugge, Graham Pressley, Natasha Adams, and Kelly Carpenter—plus one other male friend, and sometimes-drug-dealer, of Graham's.

Again, one of the girls asked Nick why he hadn't just taken off.

"I've taken self-defense and stuff. It's not like I couldn't do anything right now. I just don't want to," he told her. "I don't see a reason to. I'm going home. Why would I complicate it?"

But what neither Nick nor any of the other people in the group at the hotel knew was that after Rugge had turned down Hollywood's bribe to kill Nick, Hollywood had turned to his favorite little brownnoser: Ryan Hoyt. Hoyt was still doing menial jobs for Hollywood, trying to work off his debts from the parking tickets and the marijuana, and he would do anything to impress his idol.

"I have a way for you to erase your debt," Hollywood told him.

Hoyt was all ears.

"There's a mess that needs to be cleaned up. I need you to take care of somebody."

Hoyt agreed without question, even though his debt by that point was just a few hundred dollars—plus the one hundred dollars per week interest whenever he was short on his payments. Hollywood handed him a big blue hockey duffel bag, which was the bag that he stored his guns in. This time, the duffel bag contained a black TEC-9 semiautomatic assault pistol—the same kind of gun used in the 1999 Columbine school shooting. But semiautomatic wasn't good enough for Hollywood; he'd had the trigger shaved down so that it could be converted to a fully automatic weapon. It was capable of spraying up to a thousand bullets in a minute. And now it was in Ryan Hoyt's hands.

That day, Hollywood also took twenty-five thousand dollars out of his bank account in the form of cashier's checks and dropped off his Mercedes at a repair shop. Then he called Rugge at the Lemon Tree Inn at about 8:30 p.m., using a phone card.

Graham Pressley went to his own house for a little while to pick up swimming trunks for himself and Nick. The two of them then went to the hotel swimming pool, which Nick dipped a foot in and declared too cold.

"I think we'd better check out the hot tub instead," he said.

There was an outdoor hot tub next to the pool, with a few young women already in it. Adams and Carpenter had given Nick and Pressley some tips on picking up women earlier that night, so they found this a perfect moment to practice their new techniques—which caused a light-hearted moment of laughter a few minutes later when the women up and left.

But Nick and Pressley stayed in the hot tub, talking about girls and music and life. They spent a good deal of time together just talking, surrounded by palm trees. Nick mentioned that he now felt embarrassed about having told Adams and Carpenter about the girl he liked, but he said that one of the first things he wanted to do when he got back home was to call the girl up and tell her how he felt.

With arms outstretched on either side of him, Nick commented on how relaxing the water felt after the last crazy couple of days. He submerged himself a few times, closing his eyes and holding himself underwater. Then the two teenagers sat in silence for a few moments, watching people come and go and the last bits of sunlight fade away.

"What do you think about God?" Nick asked Pressley. It was an unexpected question, but he was serious.

"I don't know . . . I think God and the world are the same thing," Pressley replied.

"I doubt if God is there sometimes . . . but times like these dissolve my doubts." Nick looked up at the sky. "God probably laughs at us most of the time."

He talked about being worried about his family, and said he knew that his mother would be relieved to see him home again.

"My mom is the same way," Pressley said.

"But you don't know my mom," Nick told him.

It was dark when they toweled off and went back to the hotel room, where everyone was out on the balcony. The girls asked what Nick's plans were for when he got back home. Nick said that he wanted to see the girl he talked about and then he wanted to go sit and watch a sunset somewhere and think.

At around 11:00 p.m., Jesse Rugge made an announcement: "I don't mean to be rude, but . . ." it was time for everyone to leave. Someone was coming to pick up Nick and take him home. Nick and the girls exchanged phone numbers and long hugs and said their good-byes and "I'll miss you's," and then they left. Graham Pressley shook Nick's hand good-bye, but then Rugge stopped him and asked him to stay.

Back in the room, Nick fell asleep. Shortly afterward, the door opened—and in barged tall, gawky Ryan Hoyt, with the blue duffel bag that Rugge recognized as containing Hollywood's guns. Hoyt went straight to the bathroom. Rugge didn't look surprised to see him.

Who's this guy? wondered Graham Pressley. He peeked into the bathroom and saw Hoyt cleaning a gun clip. But Pressley didn't say anything about it to anyone. He was afraid for his own life. Even when Nick woke up, he didn't mention anything to him about what this "new guy" was up to.

Rugge was annoyed, because he'd thought that Hollywood was going to be there, not just send his lackey. Rugge later insisted that he didn't know beforehand that Nick would be killed—he claimed that he didn't know until the moment when Hoyt arrived that that Nick wasn't actually going home. Rugge later told police, "That's when I knew everything went sour. I was expecting at least Jesse [Hollywood], at least his ass to show his fucking face."

Then Hoyt and Rugge left together and got into a Honda

sedan owned by Hollywood's friend Casey Sheehan. This was Pressley's chance to be a hero. He was alone with Nick and could have helped him, warned him, or called the police. But he didn't.

Earlier that day, Hollywood and his girlfriend had gone to Sheehan's apartment and, after a few beers, had asked to borrow his car. Sheehan later said that he thought they needed it to move more things out of Hollywood's house, so he handed over the keys to his mother's red Honda Civic, asking only that they make sure he had a ride to work the next day. Hollywood said he'd take care of it.

Casey Sheehan also knew all about Nick's kidnapping by that point, but he had also decided not to get involved.

If he had really thought that Hollywood needed the car to move, though, why hadn't Sheehan emptied out the trunk?

Hollywood then left, alone. He drove back to his house and gave the car to Hoyt, who was still there doing menial chores. This was the moment it all became real. Hoyt had the weapon and the car. Now his instructions were to go to Santa Barbara—and kill Nick.

Then Hollywood got into a different car and drove back to Sheehan's apartment to pick him up for dinner. He said that he'd been taking a shower and getting ready during that time; after all, it was his girlfriend Michelle's twentieth birthday, and Hollywood was taking her and Sheehan out to the Outback Steakhouse in the Northridge to celebrate.

Hollywood was calm at dinner, telling Sheehan cryptically that the situation with Nick had been "unwound," or "taken care of," depending on whose recollection one believed. Either way, apparently, neither Sheehan nor Michelle Lasher bothered to ask what that meant or whether Nick was on his way home. At least, neither of them ever admitted to asking the question, or hearing its answer. Hollywood paid the $108.98 bill on his American Express card, established his alibi, and left. He went back to Casey Sheehan's house and slept over that night.

While Hollywood was out, Ryan Hoyt and Jesse Rugge drove Sheehan's mother's car to Barron Rugge's house, where they picked up at least two shovels from the side yard and duct tape from the garage. Then Hoyt asked Rugge to show him a spot to dig a grave.

But Rugge said he didn't know the area very well, and Graham Pressley would be a better tour guide. So Hoyt went back to the Lemon Tree and picked up Pressley, leaving Rugge behind in the hotel to stay with Nick, who slept on and off over the next hour and a half. He just kept plying Nick with alcohol, marijuana, and Valium, and later claimed that it seemed like Nick was having a good time.

Hoyt and Pressley hadn't know each other before this day, but what Pressley did know by this point was that Hoyt had a gun and had come there on Hollywood's orders to use it in some fashion. He later said that when Hoyt ordered him to go with him to a hiking trail in the mountains of Santa Barbara and start digging, he thought he was digging his own grave. Maybe because he knew too much about the kidnapping.

The trail was called Lizard's Mouth, because that's what one of the giant rock formations looked like—a lizard with a wide-open mouth. It sat on the crest of the Santa Ynez Mountains, with a sweeping view of the ocean and the city of Goleta. Popular with hikers and lovers and beer-drinking teenagers, the trail was like a grown-up jungle gym, filled with caves and trees and interesting boulders to climb over and around. Some of the caves were pockmarked on the inside like beehives. The rock formations had names like Breathless and Sudden Fear. Sunset there was said to be beautiful.

But now, past midnight, it was a difficult hike to navigate—it took almost twenty minutes to get to the spot. Graham Pressley had been there many times before with friends to smoke pot. He now dug a hole near an overarching manzanita bush, ordered to be seven feet wide by two feet deep, until Ryan Hoyt decided it was enough. Hoyt would later testify that he didn't threaten Pressley with the gun because he "didn't have to." Then they went back for Nick. They taped up Nick's hands and legs and then realized they couldn't very well get downstairs and across the parking lot like that, so they untaped him.

Now it was all four of them in the car—Nick Markowitz, Graham Pressley, Jesse Rugge, and Ryan Hoyt—back on the way to Lizard's Mouth. It was a thirty-minute trip, and his captors later said that Nick was barely able to sit up straight on the ride there because of all the drugs and drinking.

Once they reached the site, they all got out of the car and headed toward the spot where Pressley had dug the grave. Of course, no one mentioned this to Nick. Did he have any idea what was in store? Probably not. He likely assumed that they were headed out there for some more partying.

Pressley said that it wasn't until they were walking to the grave that he knew for sure it was Nick whom they intended to kill—and that he froze in his tracks, unable to continue walking with them. Instead, the other three forged ahead, and Pressley went back to the car, where he sobbed and waited. Nick was walking in front of his captors wordlessly when Pressley last saw him—he wasn't complaining or putting up a fight. He was just walking.

Along the way, the three passed a few people who were coming down the mountain. They nodded to each other and didn't say much, if anything.

By the time that they reached a rock near the freshly dug grave, though, they were alone. Hoyt told Nick to sit down. Rugge pulled out the duct tape.

"I'm not going to hurt you," he allegedly said.

"I know you won't," Nick replied.

Rugge duct taped Nick's hands behind his back, which Nick willingly allowed him to do, but as he taped over his mouth and nose, Nick cried; he couldn't breathe.

Hoyt dragged Nick over to the grave. That must have been the moment that Nick realized that Rugge had lied to him. This was when he knew he was going to die.

———

My son . . .

It was the last second I could have gotten to him. The last sand in the hourglass was just about to fall, and I was still at home, drifting in and out of nightmares and no closer to finding him than I had been that first day.

———————

One of them knocked Nick down into the grave. They might or might not have hit him in the head with a shovel; later reports would be unclear. Then Ryan Hoyt pulled the trigger of the gun, landing nine bullets in Nick's face and torso. He would have kept going except that the gun jammed. But nine bullets were enough. Every one of them landed a possible fatal wound, with the final one ripping through Nick's jaw and through the back of his head.

Nick was gone.

Hoyt wiped off the gun and stuck it under Nick's legs; then the two killers quickly shoveled dirt and leaves over his still-warm body, the ground wet with pools of blood.

Jesse Rugge later said that he "almost" vomited and had to leave most of the shoveling duties to Hoyt. Hoyt, on the other hand, admired his own handiwork. When they got back to the car, he said, "That's the first time I ever did anybody. I didn't think he would go that fast."

He turned to Graham Pressley and said, "You ever tell anyone what you saw and I'll kill you."

Considering the circumstances, Pressley believed him. They told Pressley to stay at the Lemon Tree Inn that night and check out in the morning, but he couldn't sleep, so he called his mom and asked for a ride home at 6 a.m. He told her that he wasn't feeling well.

At 9:00 that morning, he called Natasha Adams and lied through his teeth.

"I drove Nick home," he told her. She was relieved. "I'll call you later today—I have to go to work, but we'll hang out later."

In the afternoon, he showed up at her house with a new story. He said that Hollywood had shown up at the hotel and laid a TEC-9 down on the bed, and Nick started crying. But it was just to scare him, so Nick wouldn't say anything. Then he and Hollywood and Rugge got into a car and drove around Los Angeles and then he dropped them all off, and drove through the mountains, and . . .

Adams admitted later that the story was pretty vague and not a clear explanation, but at that point, she was just so happy to hear that Nick was home that she didn't stop to question the details. Jesse Rugge also called her that afternoon to say hello and to tell her that he was staying at his mom's house for a week.

"Jesse Rugge was the same Jesse that I've known," Adams said. "Just really happy and joking around."

Graham Pressley, on the other hand, was acting a little strange, and she asked him if he was OK. He said he was fine. Adams let her mother know that the kidnapping situation had been resolved and that everything was OK now.

Casey Sheehan was returning from work when he noticed that his car, which he had loaned to Hollywood, was back. It was parked in the alley, and Hollywood, Hoyt, and William Skidmore were all sitting around inside his apartment. After a while, Hoyt asked Sheehan to drive him to a clothing store—a surf shop. He had a few hundred dollars with him.

Sheehan thought that was strange, because he knew that Hoyt owed Hollywood money. So he asked him how he could go shopping now.

"I went up to Santa Barbara and took care of the problem," he said.

"What problem do you mean?"

"The problem with Nicholas Markowitz."

"What are you talking about?"

"It's best that you don't know."

Ryan Hoyt slept over at Casey Sheehan's house that night and soon bragged to his friend about having killed Nick. Sheehan didn't know whether or not to believe him. Hoyt seemed far too calm for a guy who claimed to have just murdered a kid. No remorse, no guilt. Maybe it was just one of Hoyt's stories, Sheehan figured. He was notorious in the group for embellishing things to make himself sound cooler, tougher, or more handsome—including one time when he pretended he had landed a modeling job.

Ryan Hoyt was many things, but he was no model.

The following day, Thursday, was Ryan Hoyt's twenty-first birthday. Casey Sheehan threw him a big party, with about thirty people in attendance. One of the people there was Jesse James Hollywood, and Sheehan finally confronted him about Hoyt's claims. Was it true? Had Hoyt really killed Nick?

"Just don't worry about it," Hollywood said.

Sheehan later overheard Hoyt saying "We fucked up" to Hollywood, but the context wasn't clear. What had he done wrong? Had he screwed up by leaving the gun at the murder scene? By burying Nick in a shallow grave on a popular hiking trail? Or by killing Nick at all?

Hoyt slept over at Sheehan's house again that night. He was more agitated by then than he had been the previous day. It was starting to settle in that he had actually done something serious—and that it might have consequences.

For me, that day and the ones following it were more of the same—working on a spreadsheet detailing what everyone had told me and what places we had tried. I reached one boy who gave me a troubling answer when I asked if he knew where Nick was.

"I think he's on vacation," the boy said. When I asked him to explain what he meant, he wouldn't. That stuck with me. On vacation? Did he know something?

It was getting harder and harder to stay grounded in reality. I felt my mental health slipping. People's voices were becoming mere echoes. I didn't know whether it was day or night anymore, or whether I had eaten that day.

Jeff and Ben spent their days out on their motorcycles going up and down hills and hiking trails, while I tried to organize the volunteer squad. They just kept showing up, God bless them. But none of them were turning up anything useful, and neither were the police.

I really feel you are coming home, I told Nick in my mind. *Please hurry.*

———————

On Saturday, August 12, 2000, three and a half days after Nick had been murdered, twenty-seven-year-old Darla Gacek and two of her friends set out to hike up toward Lizard's Mouth. On the path, they heard a loud buzzing sound, which they thought was from a swarm of bees. They followed the sound and instead discovered hundreds of flies . . . and the stench of death. A dead animal, maybe a raccoon? But the smell was so strong. Too strong.

The hikers kicked the sand a little and their unspoken fears materialized in the form of a pair of blue jeans and the corner of a T-shirt. Liquid pooled up around the body. The hikers didn't want to disturb the scene any further. They managed to attract the attention of some local student film-makers who were filming nearby, and they borrowed their cell phone to call police. It nevertheless took police two hours to show up.

Meanwhile, Gacek guarded the body.

"It was totally surreal," she told detectives. "I'm think-ing the world is so beautiful, but yet there's this body that someone put there."

She prayed that it wasn't a kid.

But, of course, it was.

The California heat had done terrible things to Nick's body, speeding up the decomposition rate. Larvae had bur-rowed into his mouth and nose. His hands were bloated and discolored . . . with his father's ring still on his finger.

He was found face up, head leaning to his right, duct tape wrapped several times around his head over his mouth, ears, and part of his nose, with his arms awkwardly behind him.

Detectives photographed the hikers and filmmakers, as well as the soles of their shoes, in case they had to dif-ferentiate their footprints from those of the murderers. At

6:30 p.m., the witnesses left the scene, forever changed by what they saw.

It took detectives two days to officially identify the body, which they eventually managed to do through his badly decomposed fingerprints, which were on file from the time Nick was arrested for marijuana possession. How sad it was to realize that I was actually grateful now for that arrest, because it was the only way they were able to identify him.

———————

Before they even rang the doorbell, we knew that there were men at our door. We were so hypersensitive to every sound, waiting for Nick to come walking through that door, that the slightest rustle of trees or chirp of a bird could wake us from sleep and send us running to the window. This time, it was Jeff who made it to the window first.

"Who's there?" I asked.

"Some men in black suits."

I couldn't breathe.

It had been a week of looking for Nick, and now my heart felt like it might stop. I put on my robe slowly, because this might have been the last minute I could have any hope. Men in black suits do not come before seven in the morning to say, "Your son is just fine."

I glanced into Nick's room, at his empty bed, as I reached the stairs—the same stairs Nick would race down three at a time. Clutching the railing, I tried not to fall. One step, two steps. I had to make it down the stairs.

I thought for a minute that this might be a good surprise, and maybe Nick would be on the other side of that door with the men. I whispered prayers, as nausea overtook me.

I made it to the door and opened it. I was unsure of how many men there were—three? Four? All I saw were sad, serious eyes.

Make this be a dream.

They walked in and told us that they were sorry. "Some hikers found your son's body. We've positively identified it. It was bullet riddled . . ."

Tears fell and my body trembled as I found the couch behind me. I felt gutted. This could not be real.

Duct taped, gagged, and with his arms behind him. Nine bullets to his face and torso. Execution style. Found in a shallow grave.

The detectives smelled of death. They wanted a photo of Nick. Privately, they took Jeff aside to ask why we had duct tape on our stairs, just in case it was related. They needed to go through Nick's room and our home to investigate for murder evidence. *Murder evidence.* They did this with finesse; I could not even remember them taking Nick's computer, though the receipt said that they did so at 10:50 a.m. From that, I could only assume it meant they were in my house for four hours that day. I don't remember at all.

How anyone else found out, I have no idea. People just started calling and showing up.

Ben had been out late when he got a wake-up phone call from his aunt.

"They found Nick," she said.

"That's great. Let me go back to sleep—it's early in the morning," he said.

"Well . . . no, Ben, they found him . . . but he's not OK."

She explained how the hikers had found him, and Ben was in shock. Until that moment, he had really believed that Nick had just run away to a friend's house. His screams woke his two roommates.

In a similar fashion, Leah got a morning wake-up call from her mother's mother.

"I'm so sorry about your brother," she said.

"Don't worry about him. He just ran away for a few days. I'm sure he'll be fine," Leah said.

"Oh God . . . you don't know."

———

I couldn't talk, so I tried to write something. The first words that came out were:

I am not screaming.
I am numb.
I feel nothing.
I feel hollow.
I died with Nick.

CHAPTER 10

PLEASE, GOD, THERE'S BEEN A MISTAKE

"Missing boy found dead."
"Body identified as Woodland Hills boy."
"Body identified as missing teen."

Those were the headlines the following day. I didn't want to miss any of the news, so I kept checking the television, not wanting to miss seeing my baby's face. I was still waiting for someone to tell me that they had their wires crossed and it wasn't Nick after all. The body was decomposed, so maybe the fingerprints weren't accurate. There was still a God, right?

Someone—maybe it was me—had had the good sense to put a note on our front door saying "No media, please." I didn't hate them for being there; in a way, I even appreciated that they cared to report about Nick, but we weren't in any condition to face reporters or talk coherently.

Outside my window, I could see people gathering. I walked out and went straight into denial mode, playing hostess to this yard memorial. I felt that if I stayed busy, then this would turn out to have just been a bad dream. We needed sodas for the kids, and music, and photos of Nick to put up outside. We needed candles, and people to keep them lit. I assigned tasks to everyone.

Why isn't someone telling me this is a mistake?

———

Natasha Adams's mother read the newspaper that morning and showed the article to her daughter.

"How could this happen?" Adams cried. When her parents left for work, she drove to Jesse Rugge's house to confront him, calling him a murderer.

"It's not what you think," he told her. He was shirtless, and Adams said she could actually see his heart beating.

Hours later, she went to her mother's law firm and conferred with a lawyer, who told her that she had a grant of immunity, which meant that she could never be prosecuted for any involvement she had with the crime, as long as she told the truth about what happened. Only then did she go to the police and tell them what she knew.

Just before she showed up at the police station, another young woman called on the condition of anonymity and told a detective that she knew the people responsible for Nick's murder. So when Adams arrived, the story she told was no great surprise. It matched the basic facts given by the anonymous caller.

Ultimately, seventeen-year-old Natasha Adams was the lone person, out of dozens, who chose to stand up to Jesse James Hollywood. She was immune from prosecution, but she was not immune from Hollywood's wrath.

———

I'm not sure where we would be today if those two girls hadn't been brave enough to take this step. My biggest heartbreak was that they didn't find that bravery a week earlier. Had they called police back then, it would have been the difference between life and death.

Meanwhile, I had trouble breathing; anxiety attacks stole all the air around me, making my chest feel constricted.

It felt like I was falling into nothing. With all these emotions overwhelming me, I had to do something, had to stay busy.

I should make sure the table fountain has water in it.

The music had to be nonstop, but only certain types of music. I'm surprised I didn't hire a DJ. The yard memorial went on for days, with people stopping by, coming in and out and sharing hugs and bringing gifts.

We received so many beautiful gifts, most of which were untraceable. However, I knew the origin of one that was left on my doorstep: unbelievably beautiful porcelain angels from the parents of Bernardo A. Repreza, a very handsome boy who had been beaten and stabbed to death in 1998 at fifteen years old, just like Nick. I don't think I met his parents, but if I did, I know they would understand my lack of memory.

Thank you. I will keep your son's picture forever.

A live praying mantis appeared on our table water fountain that day, and I remember being comforted by the sight of it as it drank from the fountain. The praying mantis, in my mind, was a sign from Nick. I had seen a praying mantis only once before, on a rose bush when Nick was about seven years old. He had been very intrigued by it. He had a whole set of thousands of cards called the *Illustrated Wildlife Treasury*, with pictures and information about all sorts of animals, and he read them all. The bugs were what intrigued him the most. If I ever had a bug question, I would ask him.

What do praying mantises eat? I should bring him something. Do they eat bugs?

That mantis hung around the whole week, sometimes taking shelter in our garage and sitting on flower arrangements people had brought, sometimes sitting on a chair or table. I was able to hold it in my hands, talk to it.

Is that you, Nick? Do you need me?

I waited for Nick to come put his arm around me and tell me it was all a big joke and, "Hey, by the way, I sent this little praying mantis to keep you company for a while."

But he didn't show up. He had to still be coming home, didn't he?

What the yard really needed, I decided, was more posters. And now I had a reason to make more. I got back on the computer, for hours at a time, designing new ones:

"Use, Buy, or Sell Drugs and You're Putting Another Nail in Nick's Coffin" was one of many.

Maybe, if I did all the right things, I could have him back. If I showed that I had learned my lesson, if I promised to get it right this time. This couldn't really be happening. This stuff happened on the news. It didn't happen to my child; it happened to *other* people.

Detectives interviewed Ben at our house that day and asked him about people he'd been associated with. Ben was candid from the start about his drug dealing and his past problems with gangs and illegal activities. He didn't understand what the officers were probing for, though, until they asked him what kinds of guns Jesse James Hollywood owned. When he told them about the TEC-9, the officers' eyes lit up. Ben noticed the looks they exchanged, and he realized at that moment who was responsible for his brother's murder.

Guilt or rage—I'm not sure which feeling came first, but they both came. And they hit hard, for all of us.

It had all come down to Ben. All those years of trying, of worrying, of taking him back and trying again and loving and disciplining, and none of it had worked. Instead, it had all led to this moment—the moment when Ben's latest drama got my son killed.

It was too much. How do you process something like that? I don't remember how I did. At first, it was just disbelief—I didn't want to think that Ben could have had anything to do with this, or that he could have prevented it. We were learning only bits and pieces at a time. I knew there was something about a drug debt that Ben owed, and something about a kidnapping. We overheard some of the interview and caught on to that much right away.

My dad and brothers were there, burning with enough anger that they could have killed Ben on the spot.

"Keep it together," I told them. "Don't do anything."

It was enough to deal with what was happening as it was. I couldn't imagine what I would do if a fight broke out on my front lawn. As I accepted what the police were telling us, I remember feeling betrayed in a way that was more visceral than I'd ever experienced. I didn't want to ever look at Ben again.

Ben told police about the .25 caliber handgun he had bought, and he told them that he wanted to turn it in to them so he wouldn't be tempted to retaliate—or get blamed if anyone else *did* retaliate. Police went through Ben's wardrobe with him because he couldn't remember which shirt or jacket pocket he had left the gun in. They found and confiscated it.

By Wednesday, August 16, officers had arrested William Skidmore, Jesse Rugge, and Graham Pressley. A SWAT team had surrounded Skidmore's house with guns drawn, then pulled him out of the house and shackled him as he lay facedown on the driveway in his T-shirt and boxer shorts. Deputies tackled Rugge on his father's front lawn. Pressley surrendered at the police station, with his parents. At 2 a.m. the next morning, police found Ryan Hoyt at Casey Sheehan's house and arrested both of them—later releasing Sheehan once they determined that he wasn't a participant in the crime.

Once the suspects were in custody, police searched their houses, pulling out every drawer, rifling through every cabinet, searching for weapons, drugs, notes, clues. Their parents were stunned, watching their houses get torn apart and their belongings dumped on the floor. By now, news about this local murder was all over the San Fernando Valley, but the fact that their sons were involved was a shock to all of them.

All except the Hollywoods, of course, who were well aware that their son had kidnapped the boy who had now been found dead. Police raided their home and brought out bags and bags of items—but they didn't find Jesse James Hollywood.

———————

I knew little of the goings-on at the police station at the time. Maybe Jeff knew more; frankly, I don't remember much about anyone else during those early days. I mostly remember the dizziness and the unreality of it all, and I remember just trying to hold it together. I didn't have any room left in me to take care of anyone else.

At some point, sitting around the glass dining room table, we picked out a box for our son's body. I don't remember what it looked like, but I'm sure it was nice. Someone brought up that we should have a limousine take us to the funeral. At first, that was discussed in a negative light, then I insisted we do it because I didn't want any one of us driving that day.

No one was going to ruin Nick's funeral, I thought, not even myself. I had to pull myself together. I needed a sedative, so I got a prescription.

Bob, the community's friendliest pharmacist, made a house call. For all of the children's doctor's visits that required medicine through the years, we went to Bob. Now there he was in the living room, with his blue teary eyes, warm heart, and trembling hand, offering me a little white bag along with the tightest embrace.

I slept in Nick's bed.

The day of the funeral, I was there, but not there. *Nick wouldn't want me to wear black*, I thought. What do you wear to your son's funeral? He liked color. Every color, except my pinkish-salmon sweatpants. I remember the day I tried to drive him to school while wearing those, and he—afraid I might have a reason to get out of the car—turned to me and said, "Mom, you're not going to wear those, are you?" Well, there was at least one outfit I could cross off the list of possible things to wear.

At the last minute, with the limousine waiting outside, someone told me that we could bring things to place in the casket with Nick. Feeling rushed and defensive, I thought, "Why didn't someone tell me this sooner?" I walked into Nick's room and gathered up things I knew others would consider silly. There was a family photo, plus a picture of Nick's dog, Zak.

Grandpa Pooh wanted to give Nick his Chapstick and nail clippers. Leah gave a letter and his favorite Nintendo game, *James Bond 007*. All of these items went into a Ziploc bag. I don't know who took it or why that, but that's what it was—our final memories in a plastic bag. And I included the words of a poem I wrote the night after we found out Nick had been killed. Then I argued with myself about whether or not to put in his Old Testament Bible. I thought he might want it, but I also became selfish, not wanting to part with anything of his.

"It's time to go," someone said.

We arrived at Eden Memorial Park's chapel and found it packed and spilling outside. There were about seven hundred people present, most looking as confused as we were. How could this have happened here, in our neighborhood? How could these killers have been the same kids who played Little League together not so long ago?

"There are deaths such as this when we can't shake an angry finger at God and say, 'Why?' We can only look at ourselves," the rabbi said, in a service that had to be broadcast over an intercom so the crowd could all hear.

I never saw Nick's body in the casket, so I just had to trust he was in there. I stood by the deep, deep hole and asked Jeff to hold me so I wouldn't fall in.

Piggybacking caskets. What a distasteful term for what it means; in this case, it gave me the option to be buried in the same plot as Nick. His coffin would be twelve feet down and mine would be six feet down. I wondered how soon I would join him. Quickly, I hoped. I just wanted to be with him again, no matter how that had to happen.

"Ben is such a coward!" I told everyone. "He didn't even show up at his brother's funeral!"

What I didn't realize at the time was that Jeff had

asked Ben not to come to the funeral because he thought it would upset me. I had said something about how every big event wound up being about Ben—the way he caused a big scene at Nick's bar mitzvah, at Leah's wedding—and I didn't want Nick's funeral to be about Ben, too. But I didn't remember that conversation, and Jeff didn't mention that he had asked Ben not to be there, so it just made me angrier that he hadn't shown up.

I was furious and miserable and out of my mind and every other bad emotion a person can have all at once.

After the funeral, I kept changing outfits because I couldn't get comfortable. I didn't know who I was anymore. I was a childless mother.

Is a mother who has lost her only child still a mother?

Being a mom had been my love and my job. Now I had no job. I went out into the yard and found that the praying mantis had died that day, too.

My mind wandered back to Nick's Bible . . . had I put it with the things to go in the casket, or not? I looked around and, with a pang of guilt mixed with relief, found it. My eyes, tired and weak from crying, spotted the gold bookmarking ribbon. What passage would I find there? The delicate sound of aging pages reminded me to be gentle with the book as I opened to page 282 of the Old Testament: Ecclesiastes, chapter 3: "Times and Seasons."

To everything, there is a season,
And a time to every purpose under the heaven: A time
    to be born, and a time to die;
A time to plant, and a time to pluck up that which is
    planted;
A time to kill and a time to heal;
A time to break down and a time to build up;
A time to weep, and a time to laugh;
A time to mourn, and a time to dance . . .

People interpret the things that come to them in different ways. For me, this passage was a sign. It told me to breathe, to embrace, to love, if even for just a moment. It warned me not to succumb to the darkness I wanted to slip into.

"Please don't let this day end," I wrote in my journal. "I'll have to face reality. I hear God is going to help . . . I am going to need it."

Jeff's ex-wife called to offer her condolences; we were, at that point, on friendly terms, but what I said next changed that forever.

She told me how bad she felt for me, and I said, "The only thing worse that I can imagine is being the mother of someone responsible for this . . . and that's kind of you, in a way."

She hung up on me and never spoke to me again.

It wasn't a kind thing to say, but it's what I felt.

I expressed that same sentiment to a reporter—that I thought it would be worse to be the parent of one of the killers because I wouldn't be able to live with myself—and Ryan Hoyt's mother took umbrage.

"Well, my situation is better than theirs. My son didn't do this," she said.

Before dawn, I stole the neighbor's newspaper just so that I could see Nick's face again. Then I went back to his bed and hoped for sleep. Five a.m. Six a.m. With nothing left to plan, no more obligations left to meet, there was no longer a reason for me to get out of bed—so that was where I stayed. For how long, I'm not sure, but I do recall that eventually Dr. Chris Fulton, our family therapist, had to come talk to me in Nick's bedroom because I would not leave it. I didn't feel like I could.

People never know what to say when someone has died. I think they know even less what to say when it's a murdered child. Mothers are not supposed to outlive their children; it's so against the accepted order of events. But some people truly want to make things better with their words. They want to make some sense out of something so senseless.

"God has a reason for everything," they would say.

A reason for everything but this, I thought. And the more I thought about that idea—that God had some control over this—the angrier I got. I wrote him a letter.

Dear God,

How could this have happened? Why my only child? Why not an accident? If you're so capable of miracles, now would be a good time. What was the purpose of my son's execution? I've heard that everything happens for a reason.
  Bull.
  This could have been stopped. And until there is something, anything, to hang on to . . . I've let go.

My mother made me promise that I would not commit suicide. I promised just so that she would leave me alone, but I didn't mean it. Every night, I hoped to sleep in, so that the next day wouldn't be as long. I took my sedatives and cried until I dry heaved, and eventually I just ran out of tears. I had come untethered from the world, and I prayed to die so I could be with Nick.

In the meantime, I wrote lists.

Every little personality trait of my son's went into a list. Every funny little memory, every quirk—did you know he put syrup into his clam chowder? Or that he had to lie down to have blood drawn? He had a mole on his back, handed down through generations. He hated when I brought up that he had size fourteen shoes. These were things that needed to be documented, so no one would ever forget.

Just in case God heard my prayer and took me to see Nick, someone was going to have to stay on Earth and remember my memories for me.

CHAPTER 11

ALL I DID WAS KILL HIM

By the time they sat down with Jesse Rugge, police already had a pretty clear picture of what had happened and how Rugge was involved. Rugge, however, was determined to play dumb when detectives asked him if he had read an article about a recent homicide in the area.

"Not really. I just looked at it and briefly was like, 'Whoa. Tripped out.'"

Tripped out?

"I was surprised. It's from the same area I just came back from on Sunday daytime from a wedding."

He didn't know Nick Markowitz, Rugge assured them, but he recognized the last name because he had run into Ben Markowitz in the "Valley party scene." They had talked maybe once or twice, years ago.

When the detectives asked who Rugge normally hung out with, he said, "No one, really," and then mentioned three guys, including Graham Pressley, whom he said he saw every now and then. But really, he said, he had "pretty much stopped" being part of the party scene when he was nineteen. Now he was twenty. He didn't want to be the old guy who hung around high school parties anymore, he explained.

"Do you know any other Jesses? Keep in mind we're not sitting here because we're stupid," the detective said.

"I know a bunch of kids."

"Tell us about Jesse. Jesse from West Hills."

"Used to play baseball as kids . . . I don't know Jesse's last name."

"What does Jesse do now?"

"Think he's working for a wood floor company, maybe, but I haven't seen him for a while."

"What does he look like?"

"He has long hair, I think."

"White guy?"

"No, brownish."

"Hispanic?"

"No, tan. I probably haven't seen him in a month, month and a half, so I really don't know what he looks like now."

"So, you don't remember his last name?"

"No, not really. I don't, actually."

"Do you know how that sounds?"

"Well, yeah, it sounds awkward . . . Look, I know the kid from playing baseball when we were younger. I've run into him at a party. That's really the only acquaintances I have with this man." After a pause, "You guys freaked me out pulling up to my house."

"I'm going to ask you the freakiest question in the world. Did you have anything to do with this? Anything at all? I'm not necessarily asking if you killed the kid, just if you had anything to do with it."

"Where do you get this from? No, I do not. I don't get why you're even asking me this. This is ridiculous, sir."

It was as if Jesse Rugge thought that the detectives were simply going to have a good chuckle about what a silly mix-up this was, then let him go back home to sleep. He was obviously tired—throughout the whole interview, he yawned huge, sloppy yawns. And kept asking for cigarettes.

The first little bump in his smooth-sailing road of denial came when the detectives mentioned that they had been speaking with his father and stepmother for—oh, an hour and a half or so. And they had made it clear that they'd both seen Jesse James Hollywood at their house that weekend. "You know, the guy you really don't know?" detectives asked.

"Mmm hmm," Rugge mumbled.

Still, he wasn't ready to give in, insisting that he was being accused of something he didn't do. "I don't have no idea of what you guys are talking about. Obviously, you know as much as I do."

The detectives were patient, and they worked hard for their confession. They slowly let Rugge in on more and more details of what they already knew and could prove. Among other things, they told him that they had pictures from the security cameras at the Lemon Tree Inn showing that he was there renting a room the night before the murder. Each new piece of evidence made Rugge act more miserable—he put his head down on the table, didn't know what to do with his hands.

What they explained to him was that they knew Rugge was involved, but they didn't yet know why. Was he a cold-blooded killer, or had someone put him up to this? Had he pulled the trigger, or had someone else done it? No answer.

"I think somebody else is responsible for this, and I'd hate to see you make a bad decision," one of the detectives said.

"If you think it's Jesse [Hollywood] or them, I doubt it's them," Rugge said.

"Jesse is involved up to here," the detective said, gesturing to his head. "You're there. Right there when it happened."

"No, I wasn't. I don't know what people have been telling you, bro."

"Tell me about the Lemon Tree."

Nothing.

The detective continued, "I know who was there and

you were there renting a room. Guess who one of the pictures is? The dead guy. Isn't that a coincidence? Don't you
think that's some coincidence, Jess?"

"That's some shit."

No matter how clear it was at this point that he couldn't
get away with playing dumb, Jesse Rugge still refused to
talk. The detective asked if he was afraid of what Hollywood was going to do to him.

"No, I'm afraid what jail is going to do to me. That's one
fucking thing I'm scared of. It's my life. I'm going away for
a very long time. I'm going to get hurt inside there. I'm a
white man."

Then, the first little crack of the doorway opened. "I
didn't get any money," Rugge said.

"But you got offered it."

Rugge wanted to know what a judge could "stick him"
with.

"Capital murder, kidnapping, torture . . ." the detective
said.

"Torture?" Rugge's face contorted. The first two didn't
bother him, but the last one sure did. "I didn't do nothing!"

Fine, the detective said. We know you're no cold-
blooded killer, but you know who is.

"I'm not a killer, but I don't know who was."

"I know who was in the car, what you brought, where
you went . . ."

"It makes me look like a rat. I'll get my ass stabbed in
jail."

"You're not afraid of Ryan?"

"Who's that?"

And so went round two of "Rugge Tries to Pretend the
Detectives Are Idiots." He went through great pains to avoid
giving anyone's last name at any time, and he mostly tried
to pretend he didn't know anyone on the planet. Perhaps
he'd been living in a bomb shelter for the last few years.

"All I did was hold the kid," he finally said. "Didn't hurt
him. Acted like my best friend, that's all. I didn't do anything."

"You didn't know what was coming?"

"I'm going down for something. I'm freaking out. Ben Markowitz is a good guy."

That gave the detectives a good laugh. If they had learned anything from all these interviews, it was clearly that Ben was *not* a good guy.

"What did Nick think was happening?" they asked him.

"I don't know. I wasn't briefed with anything."

"What did you think was going to happen at Lizard's Mouth?"

"I don't know."

"Why did you need shovels and duct tape?"

"I didn't put anything in the car. I did not hurt the kid."

That became one of Rugge's most-repeated catch phrases. "I did not hurt the kid." Sometimes a "fucking" got thrown in there, too—"I did not hurt the fucking kid." It came up every few minutes in various contexts. Once he even pounded his fist on the table for emphasis. Yes, he kidnapped him, but he didn't hurt him. Yes, he made him do chores at his father's house, but he didn't hurt him. Yes, he held him against his will, but . . .

Then he stopped talking about the crime. "I'm just fucking scared, dude. Where am I going to be sitting when I go to jail? LA County? I'll get ripped up in there in a second . . . Anywhere in prison I go to, there's someone who's going to know it. And I just meet up with them in the transfers."

"You could be sentenced to death. It looks like you put him in his own grave and shot him, so it doesn't matter who you're going to be afraid of," the detective told him. "I'd be afraid of that needle. Does that spin it a little different?"

After some more agonizing silence, Rugge spilled a few more details: Jesse James Hollywood had been driving the van when they'd spotted Nick and kidnapped him, then made Rugge drive. Then Hollywood told Rugge to hold Nick.

"He could have ran and I never even would have stopped to think twice. I'm not even going to run the kid down. He just obeyed everything . . . he wasn't tied down. I'd leave him alone with the phone and he wouldn't even make a phone call."

What was the plan? There wasn't any, Rugge said. As far as he knew, someone was coming to the Lemon Tree Inn to take Nick away—but somehow, the plan changed.

"You helped dig the grave, didn't you?" detectives asked.

"I didn't dig no grave. Fuck, no."

"Who dug it?"

"I don't know. You guys know who dug the goddamned grave. I'm the only one who knows . . ." A pause. "You guys talked to Natasha."

"We're not going to tell you."

But that didn't mean that Rugge wasn't going to keep trying to get more information. Throughout his interview, he kept trying to weasel information out of the detectives about what they already knew, who they had already spoken to, and what those other people had said. Before he gave his story, he wanted to hear "some of the other stories." Before Rugge named who did the shooting, he wanted the detectives to say the names of the people they already knew about. Of course, they wouldn't do that.

"There is one killer and one killer only. All I did was watch a kid get put in his grave and got [sic] shot," Rugge said.

Graham Pressley really had waited out by the car, he said, and the killer dragged Nick to his grave and shot him—one shot was all it took for Nick to die, he said.

"I only put two shovels of dirt on him, that's it. I couldn't do it."

As for what Nick was saying in those last moments, Rugge said he blocked it out.

When the detectives asked for more description of Ryan, Rugge said, "We all played baseball together . . . The Pirates. He doesn't live with his parents . . . He's maybe a little shorter than me. I'm six feet four inches; he's like six feet two inches, dirty blond hair. Ryan's a loner type, like a hang-around. Ryan is one of Jesse's friends."

But Jesse Rugge insisted that he had no idea what Ryan's last name was—right up until the moment when he messed up and said, "Hoyt came up here." He immediately realized his error and said, "I wanted to tell you that anyway." After that, he was more forthcoming about naming Ryan as the killer.

"Why did he have to tape his hands? Ryan said, 'Put the tape on his hands so he can't do anything.' I feel so bad. Nick didn't say anything, didn't fight . . . Hoyt didn't want to hear him talk to say anything. After he was taped, Ryan took out the gun. Ryan finished everything."

After he had a minute to think through the last hour of confessions, Rugge said, "See, dude? You made me a rat." He repeated that a few times, worrying that he was going to look like a "little bitch" in prison. Then he wanted assurances that they were going to leave his sister out of this, because she was a "good, loving mother" who had told him to turn himself in when he first confided in her, after Nick's murder.

"I thought all I was doing was taking this kid for a day and a half. I ruined my life. I ruined this kid's life. I ruined this kid's family's life . . . I can't believe what I got myself into. I'm so sorry. I'm so fucking sorry. You don't know what I feel," Rugge said.

With that, the detectives left the room for several minutes, leaving Rugge alone in the room with the tape still rolling. He picked his nose for a solid minute. Then he yawned, put his head down, shifted around, yawned some more.

When they returned, they told him to strip down. He took off his shirt, revealing his last name, "RUGGE," spelled out in a big tattoo across his stomach. Then came the pants—and the Joe Boxer yellow boxer shorts with the big smiley face across the front. They handed him his new prison jumpsuit, in red, which concerned him. Did red have a special significance? Was it for special types of crimes? Maybe it was meant to draw more attention to him, the new prison rat.

But he was not going to be the only new rat in town.

Shortly after Ryan Hoyt was arrested, there was a news conference on television about it, which his mother, Vicky Hoyt, saw. When Ryan called her from jail that night, she asked, "You didn't do this, right?"

"Right."

Her demeanor became manic, alternating between yelling and whispering, words tripping over themselves.

"Ryan, Ryan, you are innocent. You are so innocent. You are guilty by association."

"I know," he said.

"Who did this? You tell them right now!"

"I don't know."

"Where is Jesse? Where the fuck is he?"

"I don't know."

"Then find him! Spill your fucking guts and get out now! Do it for me, do it for your family, do it for yourself. Tell them what you know. Ryan, you tell them now, you fucking asshole. Don't defend anybody. This is your life!"

It was an instruction she would drive home again and again until he listened.

"Turn Jesse Hollywood in now! Now! You talk now! You tell the guard you want to talk to the detectives!"

"Mom, calm down," he said. He told her that he had been at his grandmother's home on the night of the murder. "The thing is, I need Grandma to say that I was at home."

Vicky would later say that her son was laughing during this phone call. "He said he did not do this crime. He's not capable of it. My family will vouch for him; his father will."

He followed the advice his mother had given him. So he called out for an officer, and the officer informed detectives that Hoyt was ready to talk.

Meanwhile, his grandmother went to check on a hysterical Vicky, who was attempting to jump out a window. She wound up in the emergency room at Olive View Hospital at about the same time her son was entering an interrogation room.

Two men, Detectives Mike West and Ken Reinstadler, sat across the table from Hoyt.

"Good evening. How you doing?" Detective Reinstadler said.

"Shitty," answered Hoyt.

After a little small talk, Hoyt said, "I called my mom and she tells me there's a news conference and people are saying I dug the grave."

Hoyt hadn't wanted to speak to detectives when they first arrested him; he had said he wanted an attorney, which they now reminded him about.

"But all this, excuse my language—bullshit—starts flying out and I don't know what to think. I'm in my cell throwing up."

The detectives again advised Hoyt of his Miranda rights: the right to remain silent, the right to an attorney, the right to have the court appoint an attorney if he could not afford one. After Hoyt signed a document agreeing that he was waiving these rights, he went on.

"I feel like I've been shit on, excuse my language . . . I honestly really do not know that much about any of this, OK? OK?"

"We have interviewed dozens of people. We know that you're involved in this killing. Too many people can't be saying the same things for it not to be that way."

"Look, all I know is this: somebody told me that this kid's older brother owed a lot of people money, OK?"

"Who's that someone?" Detective West asked.

"Someone who's still missing."

"Let's not play games. We know exactly who you're talking about. We want to hear it out of your mouth."

"The thing . . . it's going to be used against me in a court of law and I can't."

"Where you stand now is, what are you going to say that's going to help your case?"

"I would like you guys to talk to my grandmother because, one, I was Friday night home, Saturday night I stayed at Jesse's cause I've been helping him move out of that house. Sunday night I was home."

"You're talking about Jesse who?"

"Hollywood."

Then Hoyt continued his recounting of the past week—he'd been at home on Monday and Tuesday. "Wednesday through Sunday I was at Casey's house because my birthday was on Thursday. So I don't see how I can be placed as the guy digging this kid's grave and killing him."

"You didn't dig the grave. You killed him. That's a little misunderstanding there between you and Grandma. You've been identified."

As the detectives continued painting the picture of just how much trouble Hoyt was in, he seemed to finally grasp that they were serious—he wasn't going to get away with murder. And his voice got soft.

"You mind if I go back to my cell and think about it tonight and talk to you guys tomorrow? Cause I know my arraignment is Monday."

"Once you're arraigned, we can't talk to you," Detective Reinstadler told him. "That's the bottom line. If you want to tell us something, I'm being honest with you, this is your opportunity to do it. This is it."

"If I talk, does my name . . . does it get said in court that I said it?"

"There's no way to keep your name out of it . . . that's the way the law works."

"Well, I mean, what if *you* said it in court?"

"You may have to say in court yourself what you're going to tell us. It depends on what it is and the situation."

"Do you mind if I have a glass of water or something?"

"Sure."

One of the detectives went off in search of a drink while Hoyt continued. "I had nothing to do with the kidnapping." Then his voice switched to a whisper. "Then why am I charged with it?"

The detectives encouraged him to start talking. "Give

us something that we know you're telling us things in good faith. Like, where is Jesse Hollywood right now?"

"Honestly—I mean, to tell you honestly, nobody knows that. Nobody."

"But you know where you are, right, Ryan?"

"Yeah, behind bars for life. If I end up behind bars for life, I can't be behind bars for life as a rat."

"Did you bring something back to Jesse Hollywood to show him that this was done and over with?"

"No."

"Why did you do it? Do you owe him money? I know you deal dope for him, OK? We know that. And we know how it works. How much money did you owe him? How much?"

"Enough to do what I did."

Hoyt wouldn't pin down a figure—maybe because two hundred dollars sounded ridiculous in exchange for committing murder.

"You know that I owed money. I found out Tuesday of a way to erase that debt."

"And who told you how to do that?"

Hoyt didn't respond.

"Well, this has to do with your first statement, correct? When you said that Jesse Hollywood told you something about Ben, right?" asked Detective West.

"Yes. The thing was, what Ben owed Jesse didn't, in my opinion—this is off the record. I'm going to say this off the record—in my opinion, didn't justify this kid's death. It's the thirty thousand he owed somebody, it's the forty thousand he owed somebody."

"So, Ben's debt to Jesse wasn't that great, but Ben was into other people for lots."

"Lots. Still is. In fact, I think he was beat up recently for it."

They talked a bit about how much Ben owed to other drug dealers, and then Hoyt said, "In my opinion, it's a damn shame, a damn shame that this kid had to go for it. But I had nothing to do with the kidnapping."

He went on to say that an intermediary for Hollywood had pulled up in a car on Tuesday to ask if he wanted to get rid of his debt. Then the guy said, "Take care of somebody," and gave him directions to get to the Lemon Tree Inn.

"What did you take that to mean?" Detective West asked.

"Well, that I had to do something pretty serious."

"That you had to kill Nick?"

"Is that his name?" Hoyt asked. They all just called him "Ben's brother," he explained.

"How did you get the gun?" Detective Reinstadler asked.

"It was there waiting . . . it was at where we finally ended up."

When the detectives urged him to describe what happened once he got to the hotel, Hoyt said, "You guys know what happened. I think I'm going to stop there for now." But he didn't stop. He kept talking. "I have an eight-year-old brother whom I love dearly. I have a mom who depends on me. She's already got a son locked up. She's got an addict for a daughter. You see why I'm so hesitant?"

When Ryan Hoyt spoke with his mom, she had told him that she couldn't afford to get him a lawyer. "And a public defender, I'm going nowhere with that one."

"Let's put this in perspective here, OK? Who are you ultimately concerned with?" the detective asked. "Who did you feel sorry for here?"

"Not me."

"Who?"

"The kid that I buried."

"What has been going through your mind since this happened?"

"You don't even want to know that one."

"Having trouble sleeping?"

"Sort of."

"Wake up thinking about someone saying, 'Please, please.' Am I right?"

"Close."

"That was what the duct tape around his mouth was for."

"I didn't do that." That was Jesse Rugge, Hoyt said.

"You're saying he put [on] the duct tape. He said you did it."

"Really?"

"Oh yeah."

"I love this one. The only thing I did was kill him."

The detectives didn't react. They didn't miss a beat.

"You didn't dig the hole, right? You didn't duct tape him at all?"

"I put it over his mouth at the hotel, but I took it off when we left."

They tossed the duct tape in the garbage at the hotel, Hoyt said, and Rugge was the one who put more duct tape on Nick once they got out to the grave—which Graham Pressley had dug. Detectives asked if he threatened Pressley, but Hoyt said he didn't have to—Pressley had just picked the spot and done it, no questions asked. They didn't speak except to talk about directions.

And then Ryan Hoyt decided that he'd talked enough for the night.

Detectives now had confessions from everyone in custody. Now there was just one more objective: to find Jesse James Hollywood.

CHAPTER 12

THE FUGITIVE

The others had been fairly easy to find. They hadn't made attempts to flee. Jesse James Hollywood, however, had a support network that none of the others shared. Because of his father's connections and money, he also had opportunities none of the others did: hush money, bribe money, high-priced lawyers, people who owed favors.

Hollywood leased a new Lincoln LS Town Car on the day Nick was murdered, cashed out his bank accounts, and went around collecting from all the people who owed him money. Then he went to see his mom, because he didn't know when he'd ever see her again, considering he was about to go on the run. They were close; after his mother and father separated, Hollywood would call her every night to ask if she was OK and see if she needed anything.

He and his mom drove to Palm Springs to see Michelle Lasher at a modeling convention there; then Hollywood and Lasher came back to Los Angeles and visited William Skidmore. Skidmore told them that the news had just broken—Nick's body had been found, and authorities were looking for him.

"I'm [a] ghost," Hollywood said. And what better place to disappear to than the Bellagio Hotel in Las Vegas? Fountains, gambling, shows, security cameras every ten feet . . . which might have been more of a concern except that Michelle Lasher says they stayed for just one night and never left the hotel room. They argued, and Hollywood decided that they should move on.

He next headed to his old stomping grounds in Woodland Park, Colorado, where he had lived for a few years while his dad ran a restaurant. His path followed common patterns among fugitives; they tend to run to places they're familiar with first. Detectives discovered that Michelle Lasher had checked them into a motel called the Loft House—but the detectives apparently just missed them.

They had a good idea of who Hollywood would run to in Colorado: his godfather, Richard Dispenza, a forty-seven-year-old teacher and coach of football and girl's soccer at Woodland Park High School. The Hollywoods had become close with Dispenza while they lived in Colorado, and he'd even been Jesse's coach for some time. Jesse Hollywood still called him "Coach." Jack Hollywood had called Dispenza to let him know that Jesse was in trouble and would probably be heading his way.

But when investigators questioned him, Richard Dispenza claimed that he didn't know where Hollywood and Lasher had gone. He admitted that the couple had stayed with him for one night, on August 16. But after that, well, gosh darn it, wouldn't you know? They just disappeared. Strangest thing how that happens, isn't it?

Investigators sensed that Dispenza was lying, but they had no way to prove it yet. What had actually happened was that Dispenza had checked his godson into a Ramada Inn in Colorado Springs for August 17 through August 20. He did it under his own name but told the clerk the room was for someone else.

Hollywood was calling Michelle Lasher "Sue" on that trip and introducing her to people under that name. But once he was settled in Colorado, Hollywood told her that it was time for her to go home. He didn't even drive her to the airport; she took a taxi.

She returned home by plane, and she found detectives sitting on her couch. They had been there to talk to her parents and had no idea she was about to walk in with a suitcase. Once they took her to the police station, in front of her mother and investigators in the middle of questioning, Michelle began rubbing her breasts.

"I have to do this," she explained. "I just got my boobs done." Apparently the implants would cause her breasts to harden if she didn't massage them.

At first, she lied and lied, telling detectives that she had been visiting friends and had no idea where Hollywood was. After some grilling, though, she admitted she had been with him. She said he had been acting "like a shit-head," and she didn't know where he was anymore.

Hollywood left his rental car near Richard Dispenza's home, and left his two guns with another old friend, William Jacques. Hollywood had visited Jacques to drink beer and watch movies and had said that he wouldn't need his guns anymore. By the end of their visit, Hollywood had admitted he was actually on the run from police, but Jacques didn't want to get involved.

On August 20, Hollywood called Dispenza from a pay phone and found out that police had already been there and were hot on his trail. After that, Hollywood didn't return to the hotel; he just started looking for old friends who might help or harbor him.

Three days later, Richard Dispenza confessed to police that he had previously lied about not knowing Jesse James Hollywood's whereabouts. It's just that he'd wanted to give his godson a chance to go back to California and turn himself in, he explained. Plus, he hadn't known what kind of trouble Hollywood was in at the time—despite the phone records showing calls from Jack Hollywood, Dispenza claimed that Jesse had just showed up and said he needed some help, he said. Had Jack told him nothing?

Richard Dispenza was arrested on August 23 for the

felony of harboring a fugitive, then posted five thousand dollars bail and was released. He was put on paid administrative leave from his school job while he awaited a trial.

Hollywood next hitchhiked a ride to the family home of Chas Saulsbury, a friend who hadn't seen or heard from him since the Hollywoods moved away in 1995. Saulsbury said that he came to his mother's house one day and was shocked to see Hollywood standing on the doorstep waiting for him. Hollywood initially gave him only a very bare-bones explanation of what was going on—that some friends of his had killed someone, but he wasn't involved. The police were after him anyway, though, and he needed help getting out of town. They went on the Internet and looked up the *Santa Barbara News-Press* website, where they read an article about how Nick's body had been found, and they learned that the others had all been arrested.

Mexico or Canada—Hollywood wasn't sure where he wanted to go, but it was probably going to be one of the two. They tried to get Hollywood some fake identification online but weren't successful in printing it out.

What they told Saulsbury's mother was that Hollywood had been pickpocketed in Las Vegas, and he needed Saulsbury to drive him back there. But after they got to Las Vegas, Hollywood became very agitated and changed his mind—he wanted to go back to Los Angeles instead. He needed advice from a friend there. Would Chas drive him there?

It was a fifteen-hour ride in total, and Saulsbury agreed to do it, probably for money. Hollywood would later say that he'd paid Saulsbury $3,000 to take him, although Saulsbury claimed that he'd done it out of a misguided desire to help an old friend. What he learned during the ride, though, made him increasingly uncomfortable.

Little by little, Hollywood appeared to be coming unglued. Praying, crying, saying he wished he were dead. He told Saulsbury more details of the story—how he and his friends had taken Nick because of Ben's drug debt. Then Hollywood explained that he was initially "not sure" what to do with Nick until he'd spoken with his attorney, Stephen Hogg.

According to Chas Saulsbury, what sealed Nick's fate was when Stephen Hogg suggested that Hollywood should get rid of Nick and hide his body to avoid being caught on kidnapping charges. So, at that point, Hollywood told Jesse Rugge and Ryan Hoyt what the lawyer said, and Hoyt "volunteered to do it."

Did no one stop to think that murder charges might be worse?

Saulsbury got spooked about his own fate at this point and just wanted to get home and get out of the situation. He tried to connect with Jack Hollywood, maybe to hand Jesse off to him, but didn't succeed.

Instead, Saulsbury took Hollywood to the van owner John Roberts's house. Roberts was in the middle of watching a football game on television when Hollywood showed up at his back door. The two hugged and became emotional. Hollywood wanted money—particularly because Saulsbury, who was supposed to come back to pick him in a little while, had instead left with the rest of Hollywood's money, about eight thousand dollars. But more importantly, Hollywood wanted help in getting a fake passport and fake ID so that he could leave the country as soon as possible.

"I told him that I couldn't," John Roberts would later testify. "I knew people in Chicago that do it, but I couldn't do it, and I couldn't give him any money, and he could not stay at my house."

Well, that wasn't entirely true. Roberts did give Hollywood a manila envelope with ten thousand dollars in it and then claimed that he urged Hollywood to turn himself in. Quite a mixed message—why would Hollywood have needed ten thousand dollars to get to the police station? In any case, Hollywood was off again—this time, without Saulsbury to drive him around.

When Saulsbury got back home to Colorado, he spoke with a lawyer, who told him that Hollywood's could be a death-penalty case, and he needed to talk to police. So Saulsbury did, but he didn't tell much of the truth. He claimed to have no idea why Hollywood was in trouble and that he'd assumed his old friend was just on the run because of a drug debt. But he did tell police that he had dropped Hollywood back off in West Hills a few days earlier, on August 25.

On August 29, the Los Angeles Police Department's SWAT team closed off the streets in the West Hills neighborhood, surrounded and barricaded John Roberts's home, and used a bullhorn to tell Jesse Hollywood to surrender and anyone inside the house to get out.

But the only person who came out of the home was a dazed and possibly drunk John Roberts.

The SWAT team fired about 300 pounds of tear gas into the home, destroying virtually everything inside, according to Roberts. They waited, but no one else came out. After searching the home themselves for an hour and a half, they announced that Hollywood was not there.

Once again, they had narrowly missed him. At that moment, Hollywood was actually staying in a friend's borrowed trailer in a remote Mojave Desert location. He was watching television and saw the eight-hour standoff take place between John Roberts and police, which Hollywood would later say made him feel guilty. His conscience didn't seem to nag him when it came to Nick's murder, but it did bother him that his dad's friend was getting "hassled" by the police.

For two weeks, Hollywood said, he stayed in that trailer and lived off frozen food, beer, and cigarettes. According to him, the location was so dangerous that the post office wouldn't even deliver mail there.

America's Most Wanted picked up on this case early, and Hollywood saw its first episode featuring him while he was in the trailer, too. It made him even more determined to get out of the country. But first, he needed to secure a fake ID; then he hopped on a plane from LAX to Seattle to visit more friends. He stayed there for around two more weeks, then paid about two thousand to get someone to smuggle him into Canada by boat.

———

Canada was one of the places I'd heard might be a possibility for where Jesse James Hollywood was hiding. I guess a lot of American fugitives go there.

I was spending my days making more and more "Wanted" posters. I got pictures of Hollywood in various states—with a baseball cap, with surfer hair, with almost no hair, looking angry, with a goofy smile. I added a fake moustache and beard to some posters, in case that's what he looked like by then. I even put fake makeup and long hair on him on other posters, in case he was disguised as a woman. On those, I named him "Jesseca."

When I wasn't making posters, I was going onto Internet chat rooms and message boards making a nuisance of myself. On a good day, I could hit more than three hundred of them—just signing up and popping in with my message, which I would cut and paste over and over again.

$20,000.00 REWARD for Jesse James Hollywood
AMERICA'S MOST WANTED—WANTED BY THE FBI

Please pass this on to others to help me find this
5' 4" coward. He is responsible for the execution of my
only child, Nicholas Samuel Markowitz, 15 years young.

You can remain anonymous,
and will not have to appear in court.

http://www.fbi.gov/wanted/topten/fugitives/fugitives.htm

If you have information, please call 911
or 1-800-CRIME TV.

I'm sure some people saw me as a spammer, but at the same time, if it were your child . . . what would you do?

Even though I was doing all the things that one might do if one believed that her son had been murdered and his killer was on the run, I wasn't always very clear on that belief in my own head or heart. Plus, I started taking a lot of pills and drinking more than ever before, just trying to make the days go away. Trying to dull the pain, or keep myself as far removed from reality as possible.

My mom's birthday was August 27, but we were unable to even think about celebrating. We had just taped a segment for *America's Most Wanted*, and that in itself was draining, even though it made us feel good that someone cared to find Nick's killer. The trouble was finding the energy to put on makeup and pretty clothes and face the lights and cameras when all I wanted to do was crawl back into bed and never wake up again.

"Please shorten my day. I am feeling as wilted as my houseplants," I wrote in my journal.

In the middle of the night, Jeff's sobs woke me, piercing my heart. He would cry in his sleep many nights, unaware that he was doing it. My own tears had disappeared after the funeral and hadn't returned. I just couldn't cry anymore; crying made it real.

On September 1, I wrote in my journal, "I really feel that you are coming back, but the problem is your funeral was two weeks ago."

Every time I heard helicopters, I assumed it was someone tracking Jesse James Hollywood and that they were about to find him any minute. After all the press, I was sure he couldn't hide out for long—someone was bound to see him and alert the police. Yet day after day, there was no news.

Our therapist came to the house to see us every couple of days. My mental state wasn't improving; it was deteriorating. I wrote letters to Nick asking him to help guide me. I missed everything about him—the way he would sneak around the house and pop up to scare me, his celebrity impressions, his dirty cereal bowls in the sink. I smelled his laundry and sprayed his cologne on myself.

I could not stop laughing on September 10, 2000, the first time I was admitted to Pine Grove Hospital's mental health clinic. It wasn't because I thought anything was funny. In fact, nothing was funny. All I wanted to do was die, but I couldn't stop laughing.

Dearest Nick,

Guess where I am? Visiting Pine Grove—and no, I'm not camping. I don't think I will ever go camping again without you. It just would not be the same.

I was thinking you could somehow get a hall pass like the one you did in high school, and come see me. I really need to see you. I know, or so I think I know, that you're not really coming back. I am having a very difficult time in coming to reality with your disappearance, let alone your execution.

How is it that I am supposed to go on living? For what?

Your memories are so sweet and funny, but I feel it is OK to be selfish and want more. Like just one more hug or even a good-bye. They would not let me see you. I miss you terribly.

Please, please do not let this be real.

Your birthday is coming up next week. What am I going to do? You would have turned 16 years young. I am torn apart at the thought of instead of a car for your birthday you ended up with a coffin. Please help guide me in what to do on your special day. It will always be my special day, giving birth to you 16 years ago. It was too short a time with you. You were robbed of the best years of your life. I am so sorry.

XOXOXO
Mommy

One pill was not enough to help me sleep. It's likely that I sneaked another. Sleep might give me strength, I thought.

In the morning, we had a group therapy session. All the people there went around the circle telling us about their problems. Their stupid, stupid problems. This one was having a career quandary; that one thought she might still love her ex-boyfriend, whatever. Then it came my turn . . . and after I spoke, suddenly everyone wanted to leave. They all realized they didn't have any real problems after all.

So it was just the therapist and me left in the room, and I still couldn't stop laughing. After just twenty-seven hours in the mental health clinic, I was discharged and back home again, where I took some more pills and tried not to think about how much that experience was going to cost us in medical bills. What a waste.

A double dose of something or other helped me sleep for four hours in a row, a rarity. I always looked for Nick in my dreams, hoping he'd show up and talk to me, give me a sign, something. But the only time I caught a glimpse of him, it wasn't a good glimpse. He was wearing black pants and a dragon shirt that Ben had helped him shop for, and he looked handsome except for the expression on his face— very angry. He was walking all alone toward me with his fists clenched, tight lips, and glaring eyes.

Why was he so mad? Was he angry about what happened to him? Was he angry with me for how I felt about Ben?

I just need some time. I know in my heart that if Ben could have saved you, he would have. Please come back to me in my next dream with a smile. I need to see you.

I made it to the therapist's office twice more that week. Afterward, I would always go to the bar across the street and have a drink . . . or two or three. And then I would drive home. It's a miracle that I didn't create another tragedy.

Three days after coming out of the hospital, I sat at that bar and lost myself in the drinks. Then came the pills. My funeral arrangements had already been made along with Nick's; I already had the plot, so why not use it? I prayed that there really was a heaven and that I'd get to see my son again, and then I took some more pills. I don't know how many, but I knew it was enough. I felt myself slipping . . . and then I thought of my therapist, Dr. Fulton.

The guilt set in. I had done this just after leaving his office. How was he going to feel? Not wanting him to have my death on his head, I walked back across the street and told him what I'd done. He called Jeff at work to come get me, while I passed out in the waiting room.

The black tar that was crammed down my throat in the emergency room made me think I surely would never try that again.

I was admitted to Northridge Hospital that day because UCLA's Resnick Neuropsychiatric Hospital didn't have a bed available. I guess there were a lot of us crazies out there. I think this was the place where I saw ants crawling across my bed. That didn't freak me out; it actually comforted me. I talked to them, out loud, telling them that everything was OK and I would be their "Auntie."

When they discharged me less than a day later, they wrote on my chart, "Patient is less depressed, denies feeling suicidal at time of discharge."

Ha!

And there went another month's salary for Jeff. Maybe more. Probably more. It was difficult enough for Jeff to work those days; for several months, he couldn't hold it together in front of his employees. In the middle of a job, he would just burst out crying. For the most part, people left him alone. There were no words that would fix this.

Jeff tried hard to be the stable one. He had to keep working and try to keep some sense of normalcy in our lives. After this time, he would say that it was good for him to have a routine and a sense of responsibility. In a way, it was a detriment for me that I had no responsibilities that would force me to get up each day and get back on track.

I had difficulty remembering the details of the funeral, and of Nick's sixteenth birthday, which was held at the cemetery. My sister Brenda and her husband bought Nick a star in honor of his sixteenth birthday. It was inspiring to look up into the sky and know that I could actually wish upon his star. I promised Nick that I would not abuse this privilege and save some room for the wishes he might need up in heaven.

At the cemetery, Nick's friends each signed a white balloon with an attached memorial key chain, cut the strings, then watched them disappear into the blue sky, up to Nick. I don't remember doing it, but I'm told I did. We brought Cokes, umbrellas, and blankets. We all left flowers and tears behind.

Nick's best friend, Ryan, was so distraught, cheated out of his best buddy. I didn't want to be selfish, so I asked Nick to please help Ryan through this, too. It was hard seeing him like that, sweet Ryan, who was now the closest thing I had to Nick.

Inappropriately, I also approached Nick's former girlfriend at the cemetery, and I whispered in her ear, "I wish he had gotten you pregnant so there would be something besides memories left."

Immediately I knew it was extremely wrong for an adult to say such a thing to a teenage girl, let alone place that kind of burden on her heart. The "what could have beens" had gotten the best of me. We cried together, and she told me how much she missed Nick. I gave her back the two rings she had given to him.

A few days later, I awoke to bright lights and strange voices.

"How many did you take?"

The nurses and doctors were bothering me. They wanted to know about the pills. I told them to go away, but they didn't. And neither did I.

Please just let me sleep. Please just let me die.

They didn't let me. They admitted me at the UCLA Resnick Neuropsychiatric Hospital. I guess this meant that someone else had gotten sane enough to give up a bed.

In an evaluation room with a dozen or more doctors and

interns all staring at me, one doctor called out, "So, how are you feeling?"

I patted both of my cheeks, then twisted my index finger into my dimple zone. "Just peachy!" I said with a giggle.

I thought for sure they were going to bring out the restraints right then. The whole lot of them stared me down in such a way that I thought they were never going to consider letting me out of this place.

Very sternly, the doctor said, "That is inappropriate behavior!"

Yes, sir. Won't happen again, sir.

Back in my hospital bed, I began seeing things in the carpet and drawing what I saw. Two animals: a seal and a dog. Plus, there was a third animal that I couldn't make out, and two faces with closed eyes and curly hair.

Then I thought about all the potential uses for my medicine cup and wrote a list that Martha Stewart might have applauded, including these items:

- Paint it red and put a handle on it to make a doll bucket.

- Stack several together to make a miniature Christmas tree; then paint.

- Cover it in fabric and make a Barbie lampshade.

This also began my rhyming phase, where almost everything I thought came out in a singsong rhyme. Brains can be weird things after trauma. Even I knew that I was nuts. Where are those nice young men in their clean white coats, anyway? Shouldn't they be strapping me to the bed or something?

With limited poison available, I also took up smoking while at the hospital. We weren't allowed to have lighters, of course—being that I was on suicide watch, I wasn't allowed to even have a comb unless supervised—so we'd have to go outside and stick our cigarettes into this particular hole in the wall and press a button, which would ignite the flame. It looked like a car cigarette lighter. After our therapy sessions, we'd ask each other, "Are you going to the wall?" We'd meet up there and borrow each other's cigarettes and talk. It became a welcome ritual, and I enjoyed the company.

Our days were highly scheduled and regimented, which was a comfort in itself. I didn't have to think about when I had eaten last or whether it was time to take a shower or take a pill. And I didn't have to do laundry or vacuum, either. It was like a vacation . . . except not at all.

This time, I was discharged after about two weeks, and I was afraid to leave. The doctors told me there would still be life to come, and that I would always have my memories of Nick, but I wanted more than memories. I still wanted to be with him.

One of the things that eventually kept me going, however, was knowing that if I died, I would also be taking all my memories with me—and that meant killing off memories of Nick that no one else could ever carry on.

The other thing that kept me going was the fight for justice. I had to stay alive. I had to stay alive long enough to make sure that everyone responsible for my son's murder was behind bars.

CHAPTER 13

HUNTING

The grand jury proceeding was coming up in November, and the prosecutor would have to present enough evidence to show that all four suspects should stand trial for the crimes they were charged with: murder, kidnapping, and criminal conspiracy. My sister Brenda wanted me to get away for a few days before then, so she took me to a cabin in Big Bear, nestled in the San Bernardino Mountains. Our objective was to take our minds off reality for just a short while and pretend that life was normal again.

Shortly after setting foot in the cabin, we lit a fire in the fireplace, and a newspaper next to the woodpile caught my eye: Jesse James Hollywood's picture was on the front page. Even here, even in this little cabin in the mountains, I couldn't escape his smug little face and what he'd done to my life and, more important, to Nick's.

More pills. More alcohol. I would not let his face ruin my day with my sister. We went to a candy store, where we bought everything. Enough to make ourselves very sick. We took it all back to the cabin and spread it out in a big pile in the middle of the bed. With our wax lips on, velvet crowns on our heads, and silly string sprayed everywhere, we dove face-first into our stomachaches.

We had fun . . . and I felt guilty for having fun. I felt guilty for laughing.

My sister is my best friend, and I knew she felt helpless and lost herself, so we clung to each other and faced a very empty world together the best we knew how. I knew I was lucky to have the kind of family I did—hugs and kisses, love and support. I cannot imagine not loving your siblings with your whole heart.

Back in hell, Jeff and I drove to a hotel in Santa Barbara, where we would stay during the grand jury proceeding. He'd bought Ben a new pair of shoes for court; this bothered me in a way it was hard for me to express. I didn't want Jeff to ever do anything nice for Ben again.

Why hadn't Ben come to me on his knees? Why had my son died looking up to a coward?

I'm sorry, Nick, I would think after these thoughts. *I hope it doesn't make you angry with me. Ben's connection in your being gone forever is more than I can forgive or forget.*

Forever is a very long time. I sat in room 54, above the workroom of the hotel, and thought, "This is the last chance to tell me that this is all a mistake. It was really someone else's body they found."

But no one said that, and on October 23, 2000, John Roberts became the first witness to testify in court about my son's murder.

He talked about the meeting that he and Jack Hollywood had with Jesse after Nick had been kidnapped. Jesse hadn't given them any information at all, Roberts said. "It was almost like he did not, at that time in front of us, regard it as being a terribly serious thing."

But when Hollywood showed up at Roberts's house after Nick's body had been found, he was "absolutely terrified. He knew his life was over." Roberts claimed that he didn't know where Hollywood was now.

"Would you tell us if you did?" the prosecutor asked.

"Oh, God. I don't know. I'm trying to answer you truth-fully, but I don't know. And I pray to God I never get a phone call from him."

Court was adjourned. One day down. How many more to go? I was standing at the bottom of what appeared to be a very long staircase, and this was only the first step. Somewhere at the top was my image of Jesse James Holly-wood serving a life sentence in prison, or being sentenced to death.

Stay alive for tomorrow, I told myself. *Stay alive and look these witnesses in the eye and don't let them lie. Don't let them forget about Nick. Let your face haunt them.*

I was one of the lucky ones—in fact, I've never heard of it happening this way ever again—who got hooked up with a victim's advocate immediately. Her name was Joan Fair-field, and she would be with Jeff and me every day of every trial. When things got to be too much, Joan would walk out with me. When I needed to have something explained, she would explain it. In a situation this horrid, you took your blessings where you could find them, and Joan was definitely one of my blessings.

It had taken so much out of me to drag myself into that courtroom on the first day that I couldn't believe I had to do it again the very next day. But I did, and faced Brian Affronti, who would tell his story about how Hollywood and his underlings had picked him up for Fiesta in that white van—with Nick inside.

"Did you come to the conclusion at some point or another that he was there involuntarily?" asked the prosecutor.

"Yes, by threatening remarks coming from Jesse Holly-wood, who was sitting in the front."

"The drive up from West Hills to Santa Barbara took, what, an hour and fifteen minutes?"

"Took about forty-five minutes to an hour."

"Do you recall telling detectives that the pager went off repeatedly?"

"Yes, I do."

So Nick had gotten my pages. I didn't know whether to

be comforted or even more saddened—if that were even possible. Nick had known that I was trying to reach him. If only I had known what he was going through . . .

Soon after Nick's murder, William Skidmore had called Brian. "He told me that Nick had been killed. He told me that—what had happened, and that Jesse [Hollywood] and people were talking and he was calling to warn me to either keep my mouth shut or Jesse might come after me, too."

"Did he tell you that you were the weak link?"

"He told me that that's what was involved in the conversation with Jesse. I believe Jesse, Ryan Hoyt, William, and Jesse Hollywood's father were all talking . . . he overheard them talking and that's what they were saying about me."

"Did you notice if Nick Markowitz was wearing any jewelry of any kind?"

"I remember a red ring that he talked about. When Jesse had taken away his pager, he had taken away his ring, too, and Nick asked him . . . you know, I forgot who gave it to him, but he said somebody had given it to him . . ."

"Would you recognize it again if you saw it?"

"I believe I would."

"I'm going to show you Exhibit Number 35."

"That's the ring."

Exhibit Number 35 made Jeff cry.

I had no power to help him. There was the ring his parents had given him, and he had given to his oldest son, and now it was evidence in his youngest son's murder. It was the last thing that Nick had fought for in his life on Earth—to keep that ring on his finger until the moment he died.

———

Natasha Adams (who was now Natasha Adams-Young) took the stand next, describing how she'd met Nick and helped clean up his injuries. Then she talked about what she told her mother about the kidnapping.

"I didn't give her any names or anything," she said. "I just said I know these people, and this boy has been kidnapped. And she was kind of shocked, too, because it sounds really unreal. You don't really expect kidnappers to be kids."

Her mother told her to talk to police, but "it didn't seem like a serious thing at the time, so I wanted to see what was going to happen before I did anything about it, because I didn't want to get involved."

Besides that, according to an interview with filmmaker Nick Cassavetes, Natasha's mother told him that she was high on Ecstasy the night Natasha came to tell her about the kidnapping. It was her wedding anniversary, he claimed she'd said, and she hadn't wanted to be bothered. But over the next few days, she learned more about what happened, so when she read the newspaper article about Nick's murder, she knew it had to be the boy that her daughter had talked about.

How had Adams reacted when her mother showed her the article?

"I just started crying right away," she said. "And I asked her, like, how it could happen. The normal responses to something like that."

Her father was also apprised of the situation. So, both of her parents realized by then that Nick had been killed. And they both went to work?

"Yes."

"OK. But they knew that this was the body of a person who you had seen alive in the previous days?"

"Yes."

"And they knew at this point that you probably knew who was responsible?"

"Yes. My mom said she would make an appointment with a lawyer."

Next to the witness stand was Gabriel Ibarra, one of the men who had been at Richard Hoeflinger's apartment when Jesse James Hollywood and his crew showed up and duct taped Nick in the back room. He described seeing Nick with a sock over his eyes like a blindfold, and he described how they all left to party and tried to forget about the kid who was tied up in the apartment.

Casey Sheehan spoke next, mostly about Ryan Hoyt's demeanor after he killed Nick. At first, Sheehan hadn't believed that Hoyt had actually done it, because he seemed way too unaffected, even going shopping and partying that same day. Then they'd headed to Malibu to have dinner with Sheehan's dad.

"We were just talking on the way out to see my father at the beach . . . that's when he started to kind of seem scared."

"OK. What specifically did he say at this point?"

"That Nick was dead. 'What should I do? We took care of Nick. Nick is dead.' I think he referred to it as a problem a few times."

"Did he say specifically, 'We took him to a ditch, shot him, and put a bush over him'?"

"Yes, sir."

"All right. Did you ask him who's 'we'? Who are these people you did this with?"

"Yes, sir. He said Jesse Rugge."

"Do you know if Hoyt had a weapon?"

"Yeah, I know that he didn't have a weapon in his possession. He didn't own a gun."

"Do you know whether or not Hollywood had a gun?"

"He had a shotgun and he had a TEC-9."

On the day Ryan Hoyt was arrested, he had called Casey Sheehan to ask if he could come over because his house was "hot," or under surveillance.

"Tell me why you didn't call the police, or tell somebody at that moment," the prosecutor said.

"I don't really know why."

Kelly Carpenter then talked about how she and Natasha Adams were both "very fond of" Nick and that she hadn't called police because "I was already under the impression that my friend Natasha was probably going to talk to the police . . . I was really scared and I didn't know what I would say."

In response to the prosecutor's questions, Hollywood's girlfriend, Michelle Lasher, said "I don't know" and "I don't recall" seemingly hundreds of times. She didn't know anything about the killing. She had never met Nick. She didn't remember how long she had been in Colorado with Hollywood.

"At one point, you told detectives that the car you were driving to Colorado was a black Cadillac?" the prosecutor asked.

"Yes."

"It, of course, wasn't a black Cadillac and you knew it wasn't a black Cadillac. Why did you tell them that?"

"I was just being protective."

Attorney Stephen Hogg refused to answer questions, citing attorney-client privilege. The most unintentionally funny moment in the proceedings came when Jack Hollywood was called to the stand. He was sworn in, then asked if he was Jesse's father.

"Yes, I am."

"Do you know where Jesse James Hollywood is currently?"

"Could I talk to my attorney?"

"Did you not anticipate that you would be asked this question?"

It was so silly.

Jack Hollywood acknowledged knowing that his son sold drugs and that Ben Markowitz owed his son money for drugs. He acknowledged that his son had been a participant in kidnapping Ben's brother and that they had had a meeting to talk about what to do with Nick. So, once he knew that a boy had been kidnapped, had he at least called the boy's parents?

"I don't know them. And I . . . no, I didn't. No. I mean, I never met them, I didn't know where they lived; I didn't know anything about them."

"Did you ask your son anything about that?"

"No."

"Did you open up a telephone book and look up Markowitz?"

"No."

Jack Hollywood said that he kept calling his son to talk about the situation, but Jesse kept putting him off and saying he had other things to do or he didn't want to talk about it. Jack apparently never asked where Nick was being held.

"Why didn't you ask him specifically where he was?"

"Like I said, I never really got a chance to sit down and talk to him."

"Why couldn't that be a conversation or a question asked standing? I mean, why couldn't you ask him that first thing right off the bat on the telephone? 'Where is this person? Where is he?' "

"I'm sure I could have, but I didn't."

"And why not?"

"I just didn't do it."

And when asked again if he knew where Jesse was now, he answered, "No, I don't."

I tried not to let my mind ruminate on all the "what ifs" and "should have beens," but it was so difficult to listen to person after person describe what they knew and when they knew it, only to have done nothing about it. How could so many people have seen my son duct taped and not called the police?

It made me feel so hopeless that his life had mattered so little to so many people and that there was this much selfishness in the world—dozens of people who'd decided to look out for themselves and ignore the plight of a kidnapped boy who was right in front of their faces. People who knew it was wrong and ignored it anyway.

I wrote more poems to Nick:

Shadows

As I wait for court sessions to be scheduled,
Your face comes to me.
Tears blur my vision;

I take a deep breath.
I must not give in;
This just can't be reality.

Breathe . . . my vision begins to clear.
A shadow is on the ground.
My heart pounds.

I look up desperately . . . hoping.
Disappointed, I search again for another
Shadow on the ground.
From my soul to yours,
Love,
Mom

The grand jury indicted the four culprits: Jesse Rugge, Graham Pressley, Ryan Hoyt, and Jesse James Hollywood—even though Hollywood hadn't been found yet. The Santa Barbara County district attorney's office announced to the press that they were considering seeking the death penalty for Hollywood, Rugge, and Hoyt.

It didn't fill me with joy or relief. It was what I'd expected to happen, and if anything had happened otherwise, I would have been totally lost. But this—this was just another day, another step. I was glad that this part was over but knew we had so much more to endure. I hated all the things I had learned already in this proceeding, and I was so afraid of what I was going to have to learn going forward. The district attorney's office had already prepared us that the details would get gruesome.

Three o'clock was always an anxious time for me those days. It was when I used to pick Nick up from school, and now . . . there was nowhere for me to be. I'd find myself getting more and more uneasy as the time grew near, and I'd give in to the ache to get out of the house and drive.

By 3:00 on most weekdays, I would find myself in front of Nick's school, just watching. Some days it bothered me to see how life was going on. There were kids carrying backpacks, smiling and laughing. Backpacks were bitter-sweet; they became an emblem of age fifteen to me—the age that my son would be forever frozen in time. I was never going to see Nick smile and laugh again. How could they smile when the world was so cruel? On other days, seeing them still living was what I needed. One way or another, life was going on.

The bar disciplined Hollywood's lawyer, Stephen Hogg, for his "ethics violation," the first time he'd been disciplined in his twenty-eight-year career—but not the last. He was soon disciplined twice more on unrelated cases. To me, again, it was nothing. A slap on the wrist, if that. As far as I was concerned, proper "discipline" would have been prison time for failing to tell the police about a kidnapping in progress.

On Thanksgiving, Jeff and I summoned our bravery and went to see Lizard's Mouth. We needed to feel the pain that we knew was waiting for us there. We sat in the spot where Nick breathed his last breath, and then we heard gunshots—it turned out that there was a gun range next to the mountain.

Jeff chiseled Nick's name into a boulder, along with his date of birth and date of death. The date of death was actually wrong; we didn't yet know that he had been killed after midnight, making it August 9 rather than August 8. But there it was, chiseled into the rock forever anyway. We didn't want anyone to forget what happened at this spot.

The view at Lizard's Mouth was magnificent. *Nick should be here with me*, I thought. *He should be helping me see things in the cloud formations.*

Looking out into the beautiful world, yet still not wanting to be in it anymore, I felt so lost and alone. Preserving Nick's memory seemed to be the most important thing to do. Prior to Nick's sixteenth birthday, we made up silver key chains—thousands of them, with Nick's name and birth date and death date, plus the address to the website that my brother had made in honor of Nick, and my e-mail address so that people could write to me if they had anything to share or wanted to talk about Nick. I handed them out to people everywhere I went.

Most days felt like a battle just to stay alive and keep my mind intact. I drank increasing amounts—champagne and orange juice in the morning, and after I'd gone through two bottles of champagne, I'd switch to wine. Red wine if the weather was cold, white if it was hot, all through the afternoon and night until I went to sleep. Sometimes beer in the summer. When my girlfriends came over, they would bring wine. I built up an amazing tolerance, which was not so surprising considering that my father had been an alcoholic all his life. He was a funny drunk who'd liked to sing country-western songs, but there was nothing funny about me anymore. I was just a sad drunk.

Jeff had gone right back to work within a week or two after Nick's funeral, leaving me alone in the house much of the time—but I didn't mind that. It gave me more time to drink and drug myself without anyone noticing. Mainly, I stayed settled at home, but I did go out for lunch some days, drink some more, then drive home.

I was so drunk that I tried to drown myself in the swimming pool one day, with the telephone still in my hand—I had called my therapist. It's very hard to drown yourself. Your head keeps bobbing back up, so you have to really force it to stay down. I could still hear my therapist's voice on the phone: "If you don't answer me right now, I'm calling 911," he said.

"Oh, fine," I said, and I gave up and got out of the pool. There had to be an easier way to kill myself. I wondered about the "never-wake-up berries" from the movie *The Blue Lagoon*. You just ate a branchful of crimson arita berries and went to sleep forever—how neat and simple.

I kept thinking that there had to be someone else out there like me, someone who would understand what I was going through. But each time I spoke to a parent of a murdered child, I would eventually hear the words "my other child" or "my children." Could I have been the only person in this unbearable situation, having my only child murdered?

I felt that Jeff had more to live for than I did—he still had his two other children, plus his grandchild and another one on the way. Leah was pregnant again. It hurt too much for me to be very near them . . . my realities hit me more each day. I was never going to have a grandchild of my own.

After Nick was born, I had two more pregnancies. One ended in miscarriage, and the other . . . well, the other was Sarah. In my nineteenth week, well after I could feel her kick, we found out she had a neural tube defect and had no chance of survival. I thought nothing was ever going to compare to the agony I felt when I sat in a room full of habitual aborters who made jokes about their unwanted pregnancies and knew that in a few minutes, this very wanted life inside me was going to be taken away from us. I couldn't stop crying; I would never get to meet my daughter.

That made Nick even more important. Having another baby just wasn't going to happen for us, so all of my hopes and dreams lived with him. With him gone, all the meaning in my life was gone, too.

I spoke to God a lot in those days. Wrote him letters, too. Most of them were similar.

Dear God,

This is Susan Markowitz. There has been a mistake. You see, Nick was a good boy. I was trying to raise him right. I am so sorry if I did something wrong. Could you please send him back? I promise to do better. I'm begging you: Please send him back and take me. There is a word called miracles; only you can do them. I have never asked for one before. Actually, I haven't asked you for anything except to have a child. Could you please undo what those boys did to my son? I looked at

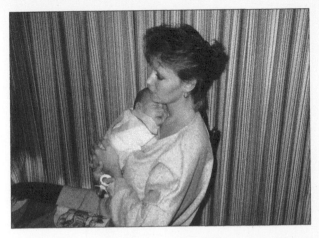

Nick and me in 1984. I now knew what having it all truly meant.

Jeff with Nick, Leah, and Ben in 1985,
enjoying one of our many trips to Catalina.

Unless otherwise noted, all photos are courtesy of Susan Markowitz

Nick helping his dad to pilot the boat, not a care in the world.

Nick and me in 1987.
This photo is one similar to the one on Nick's headstone.

Jeff and me in 1991. Taking time to be together.

Above: In 1991, I surprised Nick with a dog he named Zak.

Left: This picture accompanied a poem Nick wrote, which was hung up at his school during open house in 1993.

Nick with his very proud brother and sister,
Ben and Leah, at his Bar Mitzvah in 1997.
Wachsman Staley Photography

Left: Nick's Bar Mitzvah was one of the most emotional moments
in his Grandma and Papa's lives.
Wachsman Staley Photography

Right: Nick and his girlfriend, Jeannie, in 1997.
Wachsman Staley Photography

We found this photo of Nick on Leo Carrillo Beach,
c. 2000, in a camera after his funeral.

The only known photo of Nick with his motorcycle.

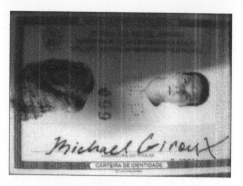

One of the false IDs Jesse James Hollywood used in Brazil
and had with him when he was arrested.
Courtesy of Mark Valencia

The Brazilian police precinct where Jesse James Hollywood
was captured and deported.
Courtesy of Mark Valencia

Booking photos of Rugge, Skidmore, and Hoyt when they were first arrested, and a photo taken of Hollywood shortly before he went on the run.
Courtesy of the Santa Barbara County Sheriff's Department

Photos taken of each of the criminals—Rugge, Skidmore, Hoyt, Pressley, and Hollywood—a few years later, after they were all in police custody.
Courtesy of the Santa Barbara County Sheriff's Department

Jeff memorializes the spot where Nick's life was taken.

For Nick.

the calendar, and it has been four months. I really need
him back. I try to get by with just his memory; it is not
enough. I will trade everything including my soul just
to say good-bye.

P.S. Waiting in West Hills, California

———————

The hearings and jury selections and trials overlapped each
other; we were at all of them, though. The first to make it
to an actual trial was Richard Dispenza, the teacher from
Colorado who'd lied to detectives about his godson Jesse
Hollywood's whereabouts. It turned out that Dispenza was
very popular in his hometown; students and faculty packed
the courtroom and overflowed into the hallways during the
weeklong trial. The judge even reminded them, "This is a
trial, not an athletic event."

The defense attorney told the jury that Dispenza hadn't
known that Hollywood was a fugitive when he'd showed
up at Dispenza's house and that he'd kicked Hollywood out
the next day because he reeked of marijuana smoke. But
he had driven him to a hotel, because he didn't think Hollywood should drive in his stoned condition.

Dispenza knew that Hollywood was in trouble, but not
that he was wanted for murder, said the defense attorney.
It was just an honest mistake! And when detectives had
asked where Hollywood was and Dispenza lied, that was
just because he wanted to give his godson a chance to do
the right thing and turn himself in. Detectives, however,
said that Richard Dispenza's story about what he knew and
when he knew it kept changing.

"To this day, Jesse James Hollywood is a fugitive from
justice," the prosecutor said. "The help from this defendant
was not a mistake—it was a crime."

The jury agreed; they convicted Richard Dispenza
of harboring a fugitive, a felony that carried up to a six-
year prison term. In addition, he was convicted of false

reporting to authorities, a misdemeanor. But it would be up to the judge to decide what kind of sentence to impose.

When he left the courtroom that day, reporters asked Dispenza if he was going to lose his teaching license. He said he didn't think so, because he viewed the crime he committed to be relatively minor. And he planned to appeal the verdict.

After a verdict was announced, the victim—or, as in our case, the family of the deceased victim—was allowed to take the stand to give what is called a "Victim's Impact Statement." It's a rite of passage I don't wish on anyone. It's a time meant to remind the court of the human side of crime—after the evidence is weighed impartially, then it's OK to remember that the "body" is a real person, and the crime has left a family in ruins. You have to figure out a way to put into words how, exactly, this crime has hurt you and why a judge should carry out the kind of sentence you believe is appropriate. A sales pitch for justice, based on just how shattered you are.

After my morning mimosas, I took the stand and begged the judge to make sure that Richard Dispenza saw some jail time. I knew there was a risk that he wouldn't spend any time in jail at all, and I wanted to convey an important point: were it not for Dispenza's lies, one of the FBI's "Ten Most Wanted Fugitives" would be off that list and in prison right now.

But others painted a glowing picture of Dispenza. His supporters wrote two hundred and forty-nine letters to the court, and his neighbor took the stand to say what a great and selfless man he was and how students were always coming to him for advice.

The judge said, "We've got an exceptionally fine citizen and an exceptionally generous man who has committed an incredible lapse of judgment." Jailing him would waste taxpayer money and serve no purpose, the judge declared, so the sentence would be three years of probation, four hundred and eighty hours of community service, and victim empathy classes.

Throughout the courtroom and outside in the halls, the students and other supporters cheered and high-fived each other for the slap-on-the-wrist sentence. I felt like they were all cheering for letting Hollywood get away with murdering my son. "Hooray for harboring a fugitive! Gimme a high-five!"

It was a tough day.

Richard Dispenza resigned from his teaching job before they could fire him, but he was soon teaching and coaching again. Just a small hiccup in his life.

––––––––––

Back we went to California, where *America's Most Wanted* did a long segment on Jesse James Hollywood that generated a flurry of new tips. People claimed sightings of him across the United States, Mexico, and Canada . . . plus the inevitable callers who would say, "He's on television every week! Are you guys nuts? He hosts that show *Monster Garage*! How could you not find him?" Of course, they were talking about the Jesse James who eventually married Sandra Bullock, not Jesse James Hollywood. Every time *America's Most Wanted* aired, hundreds of calls would pour in, and some were solid tips. The Santa Barbara County Sheriff's Department and the FBI were not allowed to tell me anything about their investigation at this point except that they were going to do their best to find him.

That wasn't very reassuring to me. It was hard for Jeff and me to sit still and wait for people we didn't know to track down the man who'd ordered my son's execution, so we followed some of those tips ourselves, putting up signs and posters in areas where people claimed to have spotted him. One person e-mailed me a photo she had taken of a guy we were both sure was Hollywood. She told me that she had tried sending this information to the police, but hadn't yet received a response. I excitedly passed it along too, only to learn that it was a lookalike. The resemblance was amazing, but the person in the photo bore no relation to the Hollywoods.

In June 2001, Nick's purebred Australian shepherd, Zak, died. He hadn't been the same since Nick had been gone. I wondered if they would be together now.

———

After Nick's death, Ben had gone into a freefall. Where before he'd sold more drugs than he'd actually used, soon it became the opposite. He went off the deep end. Many times he told the press, "It's my fault that my fifteen-year-old brother is dead." I could not understand how he wouldn't straighten up after Nick's murder. What other wake-up call could a human being possibly need?

I seethed with anger at how Ben was disrespecting his brother's memory. I seethed when Jeff wanted to visit him. If I could have made Ben disappear from the planet, I would have—to me, he was worse than worthless; he was trampling the flowers on Nick's grave by continuing to do drugs and to hang out with the same kinds of evil people who killed Nick.

Ben committed a string of crimes during this time. He later said that he was on his own suicide mission, not unlike mine. I drank and took prescription pills; he broke into drug-dealers' houses and tried to get himself shot.

In December, Ben got arrested.

He was picked up for two separate instances of home invasion and armed robbery, but that didn't begin to cover what had actually happened. First, Ben and a male friend had gone to visit his friend Heather, who had a three-year-old daughter. Another guy and Heather's sister were already there, and they began passing along a glass pipe. Heather's little daughter was walking around in clouds of crystal meth smoke.

Even though Ben was high, too, he was appalled. "Get the baby out of here," he screamed to Heather's sister.

She did, and then he pulled out a gun and proceeded to teach the other two meth addicts "a lesson." He forced Heather and her male friend to strip naked; then he tied them to chairs, just to humiliate them. He took away

Heather's cell phone and left them there, wriggling in their chairs.

The following night, Ben went to collect some money a marijuana dealer owed him, with his partner-in-crime in tow. They broke into the man's house with guns in hand. Despite his threats, Ben left with only five dollars and the guy's driver's license.

"You'll get your license back when you pay me," Ben said.

The drug dealer and Heather each went to the police and filed reports. The police came looking for Ben and found him. His mom hired a good attorney, while Ben sat in the Los Angeles County Jail for six months awaiting trial. The deputy district attorney told him that if he were convicted of all charges, he would face sixty-four years in prison.

At the trial, Heather testified about what Ben had done, but when Ben's attorney cross-examined her, things got interesting.

"Have you ever had sex with Ben?" he asked.

"Yes."

"And was that before or after the incident took place?"

"Both."

"So you had sex with Ben after this. About how long after?"

"The following night."

That was the end of Ben's first hurdle—the prosecution's case had obviously suffered a big blow. At lunch, Ben's attorney worked out a deal with the district attorney's office: two years for a simple robbery charge, less time served, which was six months by this time. Ben was looking at eighteen months of hard time, but it sounded a lot better than sixty-four years, so he jumped at the deal.

Then came time for the drug dealer to testify about the second case. During an earlier hearing, he had changed his mind about testifying, saying he didn't want Ben to go to prison, but the police arrested him and forced him to show up as a witness at the trial anyway. He pleaded the Fifth Amendment.

Ben was headed off to Corcoran prison.

Ben had been arrested before but only as a juvenile. This was the first time that he was going to be sent to "Big Boy" prison, and the thought of it scared him to pieces. Oddly enough, it probably saved his life.

In prison, Ben made a promise that if God would get him through his ordeal, he would never hurt anyone or break the law again. It was the truth. Finally, finally, it was the truth. At the time, though, I would never have believed it.

I was too busy worrying about my own survival to think much about Ben's plight, though. I continued writing poetry and letters to Nick and to God, though sometimes the words jammed up worse than others.

What happened?
. . . I want Nick back.
His breakfast is getting cold.
Can you send him home now?
Nick's Mom,
Susan

Jeff and I would attend Parents of Murdered Children meetings, a group no one wanted to belong to. There, we would share in being lost. We would see the hollowness in each other's eyes and know that we were not alone in our grief. So many people in the group had even less than we did, though—their children's bodies were never found, or the killers were never identified, or they were let off the hook because of insufficient evidence.

I found reasons to thank God for the small blessings we had—at least we had Nick's body. At least we knew who had done this and why, and most of the criminals were in custody awaiting trials.

Before the trials, there were all sorts of motions and hearings that went on for months. It seemed there were court procedures of some sort relating to Nick's case nearly every weekday, and I vowed to make it to every one of them. It was a difficult vow to keep because it meant that I would learn things I never wanted to learn about my son and his brutal death, and the callousness of others, and even about myself. I worried about my own anger. I worried I might get so angry that I'd want all of them dead. But for the most part, it wasn't anger that I felt. Still, after all these months, it was disbelief and shock.

Frequently, I'd space out entirely, both in the courtroom and out. For a minute or two, I'd just be gone, floating in some otherworldly place where no one had been murdered and I was not Susan Markowitz, mother of the victim. I couldn't even say what I was thinking in those moments. It wasn't like normal daydreaming or losing myself in thought for a minute and then snapping back to reality. It was like I was really taking a total break from consciousness—my senses had just overloaded, tripped a switch, and my brain turned off.

Other times, it was a purposeful decision to put my mind elsewhere. During the more graphic moments of trials, I would give myself something else to think about: the way Nick had let me shave his face just a few weeks before his death; the way he was so proud of himself when he was about six years old and had stopped a neighbor, "Little Nick," from running into the street. I would think of those memories and try not to hear the graphic evidence. I had anxiety attacks every day—attacks that left me feeling like I was falling down a bottomless hole.

There were so many people who would never be prosecuted for their involvement in Nick's death, so many people who received immunity early on so that they'd testify against the most egregious offenders. But people who, nonetheless, had known that Nick had been kidnapped and was in danger. I wanted them all to be held responsible for what they'd done, and what they'd failed to do. Although the district attorney's office might have been handing out legal immunity like cupcakes, we didn't want anyone to feel morally absolved. Every one of them had failed Nick.

Jeff's best friend, Richard Stanley, his longtime tennis buddy and doubles partner, was our attorney. He and another attorney, Richard Tarlow, took the daunting task of filing a civil lawsuit on our behalf with a mediator, naming thirty-two defendants—the Los Angeles Police Department for failing to investigate the 911 calls, John Roberts, Natasha Adams, Kelly Carpenter, the Lemon Tree Inn, Jack and Laurie Hollywood . . .

We reached a settlement on the suit, totaling $330,200. The money was split among the defendants based on their involvement and ability to pay: Casey Sheehan, for instance, was ordered to pay $1,000; Michelle Lasher and her parents, $35,000. Of course, we would never see anything even approaching that kind of money. What we actually received was about $193,000, plus the rights to Jesse James Hollywood's house, which we sold for $90,000.

Talking about money in relation to Nick's murder made me queasy. There was no price tag that would make this better, and I didn't want anyone to ever think that we were profiting from his death. At least, however, perhaps it could help alleviate some of my guilt about my mounting medical and therapy bills—and indeed, in the end, the entire settlement would go straight toward paying these bills. Emergency rooms and mental hospitals were not cheap places to vacation.

I was even charged for their mistakes. One time, they gave me the wrong medication—a strong painkiller—which I turned out to be allergic to; within a few minutes of taking the pill, I was sweating profusely and the room was spinning. Next thing I knew, I was on a bed strapped to a heart monitor . . . and we got a bill for that electrocardiogram, too.

Jeff never made me feel bad about any of it, and he didn't show me the debts I was accumulating on our behalf, but that didn't mean I wasn't aware of them. By the second time I got my stomach pumped, I knew the bills would be astronomical. I became so familiar with the hospital routine that I knew just what to do. I'd drive myself the thirty or forty miles to Pasadena from West Hills, and my therapist would call ahead so that the hospital would be expecting me.

Then I'd sit in the parking lot for a minute figuring out what I could and couldn't bring inside. My picture of Nick would have to stay in the car because it was in a glass frame, so I'd leave it on the console, where others might be able to see it. Then I'd sneak a few pills into my rolled-up sleeve, just in case I needed them later.

Once I was inside, all of my belongings would be put onto a table and sorted through. Contraband was taken away, questionable things were held at the desk. My hairbrush had a pointed end, so it was held. They'd put tape with my name on it, and I'd have to ask for it when I needed to use it, under supervision. Then they'd take my vital signs and ask me what pills I'd taken and how many of each. Who could keep track?

If I couldn't stay alert, they'd send me by wheelchair to the emergency room to pump my stomach, then send me back to the mental health ward. I'd stay there until someone pronounced me stable enough to go home again. In the meantime, Jeff would call my family and say, "Susan's in the hospital again," and they would all worry and wait and visit when they could.

My younger brother Ed couldn't handle seeing me in that environment. He came to visit me at UCLA's hospital the first time and understood at that moment that I was never going to be the same. I just wasn't there anymore. All he could do was to hope that I wouldn't succeed on my next suicide attempt.

Each time I didn't succeed, though, I was glad a few days later. *What if there is no afterlife?* I thought. *I would have killed myself for nothing—I won't get to see Nick no matter what. At least now I get to see him in my dreams sometimes. It's better than not seeing him at all.*

Plus, I had to remember that I still had a job to do. I

had to make sure Nick's killers didn't get away with their crime.

———————

It's illegal to drink on the beach at Paradise Cove, but that didn't stop me. Were cops going to arrest me? *Make my day*, I thought. It would just put me closer to the people who took my son's life. Why was I so drawn to the beach? Was it to reminisce about happier days with Nick and Jeff? Or to fantasize about drowning myself? I never even knew; I would just end up there some days, always with drinks in hand.

One day in August 2001, I sat outside the Paradise Café thinking about how senseless everything seemed. What was the purpose of my having lost Nick? I felt like life was forgetting us both.

"I hate life," I repeated to myself, when I noticed the most beautiful little blond girl approaching me. She was maybe three or four years old. As she swung on the thick chain border that separated the café from the beach, she asked me, "Are there ghosts in here?"

"I don't think so," I said.

"Do you have any kids?"

Sadly, I shook my head. "No."

She looked at me and replied slowly. "Oh . . . I thought for sure you had a kid." And off she ran to play with her friends, leaving me dumbfounded.

I decided to take it as a sign that Nick was with me. Hey, when in my position, you took anything you could get. Even if it meant nothing, it made me feel good for a moment.

It was getting more rare for me to feel much of anything aside from my default depression. On September 11, 2001, I sat by my television set like everyone else, frozen in time and in disbelief about the acts of terror that had just claimed the lives of thousands of Americans. Yet I did not cry. I felt a disturbing lack of emotion. I watched the events unfold with the detachment of a clinician; of course,

I knew it was a profoundly sad thing, but I could not find a personal connection.

This bothered me. Here I was, a person who used to cry over touching commercials, yet on this day of national tragedy, I still felt only my own tragedy. *This is so unlike me*, I thought. It made me realize I was still in a state of shock, still preserving myself. For what?

For the day we find Jesse James Hollywood, I told myself. For the day I could look him in the eye and say to him, "You are not getting away with murdering my son."

CHAPTER 14

THE WORST OF ALL CASES

Ryan Hoyt was the next person to go to trial. His mother, Vicky Hoyt, walked past me on the way to the courtroom and said, "Stay away from me!" As if I were going to do anything else. She was acting like she was on some kind of drugs—prescription or not, I don't know—and her testimony was rambling and very strange.

On the stand, Hoyt disavowed his taped jailhouse confession, claiming he didn't remember it. He said he didn't remember ever having a conversation with those detectives at all. Literally, he was claiming amnesia. He was just covering for Hollywood then, he said, but in actuality, he hadn't even been there when Nick was murdered. All he'd done was bring a duffel bag to the hotel, and then leave. Hoyt said that he thought the duffel bag had marijuana in it. Days later, he found out that the package had contained a gun, and that someone had used that gun to kill Nick. That was his new story.

What would have brought on this convenient bout of amnesia? Sleep deprivation, Hoyt said. He claimed not to have slept for about a week. "Prior to my arrest, I was partying so hard I don't believe I slept at all . . . I was drinking, snorting coke, smoking weed," he testified.

An expert psychiatric witness for the prosecution testified that something was fishy about Hoyt's newfound amnesia defense; total memory loss is very rare, he said, and wasn't consistent with the way Hoyt acted during the three-hour evaluation that the psychiatrist conducted.

"His memory was crisp. It was solid," he said. "But then there's that blank two-day period. That's simply not consistent with how the brain works."

However, the psychiatrist explained, fake amnesia was a "fairly common" tactic among defendants in murder cases.

This courtroom scene was different from the one with the throngs of supporters for Richard Dispenza in Colorado. Here, Hoyt had few family members, including an aunt who cried intermittently. His mother leaned her pink cheek on the shoulder of a man sitting next to her. I don't know who he was, but the way she stiffly clutched his arm was unsettling. When she looked my way, she did so with a sarcastic smile through clenched lips and eyes that looked distended, showing no sympathy.

What have I done—and more important, what did my Nick do—to make you look at me this way? I wanted to ask.

Aside from his few family members, most of the people in the court were members of the media or there for Nick, not Hoyt.

The defense painted a pitiable picture of Ryan Hoyt. His mother testified that his father had beaten her while she was pregnant. By all accounts, Hoyt had grown up in a violent, unstable household. This, apparently, was meant to make the jury take pity on him. It wasn't his fault; he'd had a bad childhood. Who could blame him for just one little murder?

———

My older brother Buster had set up a little website dedicated to Nick by then, and it had a free guestbook people could sign. Almost all of the early entries were from people who'd known Nick well—our family and his friends. It was a place where we could gather, at least in cyberspace, to symbolically hold hands and talk about our loss. The beautiful words that people left about Nick did fortify me. My cousin Rose wrote to Jeff and me, "I wish I could take some of the pain away from you, but I know nothing in this lifetime will do that. Just remember when you are weak and down and don't feel like going on, Nick is watching over you. He would want you to stay alive and healthy to see that justice is served with these people who took his life. His life now lives on through you. Let him shine!"

That's what I tried to do. Every day, I brought Nick's leather bomber jacket to court with me, and I held it to feel his presence.

The prosecutors warned us that they were going to show some pictures that would be upsetting to us. We didn't have to be in the courtroom to see them, they said, but they wanted to give us the option to look first.

My son in his grave. His skull, torn open by bullets. His body, far away and fuzzy, half covered in dirt.

How much do you have to drink to unsee what you have already seen?

Ben was still in prison during Hoyt's trial, but since he would have to be in Santa Barbara to testify, he was moved to the Santa Barbara County Jail for six weeks. It was the same jail where Hoyt was being held. Ben had to walk by him every day.

The trial lasted until November 21, 2001, when Ryan Hoyt was convicted of first-degree murder after just one day of jury deliberations. His parents were not there for the verdict. He sat stone-faced, and his grandfather later said that he knew what was coming.

During the penalty phase, we played a portion of video from Nick's bar mitzvah speech. In each bar mitzvah ceremony, the young man reads a portion of the Torah. Nick's reading was Shoeftim, from Deuteronomy, and it was a farewell speech from Moses just before he died, as the Jewish people were about to enter the Promised Land. The speech was all about justice.

In his speech, Nick said, "Moses told the people that there must be justice for all. He said, 'Justice, justice must you follow.' They were also told that no accused person should be condemned without being provided a fair trial, to include testimony by dependable witnesses."

Later, he added, "Preparing for this bar mitzvah has been a real eye-opener for me. I have really grown in the past few months, and I don't mean my height. I don't know how to explain it, but my Judaism has really started to mean something to me.

"I never realized how much Jewish law applies in today's world. For instance, my Torah portion mentions justice. Justice and a fair legal system are the basis of any democracy. The American justice system is far from perfect, but it definitely beats the alternative.

"I found it interesting that over three thousand years ago, God, through Moses, expressed the importance of a fair legal system. I know that many of you think I'm perfect"— this drew laughter from the bar mitzvah crowd—"but believe me, I am far from perfect. However, I do think I am developing a strong sense of what is right and wrong, and how to treat other people. The Golden Rule in Judaism is 'Treat other people as you would like to be treated.' That is a rule I will try to live by."

Given the first-degree murder conviction, there were only two options for sentencing: Ryan Hoyt would either get life in prison or the death penalty. I wondered if Nick would think less of me for really needing the death penalty. *An eye for an eye*, I told myself. *It's time for our justice system to really mean "justice."* I didn't want to react out of spite or hate or even anger, though. I wanted to feel the way I did because it was the only appropriate form of punishment for the crime. One of the most difficult things I've had to do was to get up and speak during the penalty phase of Ryan Hoyt's trial.

"Ryan James Hoyt, you shot my child in the face and did not even know his name! His name was Nicholas Samuel Markowitz," I said.

I told the court about what had happened to all of us since Nick's murder—about how it was tearing Jeff and I apart, about how my mother had a heart attack during the grand jury trial, about Nick's half-sister Leah's emotional roller coaster knowing her children would never know their uncle Nick.

Then I described what had happened to Nick's best friend, Ryan, at Bryn Athens: "A school that has been dealing with boys for over one hundred and fifty years suggested his mom come to get him." Ryan had been unable to pull himself together without professional help, and the two of us cried every time we saw each other.

"I can only imagine Nick's last breaths that were spent trying to plead for his life through the duct tape that muffled his cries. Game that is hunted and killed receives more dignity in its death than Nicholas did. This vision has haunted me every minute for the past four hundred and seventy-three days.

"Holidays are something I try to pretend are not there, but Mother's Day collapsed me. I lay face first in the grass over my son's body begging someone to tell me I was having a nightmare."

After court that day, I crawled back into the hotel bed, where I would try to sleep as early as I could to make the day shorter. I wrote another note to Nick.

I will be with you soon, my son. Love, Mom

P.S. Dad says for me not to hurry.
You probably need the break.

In his closing remarks, the prosecutor argued that "the death penalty is saved for the worst of all cases. This is the worst of all cases."

On the day of sentencing, I sat up front as usual. The

victim's advocate, Joan, held my hand. The court had appointed her, but to Jeff and me, she had become family. She checked on us frequently to see how we were doing, even beyond the scope of her job. We went to lunch with Joan and her wonderful husband, Pete; we transcended the relationship we were assigned to have.

Just a few feet in front of me sat Ryan Hoyt, handcuffed and sitting in a cushioned, swivel-rocking chair. He was dressed in slacks and a sweater, with gel-slicked hair, his patent-leather shoes tapping, even though his feet were chained. His eyes were black and hollow; they were the eyes of a killer. His shoe tapping bothered me.

Has he made us the same now? I wondered. *Do we both feel nothing?*

"Another day in court—that's all this is," I told myself, and I remembered some of the meditation techniques I learned from a therapist. Leave the darkness; go to the light.

In my visualization, I saw the stairs that led down to a hallway with many doors. I had traveled this path in my meditations before; I knew what was behind each of those doors. I passed up the one that would lead to my beach cottage, as it wasn't the warmth of the sun or the sound of the ocean I needed right then. Instead, I kept going to my favorite door: Nick's nursery.

It was 1984, and as I opened the door, I heard "The Muffin Man" playing from his tape recorder. The room smelled like baby oil. I grasped the handle of the top drawer of his dresser and looked at his little pastel undershirts, jammies, and blue booties. They cried out with sweetness.

Little bears with red bows smiled down on me from the wallpaper border. The room was nice and tidy, with his books lined up by size. *The Little Engine That Could, The Very Hungry Caterpillar, The Wheels on the Bus . . .*

Sitting proudly on the top shelf of his bookcase was a wooden alphabet train that spelled out "NICHOLAS." Little Boy Blue was fast asleep in the hay in a framed picture on the wall. But as I got to the crib with the baby blue blanket, I felt emptiness. My baby was not there.

In the corner of the room was a pair of shoes, size fourteen . . . what were they doing there?

The sounds of the courtroom rose, and I told myself I had to leave this place. As I walked back through the hallway, I stepped on something. I looked down and picked it up—Nick's teddy bear. I caressed its familiarity against my cheek and I thought I heard . . . "Mommy?"

"All rise. The Honorable Judge William L. Gordon presiding."

We rose. I didn't know where I was anymore.

"The court is now in session. Please be seated."

First came the motions, the penal codes, the procedural babble that made my eyes glaze over. Three hours later, the judge said the first thing that mattered to me.

"I have taken into consideration the defendant's age and lack of prior convictions."

My heart sank.

"I must also think of the vulnerability of the innocent victim . . . I also thought of how many opportunities [the defendant] had not to go through with this heinous crime. The planning and brutality of Nicholas's murder warrants a death sentence. He killed a defenseless teenage boy who had done neither the defendant nor any of his cohorts any harm. Moreover, the evidence shows Mr. Hoyt murdered out of a desire to please Jesse Hollywood's coterie of friends. There is no way I can justify the cruelty, and I sentence you, Ryan James Hoyt, to death by lethal injection in the San Quentin Prison. That will be the order."

Frozen in my seat, I attempted to make eye contact with the judge, but he would not allow it. He had never allowed it. He was the judge for Hoyt, Rugge, and both of Pressley's trials. After sitting in his courtroom for more than a year, I knew he always made his decisions confidently without the need for acceptance. Still, I wanted to convey my gratitude to him—he had given the ultimate punishment for the ultimate crime. Nick's life meant no less than Ryan Hoyt's did.

I heard whimpers from the other side of the courtroom. I had no desire to look.

People came over to us and hugged us, congratulated us on the verdict. So many people whose faces I knew only from the courtroom day after day.

I wrote a letter to the *Santa Barbara News-Press* that they shared with readers:

> *Santa Barbara is a place that I have very mixed emotions about due to the circumstances of my son's death. However, I want to make it very clear I have full intentions of coming back when these proceedings are over to thank each of you for embracing me along with my son's memory. My hopes are that I can look at your beautiful community and not link it to Nick's death.*
>
> *We believe that all the jurors took pride in their duties, and with great distress came upon their decisions. I can only imagine what a challenge it had to have been, obeying the law, organizing evidence, and suppressing the emotions. We would like to thank each of them for being able to sit through some very tough moments.*

I thanked the prosecutors, the victim's advocate, and all of the Santa Barbara Sheriff's Department for devoting such a large part of their lives to helping get justice for Nick, I thanked the Hotel Santa Barbara staff for being kind to us while we stayed there during trials, and I thanked the media for being very decent and giving us space and compassion.

Then I sat by Nick's grave and told him the news. I wondered if it brought him any peace. As for me . . . I guess I was hoping for it to feel better than it did. Getting that verdict and that sentence was important, but it didn't erase my suicidal thoughts. In fact, it brought me one step closer to feeling like my work on Earth was done.

Every step like this made it feel more real and more final. Nick really wasn't coming back.

I had to remind myself of that daily. Where was the guy with the hidden camera who was supposed to pop up at the trial and tell us it was all a joke and we could go home now with Nick? But now a jury had decided that someone really had killed Nick . . . Did that mean it had to be true?

On days when I felt particularly suicidal, I would call Jeff and tell him that I needed to go to the doctor to have my medications adjusted, or some equally smallish thing. Then I would go to the hospital and tell the truth—that I still wanted to die, and I needed help.

But really, what could they do for me? They could take away my sharp objects and put me in a room with someone else who also wanted to die and tell me that things would get better, but did anything really get better? When, exactly, were things going to get better?

You weren't allowed to just stay in bed in the hospital. They made you get up and do things all day. But there were some days I just couldn't, no matter what they told me. On those days, I would get what amounted to a bad report card. They'd make me feel like I wasn't trying.

But I was trying. I'm not sure if they understood that sometimes I had to *try* just to open my eyes. Just to sit up. Just to speak three words. Just to not break into the nurse's station and steal whatever little white pills they might have stacked neatly behind the desk and swallow all of them at once.

I told the other patients that if they didn't want to take their pills to please save them for me. If they found any on the floor, I'd take those, too. I was not picky: whatever they had, I'd take. But it didn't work that way—it really was a lot like the scene in *One Flew Over the Cuckoo's Nest* where someone called out "Medication time!" and everyone lined up at a desk to get a little cup with a pill in it. You had to stand there and open your mouth and put the pill in and swallow it before you left the station—no throwing it away or saving it for later. They didn't have to worry about me throwing away any pills, that's for sure, but they did have to worry about me stockpiling pills to take all at once.

There was some kind of comfort in being in a hospital; you do get taken care of in different ways than you might at home, and there's nothing for you to concentrate on other than your own mental health. But then I'd have to go back home and wonder what was going to make me not do it again.

———

Perhaps, given my stints in the mental hospitals, it comes as no great shock that I also tried using a Ouija board to contact Nick.

It wasn't my idea. My neighbors, who I barely knew before Nick's death, made the offer. They believed they could communicate with spirits using a Ouija board, and I thought, *Why not*? I soon found that after Nick's death, I believed in *everything*. I no longer cared to figure out which religion or lack thereof had it right; I was open to believing in anything that might give me a connection to my son.

So I would walk over to my neighbor's house and take notes while they used the Ouija board. I tried to write down everything they said—which was a challenge, because some sessions lasted for hours.

I would ask the questions:

"How do I communicate with you, Nick?" yielded the response, "You have to think of Susan; otherwise, there are two of me and none of you . . . You are so busy thinking your thoughts that you can't hear mine."

"Can you tell me where Hollywood is?" I asked, and the response came back: "He is in a cage that he made for himself. He's not getting away with it."

I left these sessions feeling good. I don't know whether I was really communicating with Nick, but it felt real to me—and I'd rather have that than let my cynicism rob me of experiencing it. My new motto became, "Embrace and acknowledge whatever comes your way." One time, Nick's best friend, Ryan, came along with me. I thanked Nick for each of these sessions and kept them in my heart, needing to believe that there was still a way for us to talk.

———

Right after Ryan Hoyt's guilty verdict was announced, the Los Angeles Police Department declared that two of their officers, Donovan Lyons and Brent Rygh, would receive written reprimands. The LAPD Board of Rights had found them guilty of failing to properly investigate the 911 calls about the kidnapping . . . narrowly. The board called it a "minor technical breach of policy" because the officers had interviewed the first 911 caller only by cell phone and never followed up with an in-person interview. But the board concluded that the officers' lack of investigating had no effect on Nick's death.

In fact, one of the board members wanted to reassure those two officers that they hadn't really done anything *wrong*; they just hadn't done their *best*. "This decision should in no way [imply] that your actions or inactions were connected to what later occurred," he told them.

Come again?

The officers had had the license plate number for the van, and although they had run the plates, they had decided not to even visit the van's owner, John Roberts. They said that they had simply looked around town for a victim wandering the streets, and when they didn't find one—oh, well. If they had visited John Roberts and asked who had his van, and then gone and tracked it down, I felt strongly that Nick *would* be alive today. John Roberts lived only a few blocks from where Nick was abducted. One of the reasons that the officers said they didn't go to the address was that they thought it was "miles" away. Perhaps they didn't feel like driving that day.

The 911 operators who'd bungled the calls and coded them as an assault and an information-only broadcast, respectively, were each disciplined, too . . . three days' suspension. Somehow it didn't seem right that their errors had led to my son's murder, and yet they were basically given mini vacations from work.

I tried not to focus on that, though. Nick's high school wanted to do something to memorialize him, and Jeff had spent many hours making a marker for future generations to admire. There would be a tree-planting ceremony in his honor on December 28, 2001, which gave me a way to get through Christmas, a little. I asked for his friends to bring letters, poems, or prayers to share.

That day, his grandma wrote, "Well, Nick, we planted your tree today, as you know, because as soon as we finished, you watered it." It had rained. "Nice touch. Only you would think of something like that to let us know you were watching. I love you and miss you."

Then something happened that really threw me: it seemed the whole world knew that Ben had gotten out of prison, except me.

In a therapy session months earlier, I had told Jeff that I needed to know when Ben got out or when Jeff spoke to him. I never wanted Ben to be anywhere near us again; my mother was now living with us, and I felt that anyone who was associated with Ben was in serious danger. But Jeff had kept it a secret from me for three weeks. I found out through other family members who were also trying to keep it from me.

I felt so betrayed.

I really just want to be alone, I thought. Jeff's life was always going to include Ben, even if only in his thoughts, and that would crush me. I began separating myself from Jeff in my mind, preparing myself for what could come. Almost no marriages survive the murder of a child; I knew the stats. I knew the stories from the Parents of Murdered Children group. The trauma put such a strain on the marriage that it almost always broke, and in our case, there was the added element that surely created much more stress— the "Ben factor."

I told my therapist I was considering spending time apart from Jeff—which was kind of a funny notion, considering that Jeff was rarely around those days anyway. Time apart would not be that different from what we were doing now. I thought about it and thought about it, but I didn't act on it. It remained another sadness hanging over me, the looming threat that my marriage might be over, too.

I realized that I was starting to think of my life in terms of deaths and trials. This was the month that so-and-so died. This was the month this trial came to an end. This was the month of so-and-so's sentencing. In February 2002, my father died. He was a great man—which is exactly what it says on his headstone: "A great man." He was never able to talk about Nick, and I tried to respect that; I didn't come around or call as much as I usually would, and I tried not to talk about Nick when I did. But when it was clear that he was dying and no longer conscious, I had told him, "Don't be afraid. We're all with you, and Nick is waiting."

Somehow, I was supposed to get myself together and make it to Santa Barbara again for Jesse Rugge's trial in April 2002. But before it even began, we were hit with a punch in the stomach: the judge ruled that the jury could not hear Jesse's confession.

It had been coerced, the judge said.

The ruling was all based on one statement that a detective had made in the middle of Rugge's confession, when Rugge was still hemming and hawing about how he was afraid of prison: "You could be sentenced to death. It looks like you put him in his own grave and shot him, so it doesn't matter who you're going to be afraid of. I'd be afraid of that needle. Does that spin it a little different?"

"I'd be afraid of that needle" was considered coercion. It didn't make any sense to me, but that's what the judge ruled. It meant that a jury would never hear a word of what Rugge said, before or after that moment. Those detectives had worked so hard for that confession, and I didn't see a thing wrong with it . . . and what made me angrier was that jurors would never even know that it existed. They'd never get to weigh it with the other evidence. *Why not let the jury decide if it was a real confession?* I thought. How were they supposed to come to a fair decision if they couldn't even see all the evidence?

Regardless of the anguish I felt, the trial was about to start, and I had to put on a confident face for the cameras.

"Excuse me, Mrs. Markowitz, can I have a moment of your time?" "Mrs. Markowitz, how are you coping?" "How do you feel about seeing Jesse Rugge here today?"

Flash, flash. The cameras went off. Did they expect me to smile? Cry?

The Santa Barbara courthouse was one of the most beautiful Spanish buildings I had ever seen, and also one of the coldest. Polished terra-cotta floors, stone walls, high ceilings with heavy beams, and open-air veranda staircases make it impossible to keep warm. On the other hand, this also made it a great retreat from the summer heat.

Every morning, I would have to leave hours early to save a seat in the courtroom. You could not put your belongings on a seat or ask someone else to save one for you. My family would travel for hours only to be turned away when they got to the courtroom because not one person would give up a seat for them. It was a media frenzy.

I had met Barney the bailiff when we'd first arrived in the Santa Barbara courthouse, in 2000, and I had been trying to forget him ever since, but there he was again. That wasn't his real name, but it's what I nicknamed him in my mind because he looked so much like Barney Rubble from *The Flintstones.* You could not miss him, with his wad of freshly polished keys dangling at his side. The shine reflecting off his shoes was just a bit less bright than staring directly at the sun.

Every trial day we had to get up by 4:00 a.m. in order to leave home by 5:00 and make it to court by 7:00 to stand in line. The doors would open at 8:00.

But just before the first day of Rugge's trial began, at 10:00, Barney stood in front of our seats and proudly announced it was time to take a break and we would not be allowed to leave our belongings in the courtroom—so the seats I just saved for Jeff and I were back on the free market. I walked out the door and turned around, making myself the first person in the "new" line.

Then, when break time was over, Barney opened the *other* set of doors . . . making me the last in line. I asked him if he could let me know which door he was going to open for the lunch break, so I wouldn't lose my seat again. With one hand on his keys and the other on his hip, he looked away and said, "You know, it still remains a mystery even to myself as to which door I'm going to open."

His moves were meticulous. He would pick a piece of lint off his chair, untwist the telephone cord. When he stood, he stood at attention as if he were holding up the wall behind him.

When I asked to speak with the judge about allowing us to save regular seats—considering that we were the victim's parents and were traveling two hours to get there every morning, he said no. "Those are the judge's rules."

After many more such encounters, I thought to myself that I had to find the humanity in this man. I don't know why it became a challenge to me, but it did; he seemed so utterly without compassion. One day, I heard him whistling and told him that it brought back comforting memories of my father, who recently passed away.

"I'll see if I can't whistle for you more often," he said. He never whistled again.

———

With the confession thrown out, Jesse Rugge was able to completely change his story without the jury knowing any different. So he claimed that he wasn't even present when Nick was killed: "I took off running once I heard the gunshots," he said.

Studying the jury's faces concerned me. They looked like they were buying it.

The months and years of sitting in courtrooms and listening over and over to how my son was killed got to me. I couldn't contain my tears, so I left the courtroom and stood in the cold hallway. There, I reminded myself that if there was a tear to be shed, it should be for my son.

In all three trials so far, I had been flabbergasted by the lack of compassion on the "other side" of the courtroom. At best, they ignored Jeff and me and our families. At worst, they shot us dirty looks, grinned menacingly at us when something went right for them, and insulted us.

The only people who even said, "I'm sorry this happened to your son" were Graham Pressley's parents. Aside from them, *nothing*. None of the other families uttered a single kind word to us. We sat in the courtroom every day next to these people. They watched our pain, our tears, up close . . . and they didn't say a word.

It didn't matter to me whether a lawyer told them to keep their mouths shut. I didn't care about gag orders or legal strategies or whatever else they used to excuse themselves for their behavior. Nothing should ever have prevented them from doing the right thing and showing some human decency. What rule would it have broken to walk over to me and say, "I'm sorry for your loss"?

I would have. I know, without a doubt, that I would have carried that guilt with me until my dying day and would have done anything I could to ease the other parents' pain had my son had been on the other side of this equation. To be so callous was foreign to me; I grew up in a family of warm, loving people who knew what it meant to care about others. This felt like getting slapped over and over again at a time when I was already so vulnerable.

I tried not to let it get to me, but it hurt. It really hurt. And it made me see a little more clearly how the children of these families had turned out the way they had; none of them had learned to care about anyone other than themselves.

Sometimes the press would put words in their mouths to make them more palatable. Articles would say things like, "Of course they felt terrible for the family whose son had been murdered, but now they were worried about their own son's future, too." Of course they felt terrible? You could have fooled me. Many of them acted as if my son's murder was a terrible inconvenience in their lives. Like they blamed me, and him, for the predicament they found themselves in.

These thoughts could have knocked me flat if I had let

them stay in my brain too long. So I tried hard to focus on the good people in that courtroom—many of whom were strangers to me, who just heard the story in the news or through their kids, and who had shown up just because it affected them. One woman, Jennifer, often brought me leis that she had made from flowers in her garden.

It is now time to get over those who just don't get it.

The jury convicted Jesse Rugge of kidnapping for ransom, but they acquitted him of murder.

It would take months before the judge would sentence Rugge, and in the meantime, I had to live with the knowledge that he'd gotten away with it, that he had beaten the murder charge. My son's flesh had been left to rot in the stifling heat on the mountains, while this subhuman got away with it because the jury never even heard his confession.

Before the sentencing, his attorney argued for probation only—no jail time—because the jury hadn't convicted him of aiding and abetting in the murder. Plus, the attorney said, Rugge was a misguided guy whose parents were divorced, and he was a well-behaved inmate who was remorseful. Also, his safety in prison was in question because Ryan Hoyt had openly threatened to kill him.

But the judge denied that motion.

"He lured Mr. Markowitz into a sense of security, which he had no right to feel," the judge said. And Rugge had done nothing redeeming even after Nick was killed, instead helping his cohorts to cover up the crime. As a result, the judge sentenced Rugge to the mandatory sentence for kidnapping for ransom: life in prison but with the possibility of parole after five years.

"What does that mean?" I asked Joan.

"It means that every two years, a parole board will review the case and his behavior and decide if he should stay in prison or not."

"Do we get any say in that?"

"You can be there and address the parole board if you want to, but you don't have to."

"We'll be there. We'll always be there."

It was never going to end, I realized. Even after the trials were all finished, this nightmare would not truly be over until every one of them died. There would always be the possibility of more appeals, of parole, of mistrials, and so on. In Jesse Rugge's case, every two years, we would have to sit in front of the parole board and argue once again that this man should not be released to the public. If we didn't do that, I would feel that we had missed an opportunity to do the right thing for Nick.

I hoped that Rugge would die in prison so I could be released of my obligation sooner rather than later.

———————

The only person involved in the crime whom I felt at all hopeful about was Graham Pressley. There was something in him that was not in the others: a soul. I could see it in his scared, sad eyes the first time I saw him. I just didn't know how to process that. How could a person with a soul have done what he did? Was I just being fooled because he had such an innocent face?

Pressley's parents had posted his bail money, so he remained free until his own trial. It hurt to see him in the court hallway, being comforted and taken home by his mom and dad. I missed those hugs. Sometimes, now, when I saw a boy who looked about Nick's age, I would ask for a hug just to remember how it felt.

For Pressley, there were actually two trials. The first one, which lasted for three weeks, deadlocked and ended in a mistrial in July 2002 because the jurors were split on whether to convict him on murder charges. They had heard a remorseful teenage Pressley tell them that he felt responsible for Nick's death. "I am ashamed of what I did, and what I did not do," he said on the stand. But his lawyer, a public defender, said that his client "wouldn't hurt a fly."

I understood why the jury had deadlocked. Pressley's defense for his actions was that he was under duress, fearing for his own life the whole time he was involved with Nick's murder. Prosecutor Ron Zonen, a senior deputy district attorney, said that it was difficult to prove that someone was *not* in fear of his life, so he knew it would be a tough decision for the jury to agree on.

Pressley was freed on fifty thousand dollars bail and had to abide by a 10:00 p.m. curfew and refrain from using drugs or alcohol while they awaited a retrial. The defense attorney had tried to make it sound like his client really wasn't involved and hadn't known anything about Nick's murder before it took place, but that was blown apart in the second trial, which took place in October 2002.

The prosecution described every time that Pressley could have told Nick about the money Hollywood had offered to have him killed—he did not tell Nick in Natasha Adams's car before they went to the hotel, nor at the hotel party, nor in the pool, nor back in the hotel room before Ryan Hoyt got there, nor after Jesse Rugge and Hoyt left to get shovels.

The defense described a terrified teenager who was normally easygoing and compassionate, and they said that Graham Pressley had not taken the walk to Lizard's Mouth with the others; instead, they claimed, he stayed in the car the whole time.

What didn't make sense to us was that if we were to believe Pressley had been so terrified of Hoyt and Rugge that he dug a grave while not saying a word about the gun to Nick, how was it that he later defied Hoyt and told him he was going to stay in the car instead of going back with them to the grave? Where had his sudden bravery come from?

Pressley would later change his story and admit that he had walked with the others part of the way, then turned back and stayed in the car—which is also what Jesse Rugge had said in his trial.

Ultimately, Graham Pressley was found guilty of second-degree murder at the second trial, and Pressley hung his head and cried as he heard the verdict. The jury said it wasn't an easy decision, but one juror explained that the moment that allowed them to come to their guilty verdict

was when Pressley and Hoyt returned to the hotel after
Pressley had dug the grave; Hoyt had left Pressley alone in
the car and said nothing to him while he went back into the
hotel to get Nick and Rugge.

Why had he stayed in the car?

This was what bothered Jeff the most. He said, "I don't
care if you were stupid, I don't care if you were scared, I
don't care if you were threatened . . . *nobody* would have
stayed in that car if he was not involved."

Although Pressley was tried and convicted as an adult,
he was sentenced as a juvenile, which gave me a sense of
relief. It was hard to imagine him in adult prison, and hard
to look at his parents and not feel sad for them.

So I didn't fight the feeling; I let myself feel for them.
Nick had sat in the backseat of Christina Pressley's
car when she drove them over to the hotel, and she had
expressed feeling tremendous guilt ever since then for not
having realized that anything was amiss. *Why hadn't she
received a sign from God?* she wanted to know.

Graham Pressley would be in juvenile prison until he
turned twenty-five, but he would have annual reviews to
determine if he could be released early. Despite my feelings of sympathy, however, I didn't want him out early. He
had failed my son terribly. He had chosen not to warn Nick
that he had seen a gun or dug a grave; he had allowed Nick
to keep walking toward that grave even when he knew
what was about to happen. For that, I wanted an appropriate justice.

And then I got a note posted to the guestbook on Nick's
memorial website:

*The Markowitzes ought to be ashamed of their thought-
less crusade against Graham Pressley. Your minds are
so clouded by sadness and anger that you have failed to
recognize your own evils as parents and citizens. Trust
me, I'm a friend of Graham's, and he is a far better person than either of you will ever be. I know this message
will be deleted because it makes you question your own*

frame of mind. I only hope it somehow penetrates your mean-spirited, vengeful, misdirected lives ...

This is coming from a child, I kept telling myself—but that didn't stop the tears that followed for two days. I didn't delete the message. I left it there, along with my response, and hoped for an apology that never came.

Most of the letters and postings were much kinder, though. Someone wrote to me saying that she prayed now that the trials were over, I could pick up the pieces. I responded by first thanking her for her love, and second by praying I would find some pieces to pick up.

In July 2003, I received a letter from Christina Pressley, Graham's mother:

I have wanted to write to you for a long time, but I did not know if it would just be touching your wounds, hurting you, and I did not want to do that because you have been through so much already. I feel like it is as fresh as if it just happened yesterday, and I want you to know that we pray for you and your family every day. . . .

I can't even begin to understand your pain, but I somehow feel responsible because I did not detect something and save your boy. I still see his beautiful young face in the backseat of my car, and I wonder why I had no warning from God, so that I could have saved him. I'm so sorry, Susan. I want you to know that I support what you are doing, I still grieve for you, and I will continue to pray for you. Graham prays for you too, every day. He asks me about you regularly. Both of us dream of Nick often. My dreams are usually that I am driving down the 101, taking him home. Graham dreams of grabbing him by the shirt on the trail and running away with him into the night, dodging bullets and making it to safety. He has been on a crusade to help kids too because of this tragedy.

I just want you to know that all of the work we do to help teens is in honor of Nick, and we will never forget him.

Blessings to you,
Chris Graham Pressley

I responded:

I am not surprised by your letter, but only in the length of time it took you to write. I feel I have known you a lifetime, but have not had the opportunity to speak to you. Our shared words and emotions in the hall-way awaiting the trials will forever be with me. I have always felt your compassion, and your letter is one of many missing pieces to my puzzled life. I appreciate it more than you will ever know.

Our correspondence continued, and we met several times for lunch. The district attorney's office was skeptical when I first told them that Christina had reached out to me; "Be careful," they told me. "Don't be surprised if she's just trying to get you to ask for an early release for Graham." But she never once even hinted at such a thing, and I felt very comfortable with her. I wanted to cry with her. Sometimes I felt that if I cried with the right person, it would make the pain go away.

CHAPTER 15

CROSSROADS

Ben had been dating the same woman since about a year prior to Nick's death. Now it was the spring of 2003, and they were expecting a baby and preparing to get married.

Give Jeff his freedom, I told myself. *Let him be the great father and grandfather I know he can be.* I could not go along for this ride, but he deserved to. There was even a point when I asked Jeff to move out. I was not mad at him, and I didn't want to split up, but I knew I was not going to be able to be a part of Ben's life again, and I knew he would always want to.

The baby came—a girl. I felt nothing but sadness. Jeff went to see her. I sat alone in our albatross of a house that was keeping me in a pattern of depression, and I wrote a letter to Ben. I'm not sure if I ever mailed it.

> *To hear you say you were sorry one thousand forty one days ago would have helped me look at you differently . . . not that it matters, not that any of this will matter. You have moved on with your life and I am trying to find a path that does not have a sinkhole.*

*I want you to know I know you loved your brother.
I know you never wanted your brother dead. Nick not
only loved you, he looked up to you.*

*Your father has chosen to reinstate himself back into
your life. Life gives and takes, but it took my world, my
purpose for living, as I know you now can appreciate.
I have heard you now have a little girl to love and care
for. I have appreciated your distance. I no longer fit in,
but I wish you many happy moments with your little
one. In addition, of course I hope she gives you some
crap along the way!*

*I would appreciate if you would not respond. My
intentions are nothing more than to move on.*

Of course, Ben probably had said he was sorry at some
point, but in my grief, I had never heard it. It was not
enough. How could it ever be enough?

Luckily, he and his fiancée married at City Hall and didn't
ask his family to come, so we avoided the question of what
I would have done had they asked us to be there. I thought
about how I would never go to Nick's wedding, never get to
kiss his children's chubby cheeks. I thought how unfair it
was that Ben got another chance and Nick didn't.

While I was still sitting squarely in that crossroads of
my life, I took my mom out to lunch at the local Mission
Burrito by our home. Afterward, on our way back to my
car in the parking lot, I noticed a teenager straining to read
the magnets on it. There were two large car magnets on
either side of my car that I had printed up with two different pictures of Jesse James Hollywood, along with the
story and the offer of a fifty thousand dollar reward.

I never knew who I was going to meet on any given day
as a result of driving a moving "Wanted" billboard, but
I had made hundreds of supporters who would ask more
about the story or express their disbelief that the police
hadn't caught this scum yet. One supporter, a Santa Barbara lawyer, asked me, "How is it that you can have this

thug's mug on your car without showing your beautiful son's?"

He was right, and I immediately rectified that. I was lucky that my local Kinko's was supporting me by providing me with all of my printing needs at their cost, but it was still expensive. I had so many handouts made up to pass around to people.

I hoped that the boy who was straining to read my car was a supporter—maybe someone who had known Nick in school. He was leaning into a white Thunderbird to talk to a woman, and as my mom and I backed up to leave, I stopped in front of him and offered him a "Wanted" card—a business card that looked just like the magnets on my car, except that the other side also featured Nick's website information.

The boy threw his arms in the air with a look of confusion and disgust. "I'm not touching that!" he yelled.

I didn't understand, but I said, "That's OK; you don't have to take it." As I pulled forward to leave, a female leaned out of the Thunderbird window and stuck out her middle finger.

"Fuck you!" she screamed, three or four times.

Fuck me? Is she talking to me?

I tried to drive off, but the shock of it just wouldn't let me leave. I circled around to the liquor store they were parked in front of and parked my car again.

"They must be friends of the Hollywoods," I realized. I jotted down the Thunderbird's license plate number, and an even clearer thought came to mind: could this be Jesse's mother?

I waited for them to leave; then I drove by the Hollywoods' house. Sure enough, it was the queen bee who'd stung me. Laurie Hollywood.

I went home and cried from disbelief. When the tears dried, we increased the reward money, again. We would have to take out a loan if anyone claimed the reward, but we knew that it would be worth it. Sometimes money makes people talk, and more money makes people talk more.

Over the next several months, I regularly drove by the Hollywoods' home. Each time I put up new posters and memorials around the city, someone would quickly tear them down. I figured it was Laurie, but I would have needed to install security cameras everywhere to catch her.

Jesse James Hollywood's parents were still playing dumb, pretending that they had no idea where their son was. I knew that they knew. And in driving by their house, I kept hoping to pick up a clue. I took note of the types of cars parked in the driveway, but nothing seemed very useful. Laurie was taking in the garbage cans one of the times I drove by, and she flipped me off again. It was the first time I got a good look at the wrathful face behind the finger.

My friend Randi drove in from Washington to visit once, and she got to witness an even rarer treat—this time, not only did Laurie give me the finger, but she threw in a bonus: she stuck her tongue out at me. I hadn't realized adults even did that.

I began seeing a new therapist, as I didn't feel I was making much progress. Dr. Fulton had been the same doctor we had seen with Nick when he was angry with us because we weren't letting him see Ben. There were still those memories lingering in his office; I could still see Nick's reactions in that room. Dr. Fulton primarily treated children and teens; he didn't specialize in grief therapy.

Parents of Murdered Children recommended Dr. Larry Schulte, who was trained in treating grieving parents. The first few sessions were on my own terms. Depending on how I was doing that day, I showed up late, or stayed past the point when he told me our time was up, or left early. I felt very at home with him very quickly, and although I wasn't consciously trying to step over his boundaries, I was just trying to get my own needs met. Some days it was too much to handle, and others, I needed to just talk until all the talking was done.

At the end of one of my first sessions, I casually mentioned that my last therapist would have said that my drinking was a problem. Then I left, wanting him to figure out how to deal with that before our next session. He asked me about it. I smiled and said, "No one, not even you, Dr. Schulte, will get me to quit drinking."

It was a challenge. Of course I knew my drinking was out of control, but I also felt very justified. No one was going to say that I didn't have the right—the undeniable right—to get as drunk as I wanted to every day of the rest of my life if that's how I managed to get through the days. And yet, it was a problem. I knew it. Although I was saying the exact opposite, I just wanted someone to shake me and make me change. And if Dr. Schulte had pushed me in the beginning, I would have just walked out. He had the right touch, though, letting me get away with just enough but still acknowledging that he saw things we would need to work on.

Some days, I would arrive early and just fling myself on his floor; he didn't have much of a waiting room, which he kept apologizing for. But there I'd be, half drunk and half coherent, trying to find a place of stability to check in when he opened the door. I managed to fly just under the radar; if he had realized I was drunk, he never would have let me drive home.

Some days, I was able to summon up anger, a feeling that was usually overshadowed by depression and confusion. Anger was a better feeling because it was active; the depression just made me want to hide in my house all day, whereas at least the anger propelled me to get back out there and hunt for Jesse James Hollywood.

Anxiety attacks rendered me housebound on and off, but my anger gave me the will to keep fighting. I attended a retirement party for someone I didn't even know, just because someone told me that important people would be there. So I went with a stack of "Wanted" cards and key chains in memory of Nick. I handed them out to police officers and the president of the city council. Everything I passed out was a new possibility, I reminded myself.

Maybe this would be the person who would finally find Hollywood and bring him to justice.

For the third anniversary of Nick's death, we paid four hundred dollars for a memorial in the *Santa Barbara News-Press*. It included a poem I wrote, plus an essay that Nick had written for his Hebrew school:

Acts of Loving Kindness
By Nick Markowitz, age fourteen

Everyone has an obligation in this world to make it nicer for everyone else. I wouldn't consider myself a good example, but at least I know what I should be doing. . . .

Giving money, gifts, or even your time to another individual can brighten up their day and give them a great impression of you. Giving respect and love can often be the best gift of all, as it not only enlightens the person with physical things, but emotional as well.

Even though it is expected of us all, I would still consider going out of your way to be extra-special nice to your parents is always good.

You can make donations to the local Ronald McDonald foundation, and I'm sure they could always use a buck. Also, if you plan to have a pet, you may wish to get one at the pound or an animal shelter since they're in danger of being put to death.

Almost equally important is to be kind to yourself. Spend time with yourself. Love yourself (not too much, it will make you blind).

Random acts of kindness are always welcome. "Thank you sir," for example. "How are you, ma'am?" Or, "Would you please pass the taquitos, senorita?"

I hope my examples will brighten the lives of others. This essay is an act of loving kindness all by itself.

A woman named Maggie who read the essay online wrote to me, "I have been trying to decide on the purchase of a new dog, until I read Nick's suggestion of adopting one from the animal shelter. That now will be the route I take. In honor of your son."

It was a beautiful gift, which I cherished. Letters poured in from dozens of readers who wanted me to know that they had been touched, or that they had followed the case and were thinking about us. I craved their words; it was another form of therapy for me to hear that people had not forgotten Nick. The anniversary dates and holidays were always particularly hard days—the day he was kidnapped, the day he was killed, his birthday, Christmas. Those were the days I needed the letters and the invisible support even more.

I put a poster and roses on the tree where Nick had been kidnapped. When I drove by later, the poster had been ripped down. At least the roses remained.

My dreams twisted into nightmares, often starring Jesse James Hollywood or Ryan Hoyt. In one, my cousins were cuddling up to Hoyt while I asked him questions—"What time did you kill him?" He answered, "9 a.m.," and I sobbed because the time on Nick's death certificate and headstone were wrong. (Of course, there was no time of death on Nick's headstone, but in the dream, it was devastating to me that it was wrong.) In another, I was drowning, and I woke myself up gasping for air, sitting straight up in bed. I saw Hollywood in my nightmares in all sorts of places, and it made me so angry that he haunted my sleep; I wanted to dream of my son, not his murderer!

I don't know why I still had a hard time telling even my therapist about the depth of my sadness; it was like I was still trying to make light of things and not scare anyone, so instead, I would go to the sessions wearing silly socks and flounce down on his couch and talk about sadness but not about suicidal thoughts or the desire to sleep all the time, to go home and drink some more and try to get back to sleep.

But finally, in September 2003, I told Dr. Schulte the truth—that I felt like I needed to be in a safe environment right now. He told me he would arrange everything and that I should just get myself to Huntington Memorial in Pasadena. Drunk and on pills, I did. Before I went inside, I stuck an extra pill in my sleeve in case they wouldn't give me enough later. They gave my agony a name: PTSD, or post-traumatic stress disorder, and put me on Effexor XR.

With a schoolgirl blush, I pulled out the pill I had hidden in my sleeve and handed it to the psychiatrist on duty. My sense of guilt was too strong.

I stayed in the hospital through what would have been Nick's nineteenth birthday. There was no alcohol in the hospital, so I got sober by accident. It was disorienting. I kept journal entries that said things like:

September 20, 2003

Feeling very down. It is now 4:30 a.m. and I think I can sleep now. I will tell you more later.

September 21, 2003

I have no idea what I was going to tell you.

My house seemed bigger and hollower when I returned to it. My kitty gave me a warm welcome, but all I wanted to do was pull her into Nick's bed with me and settle back in. I slept through Rosh Hashanah. For two weeks, I left the house only twice. Jeff was out working late into the nights, so he didn't know how bad things were. I didn't even go out to check the mail. I left the bed only for necessary functions like eating, and I hid from the phone and the doorbell.

But I didn't drink.

It had finally set in for me that I was going to have to be sober if I was ever to have a chance at pulling out of this depression. Understanding it didn't make the process easier, but at least I had made a decision. I was not going to drink anymore. But from the looks of it, I wasn't going to do much of anything else anymore, either.

At the end of the two weeks, I told the doctor that I needed to be back in the hospital, where they would keep me safe from myself.

Not quite safe enough, though. I'm not sure which day it was that I cut my wrist. While I did it, I was thinking, "This is harder than I thought it would be." I had never thought about killing myself in that fashion before, and I'm not sure why I did then. My previous thoughts were the less messy ways: pills and alcohol. But this time, I'd yanked out a small cosmetic mirror that came with my eye shadow, then broke it and ran it across my vein again and again, but it was dark and I couldn't see if I was accomplishing anything.

The nagging voice in my head made me pick up my hospital phone and call Dr. Schulte, the only person I felt comfortable telling the truth to.

"Please go tell one of the nurses while I wait on the telephone," he said.

"It's hardly bleeding at all," I argued. "I'm really just weak, or chicken."

"You need to tell them anyway."

Fine.

I went to the nurse's station and ratted myself out. They were not pleased that I had called Dr. Schulte, someone outside the hospital, instead of confiding in them. They immediately sent for a watchdog who was to sit with me for the rest of the night and watch me sleep. But the problem was that he fell asleep instead, and I wanted a drink of water. Instead of waking him, I stepped over him to get to the water fountain, which was just a few steps outside of my room.

The nurse looked at me and asked where the guard was.

"Shhh! He's sleeping," I said.

That didn't go over so well. They put me in lockdown the next day because it would be easier to keep track of me there. In that ward, there was no hall—just a bunch of rooms with a nurse's station in the middle. My room had a

window, through which I could nostalgically see the hallway I used to be allowed to walk down. The musty smell in
this ward seemed to indicate that the carpets needed to be
cleaned. I looked too normal to be there. Most of the others were there for drug rehab and appeared just as strung
out as you'd expect. Compared to them, I looked like Carol
Brady.

For the next two weeks, I struggled and struggled to
get myself together. The therapists were willing to try
anything with me, and one day I asked to see the last
pictures of Nick. The doctor and I went into a room, and
he prepared me for what I would see: pictures of Nick in
his grave. After each photo, we looked at Nick's last high
school photo. We talked about how funny he used to be.
We laughed. I couldn't cry.

I guess I was looking for something tangible, something
I could relate to, like his ring. But because his hands were
duct taped behind his back, I couldn't see his hands in the
photos they had sent. I wanted to see his face, but I just
couldn't make it out—the pictures were too blurry and
distant.

After I was out of the hospital, I wanted to pressure the
district attorney to let me see more descriptive pictures,
but sweet, sure-footed victim's advocate Joan delicately
held my hand and reminded me that Nick had not been
identified by his face, but by a thumbprint. I absorbed her
explanation and accepted it. I had seen enough; I had to
leave the rest alone.

I went home feeling a little better. It seemed that each
hospital stay was a little more productive than the last. And
I was still sober. I didn't think of it much, and didn't count
the days of sobriety the way I'd counted the days since
Nick's death. All I knew was that I had to remain sober if
I was going to make it. And for the first time, I accepted
the possibility that I might make it. Not the probability,
but the possibility.

Our house was still a shrine to Nick, and that wasn't

good for my mental state anymore. Not only had I not taken down the things in his bedroom, but I'd put up more pictures, took more baby things of his down from the attic, so that the entire house was like a Nick Markowitz museum. It allowed me to avoid reality; I tried to set things up to make it feel like he was still there, still coming home any minute now. But that also kept the devastation fresh when he didn't come home. After years, I was still waiting by that window for him to show up.

At the cemetery one day in January 2004, there were already two bouquets of flowers on Nick's grave when I arrived with my red roses. I talked to Nick like I always did, just as I did at home. "Are you really in there?" I asked, like I always wondered at the cemetery.

I always tried to welcome the newcomers—the people in the newly filled graves—and ask that they keep an eye on Nick. Then, after an hour or so of feeling not much of anything, even as I looked at the photo on Nick's headstone of us kissing when he was a toddler, I left. I was tired of this dissociation. I didn't know how else to live, but I also knew that these years of feeling disconnected from reality and still waiting for Nick to show up were not healthy.

At least the medication was helping by delaying my suicidal thoughts. No longer was it the first thing I thought of every morning, which gave me time to get out of bed, at least. But the thoughts still came, and I still told myself that if I ever did decide to kill myself, it was my right and my decision, and no one should feel that they could have done something different to alter the outcome.

In April, I was back in the hospital for an overdose again. This time, I wasn't trying to kill myself. I wasn't thinking about dying or being with Nick; I'm not even sure what I was thinking. I didn't know why I took extra pills so much of the time. At first, I thought I was just chasing my high—especially now that I was no longer drinking—but then it would just turn into an impulsive action. Not thinking, not feeling, just doing. I didn't want to do this anymore, but I didn't know how to stop myself. I told my therapist I thought we should increase my treatment time.

"I don't think an hour is enough for me to say everything I need to say. Can we meet for two hours at a time?" I asked Dr. Schulte, and he agreed.

Not knowing where the right help was going to come from, I tried every avenue I could think of. I began reading *The Purpose Driven Life*, which my aunt Susie had recommended to me. I wrote to the *Dr. Phil* show, asking for Dr. Phil to help guide me. A producer of his was very interested in having me on the show, but when she found out I was still feeling suicidal, they decided to wait until I was past that. I continued to watch his show, along with the other daytime talk shows, hoping to pick up a piece of wisdom here or there that might stick with me.

I asked for the help I needed. I tried to think about having a purpose in my life again. I allowed time to pass, and little by little . . . I actually got better.

Something was changing within me, and it felt very new and tentative, but it felt . . . kind of . . . good.

In May 2004, Leah and I went out to lunch. It was a time of reconnecting. So much time had gone by with each of us living separate lives because of my negative thoughts about her brother. I told her that I was going to tell her dad that evening that if he felt he needed a relationship with Ben, he could have one. Life was too short to have the stress of his wife disapproving of his love and devotion for his son. My love for Jeff, and these new feelings of hope about my own life, had changed my view on what was important. Just because I couldn't share in his celebrations didn't mean he shouldn't have them.

"Thank you," Jeff responded when I talked to him about it.

In June of 2004, I realized that I no longer wanted to die. It was a calming, comforting feeling that I was determined to hang on to—and one that would be tested over and over. First came the knock on our door from one of Nick's friends. He had shown up, with much heartache in his eyes, to tell us that Nick's memorial tree at El Camino Real had been chopped down in a senior prank. Nick's tree hadn't been singled out; it was one of five that had been chopped down.

Do not let this set you back, I told myself.

At other times, I didn't feel depressed exactly, and I didn't feel suicidal, but I kept wanting to cut myself anyway. I kept feeling that if I were to make myself bleed, maybe I could get some relief. Maybe I could feel something. Pain on the outside was easier than pain on the inside.

My therapist suggested that I wear something of Nick's around my wrist, like a watch or bracelet, so that if I got the urge to cut myself, I would see it and remember that I had to go on living in order to honor his memory. But I wound up spending four days in Della Martin Hospital nonetheless, because I couldn't stop the thoughts.

Right after I got out, my dear friend Randi and I drove from Washington to Canada, where we spent five days putting up *America's Most Wanted* posters and handing out flyers, business cards, and key chains. I loved spending time with Randi, and it felt productive to get out and do something like that. But by this point, Jesse James Hollywood had already moved on from there.

———

Canada hadn't been all that Hollywood hoped it would be—it was cold, for one thing, and it turned out that the media there picked up on the story, too. His face was all over the television, and everywhere he went, he felt like he "stuck out like a sore thumb." There have also been reports that he had arguments with his "handlers"—people who had presumably been hired by his father to keep him safe.

For six months, Hollywood had traveled from place to place in Canada by bus: Vancouver, Montreal, Calgary, and Quebec. In Quebec, he paid one thousand dollars for a fake passport that included a five-year visa to Brazil. First he flew to Mexico, then to Brazil, in 2001.

While Hollywood was moving to escape from us, we were moving, too. It had been four years of stagnating in my shrine to Nick, and I felt like I was incapable of starting a new life there. So Jeff and I decided we were going to just leave, which we did, very quickly. Before Christmas 2004, we were already in our new house.

The new house didn't mean we were leaving Nick behind; indeed, I set up a closet full of his clothes, just like the one in his old bedroom. Left his shirts and pants on hangers, and his shoes on a rack on the bottom. It would be another five years until I could begin boxing them up. In the meantime, they were all still there, for me to look through and smell and imagine him wearing as often as I wanted.

His childhood toys were put out on display, along with many framed pictures and assorted artwork of his. The point in moving wasn't to abandon him but to leave a place that felt like I had been drowning in for the past four years. Every corner of that house was filled with sadness. Maybe in this one we would find some corners of contentment.

CHAPTER 16

ALPHA DOG

A filmmaker contacted Jeff and me in 2002 and said he wanted to make a movie about Nick's murder for the USA television network. He asked if he could buy our story rights, and we agreed. Anything that would add to the publicity about this case was a good idea, in our minds—a TV movie would help us publicize the hunt for Jesse James Hollywood in a way that me handing out flyers never could.

But his movie never made it off the ground. Meanwhile, another filmmaker named Nick Cassavetes had also been thinking about our story. His two daughters went to the same high school that Nick had, though they were younger and hadn't known each other. Cassavetes already knew a lot about Nick's story just because it happened so close to home for him, so when his friend Kevin Connolly asked him for a script he could direct, this was the idea they decided on.

They called their script *Alpha Dog*, and it looked like the movie would actually be made. Cassavetes contacted us in early 2003, and I asked the original filmmaker what we should do—was it OK for us to talk to Cassavetes?

He admitted that his movie probably wouldn't get produced, especially now that this one was in the works, so he agreed that it was OK for us to talk to Cassavetes. We did; we opened up our home to him.

I showed Cassavetes Nick's room, his bar mitzvah video, some of his writing—I tried my best to give him a picture of who Nick was and what our family had been going through. I gave him personal details that he would never have been able to learn anywhere else. Later, I also went to the set to talk with Sharon Stone, who would be playing the part based on me and who wanted to meet me to understand what I went through.

Both Jeff and I were apprehensive about the whole thing—we wouldn't have any control over the movie, and who knew what they were going to fictionalize or what perspective they'd take? All we really hoped was that they'd portray Nick as he really was. But the thought of seeing our tragedy unfold on a big screen while people ate popcorn was difficult. Important, but difficult. We spoke with Cassavetes and his crew several times, and then sat back and hoped the film would carry the right tone and the right message.

The only thing I asked in return for our participation was that if the film did well, they would help us pay the reward money we were still offering for Jesse James Hollywood's capture. Cassavetes agreed.

Jack Hollywood, on the other hand, was a paid consultant on the film who even went to some of their locations and gave the actors advice on how to play their roles. He wanted to remind the actor playing the Jesse James Hollywood role that he wasn't playing a monster, but Jack's son.

Cassavetes and his story researcher also contacted each of the other defendants and their families, as well as prosecutor Ron Zonen's office. Ron was the district attorney who handled the trials related to Nick's murder. He, too, thought it might help to ferret out Jesse James Hollywood, so he worked closely with Cassavetes and his researcher, loaning them the entire library of case files pertaining to Hollywood and the five trials we had already gone through.

Connolly, the original director, had to drop out because he got a recurring role on HBO's *Entourage*, so Cassavetes ended up directing the film himself. He had previously offered Justin Timberlake a role on *The Notebook*, but Justin said he was hoping for a "grittier" character. So this time, Cassavetes cast him as Jesse Rugge, and he sent him to meet Rugge in prison.

"It was surreal to see someone my age serving a life sentence," Timberlake later told *Entertainment Weekly*. He said that they all felt they got their hands dirty working on the film, because there were no winners at the end.

We pinned a lot of hope to the film's ability to help us find Hollywood. Once all the trials ended, publicity had died down, and I worried that Hollywood was going to get comfortable somewhere, secure in the knowledge that his picture would show up less frequently in the media now.

Sonny LeGault, the lead detective who had been investigating Hollywood, was promoted to personnel, so he would no longer be active on the case. But Sheriff Jim Anderson wasn't about to let it drop. He gave one man, Mark Valencia, a full-time task: to find Jesse James Hollywood, starting around 2004. For more than a year, that was the man's entire job, day in and day out. The Department of Justice called it "Operation Movie Star." And he was given the power to take the hunt internationally—so, along with his co–case agent, probation officer Maria Bongiovanni, he followed leads first from state to state, then country to country. In several places, they just barely missed Hollywood.

The original detectives on the case had been tracking Jack Hollywood's phone calls, and they heard a lot of drug dealing. They surmised that he was a large-scale trafficker of marijuana and cocaine, but they didn't want to bust him too early and lose the ability to use him to find his fugitive son. So instead, they just kept investigating Jack and trying to learn more about how his drug business worked. Many of his friends (or former friends) and associates came forward to talk, both in prison and out, so investigators had some idea of Jack's methods. He was dealing all over the country and even in some areas outside of the country, constantly on various phones making connections.

Early in the investigation, detectives got a phone call from a religious leader in Brazil. Apparently, Jack Hollywood had come to meet him and tried to pay him off to shelter Jesse. The man turned down his offer and reported it, but Brazil was just one of many places where Jack had possible connections. Jack had also taken a trip to Canada and asked people there to shelter his son. No one figured Hollywood was still in California, which is why the FBI was involved, but it was unknown if he was still in the United States or in one of the other likely spots: Canada, Mexico, or Brazil.

Tips had come in from all over the place, from people who thought they had spotted Jesse James Hollywood at restaurants, or walking down the street, or—as in the case of one off-duty police officer—at a Chicago baseball game. Multiple people bearing Jesse's description were arrested and questioned, but none of them had any relation to him.

When Valencia took over the case, he started by typing Jack Hollywood's name into a central database—and he got a hit. A precinct outside of Santa Barbara had typed Jack's name into the database just recently, so Valencia and Maria Bongiovanni drove to the desert to find out what was going on.

It was a connection they would never have predicted.

A drug task force had done an operation where they attempted to make a huge bust—they negotiated with drug dealers to sell several kilos of cocaine. It was a "reverse" deal, which meant that the federal agents had the cocaine and they were trying to get the targets to buy it. All of the dealers spoke Spanish and were from Central or South America. What the dealers negotiated was that they would switch cars with the federal agents; then the agents would put the cocaine in the criminals' car, and the criminals would leave the money in the agents' car.

For whatever reason, the deal fell through at the last minute, but the agents did have the dealers' car in their possession. So they put a GPS tracker on the car to see where it would go; then they returned it to the dealers. The car was busy, driving all over the United States. A GPS installation warrant is valid for a limited time, however, and when the warrant's expiration drew near, the car was in Phoenix, Arizona. They decided to just pull the car over on a traffic stop to take the tracker off.

Jack Hollywood was driving the car.

The officers who pulled Jack over didn't know who he was, and they really didn't have anything on him, so they let him go after they copied the items in his wallet—which included a UPS receipt that tracked to a storage facility in Phoenix (he had several storage units around the country) and credit cards. Running the credit cards produced a receipt for a package that was shipped to New York. Valencia ordered the package to be intercepted, and inside, he found fifty pounds of marijuana.

That was all he needed; now he knew he could write a warrant anytime he wanted to. It was time to find Jesse James Hollywood.

An informant told him that Jesse James Hollywood was flying from Vancouver to Chicago just a few days before Christmas. One of his friends had also tipped off detectives that he had been entering and exiting the Canadian border dressed as a woman . . . so my "Jesseca" poster wasn't all that far-fetched after all.

Valencia tracked Hollywood's prepaid cell phone to a specific building, and then he asked local police in Chicago to check out the building and find out if Hollywood was in it. When they got there late that night, they spotted a pizza delivery man coming out of the building, and one of the officers showed the man a photo lineup.

"Did you see any of these guys in the apartment you just came out of?"

"Yes, that guy," the delivery man said—and pointed to Hollywood.

They asked to see the pizza delivery receipt. Although Hollywood paid in cash, his name was still printed on the receipt because he had called in the order. And unbelievably, the name he used when he called in the order was "Jesse Wood."

Valencia booked a flight to Chicago. Meanwhile, early the next morning, local police got a team together and secured the building, then they booted the door open and found an open window, curtains blowing in the breeze . . . and four hundred thousand dollars in cash and fifty pounds of marijuana left in the empty apartment. On the floor were giant maps of Mexico and Brazil. There was no furniture, nothing else there but the pizza box—it was a "stash house," just a place to stop from point A to point B with drugs.

Officers arrested the next two guys who came into the apartment on drug charges. The guys were two of the people investigators had previously looked at in Seattle; they were tied to the Hollywoods. But no matter how Valencia tried, he could not get them to talk. They were more scared of what would happen if they talked than they were of going to prison.

Authorities were that close to catching him, more than once. Detectives would later find out that Hollywood had snuck out the back door of a home they had come to search, or had been on a boat just before them. Back in the beginning, he had just gone out for a bite to eat from his hotel in Las Vegas, but he saw cop cars outside when he returned, so he left.

The investigation into the Hollywoods' drug operation led to a number of spin-off investigations involving the Chinese Triad, Mexican cartels, outlaw motorcycle gangs, and an illegal arms distribution organization. Detectives also assisted and provided information that solved two separate homicide investigations in two states. But Jesse continued to elude them.

I didn't know that my friends and I were working at cross-purposes with Valencia sometimes. Once, when I was in Canada putting up posters, he was quietly cringing nearby. He worried that we were going to spook Hollywood by alerting him that we knew where he was. Sure enough, that's what apparently happened. As soon as our posters went up, his leads went cold. So, eventually, Valencia came to our house with his supervisor and said something along the lines of, "Hi. I'm Mark. You don't know me, but I'm the investigator assigned to find Jesse James Hollywood . . . and I'm going to do my very best to find him. I can't tell you what I'm doing or where I'm looking, but you have to trust me."

Valencia was a big brute of a guy—"Gorilla" was his nickname—and he was a Native American former U.S. Marine. With his long ponytail and tattoos, he was not someone who fit in very well with the other investigators in the sheriff's department. He was the kind of guy who was normally called upon when they needed to break down the door of a suspect's house or scare out a criminal, not the guy who was typically in charge of investigating. We liked and trusted him immediately, though. You could tell that he cared about our case and took it seriously.

Trusting him didn't mean that I felt I could just sit back and wait, though. Aside from the times I was trying to kill myself, the rest of my days were filled with activities geared toward tracking down Hollywood.

We had twice increased our portion of the reward money, so we were now up to a total reward of seventy thousand dollars: twenty thousand of that would come from the FBI and fifty thousand from Jeff and me. I was all over the Internet publicizing that and asking for leads.

We even offered to put our portion of the money into a college fund for Jesse James Hollywood's younger brother if he turned himself in.

Once, at a Taco Bell drive-through, I refused to pull

my car forward because I was sure that Hollywood was driving the car in back of me. I wanted to trap him there, at least while I wrote down his license plate number and called the police. It turned out that the man was six feet tall and just slouched down in the seat. He looked nothing like Hollywood. It was just my brain playing tricks on me.

Sometime in early 2005, detectives told us that it was no longer a case of "if" we find him, but "when." They couldn't be more specific, but they wanted us to know that much, at least. It had been more than four years of a lot of dashed hopes, a lot of leads from all over the world that went nowhere. Hollywood kept moving, and we kept missing him. But many people in Santa Barbara were personally invested in finding him, including Sheriff Anderson, so we never felt that we were less of a priority once Nick's murder was no longer "news."

A new phone number began regularly appearing on Jack Hollywood's phone bills. The person he was calling had recently applied for a visa and was heading to Brazil. Informants tipped the police that this person was going to meet Jesse James Hollywood—so Valencia and his partner got on a plane, along with FBI agent Dave Cloney.

For a week or so, they met with Brazilian Interpol officers and were assigned two more FBI agents, who were the FBI's Brazilian Legal Attaché. Because Brazil's policy was not to extradite criminals who are charged with capital crimes, this could not be handled as an extradition. It would simply be a deportation because Hollywood was in Brazil illegally, using a fake name on his passport.

It turned out that Hollywood already had a criminal record under that fake name; he was stopped on cocaine charges, but police let him go because he happened to share one of his fake last names with a judge. He would later swear he didn't pick the name because of that reason but simply chose names that he thought were cool or belonged to childhood acquaintances.

Interpol officers would have to be the ones to arrest Hollywood and get him on a plane back to the United States. They would do it, but they wanted some rewards for doing so: twenty flashlights and Leatherman knives. Oh, and they also wanted to go to Boston to see a Celtics basketball game. They turned down the chance to see the Lakers instead because "They just traded Shaq."

When the basketball negotiations failed, they decided they'd be satisfied, instead, with a three-day trip to Sao Paolo, the richest city in Brazil. With that, the agreement was sealed with a smile. No one actually begrudged the officers those perks; they were very hardworking and dedicated cops who made do with so little that the American officers admired how they managed to conduct proper law enforcement investigations despite it all. On one day that week, the Interpol officers showed up late and bloody because they had been carjacked and in a shooting. Then they apologized for being late.

One day, a supervisor was ignoring Valencia, so he asked if something was wrong. Through an interpreter, the supervisor said, "You didn't give me a pin."

It turned out that Valencia had given Santa Barbara County Sheriff's Department star-shaped pins to the officers, but he had run out. He called his department and had them quickly mail a personalized pin for the supervisor—and then things were well again.

Investigators had tracked Hollywood's new phone, and when they "pinged" it to check his location, he answered the phone. They pretended to have the wrong number and hung up. But later that day, the investigator meant to call home, and hit "redial" by accident, calling Hollywood's phone again.

"Cuz?" he asked. "Is that you?"

"Who's this?" the investigator asked.

"No, who's this?"

It went back and forth for a minute until the investigator realized what had happened and hung up. But another minute later, Valencia realized something bad.

"You just spoke to him in English," he said.

Considering they were in Brazil, it would be highly unlikely for anyone to accidentally call a wrong number and speak perfect English—twice, over the course of a few hours. They worried it might tip Hollywood off that, once again, the authorities were near. But there was no time to waste worrying about it. The agents knew, based on tips, that an American cousin was going to meet Hollywood at a mall near the beach. They had to outrun the bus she was on, so they sped all the way, finding Hollywood smiling and waiting when they arrived.

He *had* been suspicious about the phone calls, but not suspicious enough.

After the violent scene of the standoff, with Hollywood's girlfriend screaming "Kidnapping! Kidnapping!" and military police and Interpol agents almost shooting at each other, Hollywood was taken to the police station, where he spent a great deal of time cursing out the officers in Portuguese, insisting that his name was Michael Costa Giroux and that they had the wrong guy. He had all the right fake answers to their questions about who his parents were, where they were born, which schools he attended, and so on. After some time, it looked like the Interpol officers were a little unsure . . . *did* they have the wrong guy?

When he couldn't take it anymore, Mark Valencia stood up and stepped right in front of Jesse, moving in on his personal space.

"I'm Detective Valencia from the Santa Barbara County Sheriff's Department," he said. "Now it's time to stop lying. Your name is Jesse James Hollywood."

It was as if all the blood had drained from Hollywood's face. He didn't realize that anyone from Santa Barbara was actually there, and once Valencia introduced himself, he almost fainted. At that moment, he knew he was caught. Then he shook it off and stuck out his hand to congratulate Valencia for catching him. "So you're the one," he said. "You did it. But I won't be here in the morning."

At that point, Valencia had already called his department

to make sure that Jack Hollywood was under arrest. He knew that whatever tricks Jesse thought his father could pull were not going to happen now. All the phone numbers his girlfriend, Marcia Reis, might have been given to call to get him freed were not going to get answered. There was no one left to get him out of this trouble.

And so the next day, Jesse James Hollywood was on a plane to back to California.

———

March 8, 2005, was a Tuesday, and the city was redoing some concrete work in our cul-de-sac, so I was stuck inside when I got the call. It was Jeff saying that one of the detectives had called and wanted to meet us at Jeff's shop.

"Do I really have to be there?"

"They said it was important. They said you'll want to be there," he said. And I knew it in an instant.

They had caught Jesse James Hollywood.

I hung up the phone, dropped to the ground, and sobbed.

Then I got into the shower and let the warm water wash over me as I cried out four and a half years' worth of grief. I didn't cry out of relief, though I'm sure that was mixed in there somewhere; the main thing I felt at that moment was the pointlessness of it all.

Why did this have to happen?

I cried and cried in a huge release, and then I walked half a mile down to the road where my mom had driven to meet me. She was lending me her car because mine was trapped in the driveway. I dropped her off and drove to Jeff's work.

The investigators were already waiting inside the office.

"We've got him," they said. "Right now, Jesse James Hollywood is on a plane heading back to Los Angeles."

I should have screamed or cried or something, but I had already let out all my emotions back at the house. I was drained.

They gave us the details they were allowed to share,

which were basically the same details they would share with the public. We hugged and thanked the detectives. Then I got down on my knees and thanked God that I wouldn't have to think about Jesse James Hollywood anymore. No longer would I have to study every male face I saw, suspicious of everyone at every store and every stoplight.

The boxes of wanted posters could be . . . well . . . what on Earth did one do with those?

My car would be just a car again, instead of a moving billboard. My life would be . . . My life would be mine again, and that left me reeling with confusion. I had no idea what I was supposed to do next. My only goal remaining was to see Hollywood convicted, and that seemed inevitable now. I would have to find some other reason to keep going.

The next day, a reporter from the Brazilian newspaper *Extra* e-mailed me the articles their paper had just printed about Hollywood's capture. Unfortunately, the articles were in Portuguese, but I appreciated the sentiment all the same. Brazil, it seemed, was quite proud to have helped us "get the guy."

Just after Hollywood was booked in Santa Barbara County Jail, we participated in a press conference. Jeff and I stood behind glass doors across from the courthouse while we waited to be introduced. We looked out and saw a massive display of microphones and people, and it made my knees buckle. The investigators introduced themselves and gave the information they needed to give; then they brought us out to the podium.

Jeff spoke first. "We thank those who have never given up on us, never given up on Nicholas. We thank you all from the bottom of our hearts. You'll never know the depths of our gratitude. . . . This is a bittersweet moment. Nothing will ever bring Nick back to us, but we can rest now knowing all five of Nick's perpetrators are being held accountable for their horrific acts. Thanks to all these officers, our loving son Nicholas Samuel Markowitz will receive his justice."

It was hard for me to speak, my voice choking and quiet. It was the most nervous I'd ever been speaking in public. In my thoughts, this was the finale. People wanted to see me look happy and relieved; they expected me to talk about *closure*, a word I hated. There was no closure. There should be another word for whatever it was that you can hope to achieve after a tragedy like this.

"Since the moment that Nick was so brutally taken from us, our lives have been forever destroyed. We have been living in a constant state of shock, pain, and questions. Today, one of those questions was answered," I said.

Later that day, we visited Nick's grave to tell him the news, but someone had beat us there—we found a note on the grave that simply read, "We got him!"

On YouTube, I think, I saw a video of Hollywood getting out of a police car and being booked. The first time I ever saw him in person was in a pretrial motion; he was behind a glass window to my left as I sat in the courtroom. He looked too tan, I thought. It angered me that he had been out enjoying the beach all these years that my son had been in his grave.

He didn't look like as much of a thug as I thought he would. Of course, he had had plenty of time to surf it up and improve his image. His hair was wavy and gelled, lacking the backward-baseball-cap hoodlum look that had stared back at me from his wanted posters. And even though I knew his height, he was still shorter in person than I imagined; when he stood up, it made me think that if Nick had taken him on, one-on-one, there would have been no contest. Nick had been six feet tall . . . a full seven inches taller than Hollywood.

———

Jack Hollywood had been arrested on suspicion of manufacturing the date-rape drug GHB (though those charges were later thrown out because although he had the ingredients and a recipe, there was no proof he'd actually made it). However, he was kept in custody on a DUI warrant, because he had failed to pay a fine, and on marijuana charges. He ended up pleading guilty and serving eighteen months in an Arizona prison.

But the wheels were already in place for Jesse's legal team—Jack had hired James Blatt and Alex Kessel, two rather notorious criminal-defense attorneys known for being ruthless and aggressive. And they were obviously prepared in advance for this day to come, because almost immediately after Jesse was arrested, they began trying to have the entire Santa Barbara County district attorney's office thrown off the case, and trying to block the release of *Alpha Dog*, which was filmed but not yet released.

What his lawyers argued was that Deputy District Attorney Ron Zonen had acted inappropriately in sharing his case files with *Alpha Dog*'s producers. He had shared boxes of material—photos, tapes, reports, trial transcripts, rap sheets, contact information, notes. Zonen explained that he was trying to ensure accuracy in the film and hoped that it would be a way to get international attention to help capture Hollywood.

"I asked only that Hollywood's picture be shown at the conclusion of the film along with a phone number to call with information as to his whereabouts," Zonen said. "I asked that the audience be told that Hollywood remains a fugitive and that there is a reward for his arrest."

Two judges agreed that he had done nothing improper— there was no money involved, nothing to indicate that Zonen's motives had been suspect. But the defense attorneys appealed it until they got the decision they wanted: the appeals court ruled that Zonen be taken off the case and not allowed to prosecute Hollywood. They didn't want to set a precedent for prosecutors to share all their information with the media, especially in a death-penalty case, where the prosecution is held to an even higher standard of integrity to ensure that the defendant gets a fair trial.

It didn't end there, though. Next, the California Supreme Court took up the case and ruled that Ron Zonen should not be removed from the case and that there was certainly no reason to remove the entire Santa Barbara district attorney's office. The district attorney's office decided that Ron Zonen would step down anyway, though, just to remove that as a basis of a potential appeal down the line if Hollywood were to be convicted. It was too messy and too important a case; this one would have to be conducted with the knowledge that it was going to be in the spotlight and that Hollywood had the resources to hire lawyers who could drag it on and on through the system. They had already managed to drag it out for eighteen months.

It was a tough blow for us, as Zonen had handled every other case, and we knew he cared about Nick and our family. It had been a big mission of his to make sure Hollywood was brought to justice. But the case would now be in the capable hands of Senior Deputy District Attorney Joshua Lynn, a handsome, compassionate man with a calm and classy demeanor. Lynn had been preparing for this role; he was the "understudy," as he put it, from the moment they first learned about the motion to remove Zonen. The two men were ordered not to speak with one another about the case until the California Supreme Court finally ruled that Zonen did not need to be removed. After that point, Zonen and Lynn were allowed to talk, but Zonen had no meaningful role in Hollywood's prosecution. I'm sure it was heartbreaking for him, after all these years of waiting for the day to come, to be sidelined.

Another veteran prosecutor, Senior Deputy District Attorney Hans Almgren, would aid Lynn, and Paul Kimes was the criminal investigator assigned to the case.

The defense team's next objective was to block the release of *Alpha Dog*. Even though the filmmakers had decided to change everybody's names (Nick was now "Zach Mazursky," Ben was "Jake Mazursky," and Jesse James Hollywood was "Johnny Truelove") and locations (the Lemon Tree Inn was now the "Caliente Tropics Hotel"), it was still marketed as being based on a true story, and people in the Santa Barbara area certainly knew it was based on Nick's murder. So the defense team tried to say that Hollywood could never get a fair trial if the movie were released.

Truthfully, we were worried about the movie, too. Reporters kept coming to us and asking for our thoughts—how did we feel about the film? Well, we had no idea how we felt, really, because we hadn't seen it yet. We had a lot of fears about how it might portray Nick, and us. And we had misgivings about how it could be sensationalized. Jeff told one reporter, "How would any loving parent feel about a Hollywood movie that glamorizes their son's death and allows celebrities to cash in on a brutal, evil murder?"

But no matter how we felt, the movie was already finished and ready to be released. So Jeff wrote to Nick Cassavetes and asked if we could have a private screening.

"Of course!" he said, and told us to call and set up a date. We did . . . and canceled, about six times, chickening out every time. I didn't know if I really wanted to see this movie, if I could handle seeing this movie. Nick's best friend, Ryan, definitely didn't want to see it. I felt like it was something I would have to do sooner or later, but I stalled as long as possible, hoping I'd feel more stable.

———

In the meantime, I was hospitalized two more times, bringing the tally to about thirteen hospital stays, either voluntary or involuntary.

The final time was the one that stuck, though. In March of 2006, my sister dragged me out of the closet, where I was crying and drinking. Apparently, I had called her. I had also called my little brother, which I don't remember either. I went to Las Encinas Hospital and entered a 12-step program. This was the thing that finally made the difference for me. The program wasn't specific to drugs or alcohol—it was directed to any sort of addiction or bad habit, and for me, that included my suicidal thoughts and risky behaviors.

I felt for the first time in a long time that I had found people like me. The only other people who I had been able to relate to in recent years were the ones in Parents of Murdered Children. Here, I was in a regimented program that taught me some key principles for living my life in a more healthy way. I was able to earn some privileges while I was in the hospital this time, such as the right to walk across the magnificent grounds and enter another building where Dr. Drew Pinsky was holding a conference.

Dr. Drew was the star of VH-1's reality show *Celebrity Rehab* and the syndicated radio show *Lovelines*. But his "real job" was as the medical director for the department of chemical dependency services right there at Las Encinas Hospital. That's where *Celebrity Rehab* was filmed.

Patients had to earn the privilege to go see him speak, because once you were over there, you really weren't monitored, though the staff would get calls sometimes to note that someone from our loony ward was missing.

I didn't want to escape, though. Things finally seemed to be clicking for me. During that hospital stay, I had the dream I had long been waiting for. I often dreamed of Nick, but he was always a baby or a young boy in the dreams, never a teenager. I wanted to see him in my dreams the way he was before he died, but it just didn't happen—until then.

There he was, wearing the same shirt he wore in his last class photo. Fifteen years old.

"Mom, you look so good. You're doing great!" he said.

"So do you," I said. "You look great, too."

There really wasn't a conversation beyond that, just both of us standing before each other talking about how well we were each doing. It was all I had needed for so long. It was as if he were no longer mad at me. And something was released inside me, like letting go of a balloon and watching it float into the sky.

After I left the hospital, I kept going to Alcoholics Anonymous meetings. I had a sponsor and a good support system. I also joined a support group called Action, a parent and teen nonprofit organization. I needed structure after coming from the hospital, and this group gave me that and so much more. After March 2006, I never again had another suicidal thought. I had decided to stay alive after

all . . . and to do something positive with my life. I tried
to get stronger each day for the tasks that might be ahead
of me. I didn't yet know what I was going to feel drawn to
do, but I knew that my primary responsibility was going to
be to maintain my mental health so I would be capable of
whatever I was meant for.

Hollywood lost his lawsuit against Universal Studios to
block the release of *Alpha Dog*. His attorneys said it would
be impossible for him to get a fair trial if the movie came
out—after all, it portrayed their client as a "monster,"
they argued—but a judge saw the film and disagreed. He
refused to block the release, making it the first time that
a major motion picture about a criminal case had been
released before one of its trials had even begun. Hollywood's attorneys appealed the decision but lost, and *Alpha
Dog* was finally released in January of 2007 in the United
States and Canada.

We never did go for a private screening, but we did go to
the official premiere of *Alpha Dog*. They were going to seat
us with the celebrities, but we chose to sit off to the side on
a private balcony, so we could feel like we were watching
it by ourselves.

Parts of the film moved me to tears, but for the most
part, I remained detached from it, not really seeing it as
my reality. The first thing that struck me was that the actor
Anton Yelchin had done a terrific job of playing "Zach."
He managed to capture Nick's innocence and warmth;
the mannerisms and tone were right. About the only thing
the film didn't capture about Nick was his crazy sense of
humor, but given the context, that was understandable.

The other thing that really moved me was Sharon Stone's
scene where she donned a "fat suit" and said, "If God's got
a purpose for me, he better get the fuck down here and tell
me what it is, because I don't see it." She had really been
listening to me; I felt like she had incorporated exactly
what I told her into the role. The way she laughed, the way

she spoke . . . She said that her goal was to show people what rock bottom really looked like, and I thought she did a stellar job of capturing it. That was my rock bottom—angry and lost and laughing in a mental hospital.

Watching that scene made me feel a little better, at least, because I was a long way away from that place now. Although my recovery was still pretty raw, I was able to look back on that woman and feel sorry for her. No one who's been through a tragedy like mine should ever have to worry about hospital bills and therapy bills; the world should just scoop us up and coddle us and tell us that things will be all right.

There were, of course, things about the film that were dramatized and exaggerated for effect. Much of it was about our family.

Jeff and I never fought the way the film depicted, yelling at each other over Ben. I could actually count on one hand the number of times that Jeff and I had even been angry with each other, and none of them involved yelling matches.

Nick and I did not ever have "homework parties . . . with hats," though, on reflection, that sounded like a pretty good idea. The part about how I would sometimes just sit and stare at him while he slept, and he would wake up and see me there just smiling at him . . . well, that was true.

Ben was not a heavy drug user until after Nick's death; he was a user all along, but he was primarily a dealer. He didn't get all twitchy and sweaty and fight with his boss over a drug test, and he didn't defecate on Jesse James Hollywood's floor. He also didn't get into a big bar brawl while Nick was missing and tell everyone in the bar that he was looking for Hollywood—in truth, Ben didn't even know that Hollywood was involved until after Nick's body had been found.

Although Nick did take tae kwon do, he was not a black belt as the film depicts (in the scene where he tosses Justin Timberlake's character to the ground). In fact, he was not particularly good at tae kwon do.

The girls did not have a steamy "Marco Polo" scene with Nick in the hotel pool, and I doubted that all the sex scenes happened as scripted, but none of it really bothered me. It didn't bother me to see Sharon Stone in a horrible fat suit, even though it was an exaggeration of my weight gain. It didn't bother me to see Ben's drug use and behaviors exaggerated. None of it bothered me, because the spirit of the film felt right to me.

Jeff wasn't as enthusiastic about the film as I was—he would tell you simply that he's "satisfied" with the movie and didn't like to talk about it much—but to me, it was better than I expected. I felt that there were real lessons here, and that if teens and parents watched this movie, they might actually absorb some important messages.

Foremost, the message was about paying attention and caring enough to act when someone was in trouble. The film's poster said, "One crime. 38 witnesses. No way back." The number may not have been perfect, but it was certainly close to accurate. Cassavetes made a point throughout the film of highlighting just how many people had seen Nick during his kidnapping and murder, and that none of them intervened.

If only . . . I kept thinking.

We attended the premiere party afterward, and I got to hug Anton and Sharon and tell both of them that I thought they had done a good job. Then we went back to our lives and waited to see what the reaction would be to the movie.

———

And then . . . something amazing happened.

Each time an article had run in a newspaper, I had received some letters from people wanting to offer support and kindness, but the movie made it explode. Whereas earlier it had been a few letters here and there, now it was a steady inflow of dozens of letters at a time. People saw the movie, and then wanted to know more—they wanted to know what was real and what wasn't, and what had happened with the trials since then.

Teenagers, parents, grandparents . . . I heard from all sorts of people from all over the world. No longer was this a local story; now it was international. People wrote in broken English to tell me that they would not forget my son.

One Mother's Day, I got a letter signed "Random boy named Adam." Because he knew Nick couldn't be with me, he said, he wanted to give me a hug for Mother's Day and tell me how great I was. It meant so much to me.

The film ended up being a tremendous blessing in my life because it gave me an opening with people—instead of having to tell my whole story, I could ask the cashier in the grocery store, "Did you see the movie *Alpha Dog*?" Most of the time, the answer was yes. "I'm Nick's mom," I would say—and it earned me a lot of hugs.

I wanted to talk to people; I wanted to tell as many people as I could about Nick's story, so that maybe they would pick up something they could apply to their own lives. I wanted them to see that these terrible things didn't just happen to strangers on the news; they happened to people you meet. Real flesh-and-blood people . . . and that meant it could happen to you, too.

The reactions to the movie gave me confidence in my own voice. I began using it as an excuse to talk to strangers. I continued handing out key chains with Nick's name and information—more than ten thousand of them so far—and now I had a simple way to introduce myself and talk about Nick's story.

I would even talk to telemarketers about it. When they'd launch into some marketing pitch with me, I'd tell them that I would agree to listen to them as long as they would also listen to me afterward. They could go right ahead and tell me about their chimney-cleaning service or their political candidate, but then I was going to tell them about my son and how his murder could have been prevented.

In that way, I found my reason to keep going.

I kept abreast of all the news I could find about the movie, Jesse James Hollywood, and the upcoming trial, and people helped me do that by sending me articles from their local papers. Never really sure what I was going to do with it all, I collected all of the information nonetheless— stacks and stacks of articles to put into scrapbooks. What would it be when it was finished? Who would I give it to, and why? It was a morbid sort of collection, but it was the evidence that my son's life had mattered to people other than ourselves. His murder had been covered in newspapers across the world as well as on television programs, radio news, and websites.

I frequently checked in on websites where people were discussing the movie and the case. I became a regular on the IMDb.com (Internet Movie Database) and CourtTV.com, answering questions when I could. It was remarkable how many people would watch the movie, then immediately go to Google to search for more information. It was the kind of movie that stuck with people and made them want to know more—which made me feel good and useful.

There was so much that I wasn't able to answer, though. I had not been able to speak freely since the beginning; always, there was someone—from the district attorney's office to the judge—who asked us to hold off on discussing details of the case until after all the trials were complete and sentencing finished. That was so difficult for me! But I kept reminding myself that the day would come eventually.

The first question people usually asked me after seeing the movie was about Ben. They wanted to know if he had ever turned his life around, and what our relationship was like now.

Like everything else related to this story, the answer couldn't just be a simple one.

I had heard that Ben really had turned his life around, thanks to his children—he now had a baby son as well as a daughter—but prior to August 2005, we still did not communicate. That was when he sent me a letter. He said that he didn't know how to approach me, but that he wanted to write and tell me that, "More than anything, I'm sorry that I was in any way related to Nick's death."

"I want you to know that your letter was accepted with an open heart," I wrote back. "It was beautifully written and I so needed to hear the words you wrote."

We wrote back and forth a few times after that. It was a time of opening up—of him telling me that he had grown up with a lot of anger, and me telling him how hard I'd tried to make him and Leah feel they were part of our family. He told me how much he had needed, and still needed, his dad, and how much he'd loved Nick.

"I think it is time to say I forgive you," I wrote. "I know in my heart all the things you said in your letter were true, but for some reason, I felt it was your responsibility to step up to the plate first. I know things will never be the same and I may not be able to interact much of the time, but I will try. I know it isn't easy for you, either."

And then an occasion presented itself. My mother-in-law's seventy-fifth birthday came in October 2005, and everyone was invited. I didn't want to avoid her party just because Ben would be there, and I didn't want him to avoid it just because I would be there, either—so something had to happen. It wasn't about us, and I didn't want to take away from her celebration. I asked Ben to meet me at the cemetery four days before the party so that we could get the uncomfortable initial meeting out of the way.

Ben had never been to Nick's grave, and we had not seen each other in five years. But when he arrived, we were both ready. It was time.

Oh, good, he has hair, I thought upon seeing Ben. It was a small thing but not insignificant. He didn't look like a tough guy anymore; he looked handsome again.

He hugged me, and we talked. There were no tears, but there was emotion and comfortable conversation. We even went to dinner afterward, and talked some more, mostly about how it still all felt so surreal and how it was hard to believe that Nick was actually gone. We didn't skip off arm in arm, but it felt very natural and good. It felt like a positive step in a relationship that would probably take the rest of a lifetime to heal, if it could even ever be truly healed.

For now, we would settle for whatever this was: a quiet sort of peace, an understanding. As I walked away from Nick's grave that day, I felt that he would be proud of us both.

Ben's children had become his whole world, which gave him a better understanding of my perspective. He became the doting father I would've always hoped he would be. He even coached his son's Little League team, always wearing long-sleeved shirts to cover up the tattoos he now wished he'd never gotten. There were just too many of them to attempt to remove, though, so he did the best he could to hide them out of respect for the kids.

I still had trouble seeing Ben's family, though. It always reminded me that Nick would never have that opportunity to get married and have kids of his own, that I would never have grandchildren of my own. Maybe one day I would be able to be a better stepgrandmother, but that day hadn't come yet. It was still difficult.

Ben and I didn't see each other often; our relationship was good but still a bit delicate. We were open with one another, and I was very proud of the strides he'd made in his life. He didn't understand why I talked to the media—he would've preferred that everything about Nick's death would just disappear from the limelight. He and his wife wanted to put it all behind them and live anonymously, which I could understand—but, unfortunately, I couldn't tell Nick's story without mentioning Ben. His life would forever be entwined with Nick's death, and that was part of the message about consequences.

Sometimes people get lucky, and the dumb things they do as teenagers just become crazy stories to tell later at their high school reunions.

And sometimes they don't.

CHAPTER 17

HOLLYWOOD'S ENDING

Just short of nine years after he ordered my son's execution, Jesse James Hollywood was finally going on trial for kidnapping and first-degree murder. The pretrial motions had dragged on and on for four years while Hollywood simply sat in the county jail.

In April of 2009, the prosecution and defense met with the judge to make their requests about the trial, each side wanting to present their case in the best light. First, the judge ruled that there would be no cameras in the courtroom, which meant that it would be very different from the other trials. If they couldn't get pictures and video, many news outlets wouldn't bother sending their reporters out.

The defense also wanted to ease up on security at the trial to make sure that Jesse James Hollywood didn't appear . . . *dangerous*. They argued that there were too many sheriff's deputies in the courtroom, and "The appearance is very heavy." Two deputies were to stand behind Hollywood. The judge offered to instead move one of the deputies behind the defense and the other behind the prosecution.

"I don't want anyone behind us," said James Blatt, one

of Hollywood's two attorneys. "It's not in the best interest of the defendant to have a deputy behind him."

The judge said he understood, but that safety in the courtroom was important for all. He said he'd do his best to balance the need for safety with the need for Hollywood to have a "fair trial."

As I had during all of the other trials, I wore a special pin on my lapel—a silver brooch with Nick's picture in it. I discovered Jesse James Hollywood's trial was not going to be like any of the others when I was ordered to take it off.

The defense team argued that my brooch could "prejudice" the jury. And before the defense team was done, they would also attempt to strip the courtroom of any humanity whatsoever—there were to be no reminders of Nick in the room, and they didn't even want the prosecution to be allowed to show a photo of Nick in the middle of a poster board that included pictures of the defendants during the opening statements because the "layout of the board" might prejudice the jury. (The judge overruled that one.) And there was to be no Jeff Markowitz.

That's right: my husband, Nick's father, was barred from being in the courtroom because he was on the witness list. He obviously had not been a witness to the crime, but he was to be called to discuss Nick's disappearance, Ben's attempt to contact Hollywood, and other matters. The judge decided that he would not be allowed to sit in the courtroom even after he testified, just in case he would be called back to the stand later.

So Jeff went to work, and I stayed in Santa Barbara without him. I was never really alone, thank goodness. My friend Nadine was with me most days, and Leah came whenever she was able, as did Jeff's cousin Robyn. Our victim's advocate, Joan, was by my side as always.

I don't think it was the scene Hollywood was hoping for in the courtroom, however. While in prison awaiting trial, Hollywood had been corresponding with a man named David Woodard. I don't know why, just as I don't know why certain types of women actually flock to prisons to throw

themselves at convicted felons. Maybe it was someone he
or his father had known prior to his crime, or maybe it
was just someone who had read about the case and decided
to offer Hollywood his support. But for whatever reason,
Woodard and Hollywood had an ongoing correspondence,
and several of Hollywood's letters from prison were posted
on the Internet.

They were often about politics and about Hollywood's
defense strategies. He bragged about how District Attorney
Ron Zonen had gotten "the boot" from the trial and how
Hollywood was going to get the whole Santa Barbara district attorney's office thrown off, too. He kept saying that
things were looking up for him and that his defense team
was very optimistic. And he began calling himself "Alpha
Dog" after the movie was released.

There was also a strange element of sexuality and "fan
club" about the correspondence, where Woodard had apparently mentioned a woman who designed "Jesse James Hollywood" T-shirts and the young women who were supposedly
his fans.

One of Hollywood's letters said, "Hope you can get
together a harem of those young tender Alpha Dog supporters, pop on some Daisy Dukes and some tight J.J.H.
T-shirts for sex appeal at the trial. They already take me in
a presidential caravan with all their most expensive toys, so
it's only natural my supporters turn out for the big event,
right? The Alpha Dog Unit Team is ready for war, and
with Zonen M.I.A. we make like the Special Forces Green
Beret. As always, I appreciate your support to the fullest."

Among other things, Woodard's "support" included
sending articles, as well as apparently sending racy photos,
and offering to send all sorts of books. In response, Hollywood thanked him for the photos and asked him to send
more suggestive ones.

In another letter, Hollywood wrote:

> I'm trying to get some funds together here for vari-
> ous reasons, and I was hoping you could help out by

sending a couple of bucks my way. Western Union sent directly to my address goes on my books in 30 minutes. Any contribution would be greatly appreciated and of course used only for the most noble purposes.

He ended his letter:

Tell all my girls in Nepal I love them and Daddy will be home soon.

Love and Respect,
Alpha Dog

P.S. If I ever get outta here, I'm going to Katmandu!!!

When he didn't sign his name "Alpha Dog," he sometimes signed it "JJH," followed by "818 SFV outlaw," "Irish," and a shamrock with a penis. SFV stood for "San Fernando Valley," and 818 was the local area code.

Finding those letters online had really blown my mind. Learning that Hollywood was allowed to receive gifts of racy pictures, books, and money in prison bothered me. It bothered me that murderers and rapists were allowed *any* sorts of entertainment or luxuries; as far as I was concerned, they should be stripped to the bare essentials.

Up until the last posted letter in 2008, Hollywood expressed his confidence that the district attorney's office would be thrown off the case and that he would prevail. As he put it, "I continue to be positive and never stray from my program. I know I'll be blessed when it's showtime." And that's what it was to him: a big show.

His calls in prison were recorded, and when prosecutors reviewed them, they were even more bothered by Hollywood's callousness. He would purposely mispronounce our last name, calling us "the Lefkowitzes" and saying insulting things about us. Never once did he show any remorse or express any concern about what we were going through. He never called Nick by name, only "the kid" or "the boy." His pity was reserved solely for himself, as he regularly complained about his predicament and how unfair it all was.

The trial started in May of 2009. Hollywood wore a black suit and red tie to court and sat in between his two lawyers. It had taken two weeks and three hundred potential jurors before both the prosecution and defense came up with their final selections: nine women and three men who would now decide Hollywood's fate.

My job, as I figured it, was to make eye contact with Hollywood and not let him forget that I was in the room, watching him. Every time he turned to smile at his parents, he was going to see me—and the smile would fade. I wanted to keep him uncomfortable. If there were anything human in him, then it would be difficult for him to look into the eyes of the woman whose son he'd ordered to be executed. I was hoping it would be difficult to look into my eyes and lie.

"Ladies and gentlemen, that's Jesse James Hollywood," prosecutor Josh Lynn began. "Jesse James Hollywood murdered fifteen-year-old Nicholas Markowitz like he pulled the trigger himself."

In what he called a "highly low-tech presentation," Josh put up his picture board showing photos of each of the defendants, plus Ben and Nick. He referred to it throughout his presentation to the jury to let them get an idea of who each person was.

But then came a shocking tactic from the defense: they sank lower than even I'd thought possible. They were prepared to argue their case by attacking . . . me.

The strategy the defense came up with was to make it sound as if Nick hadn't really been kidnapped after all. Well, he'd been kidnapped at *first*, but then he could have left at any point, yet he'd *chosen* to stay because he hated Jeff and me so much that he'd rather be anywhere than at our house. Which meant that Hollywood had really been doing Nick a favor by having him beat up and thrown into a van—getting him away from his awful parents.

We were thankful when the judge said that he would not allow that line of argument because it was irrelevant; never in the three days that Nick was kidnapped had he said anything about not wanting to return home because he hated his home life or his parents. In fact, he'd talked positively about wanting to go home. So the defense team wasn't allowed to attack us directly, but that didn't mean they were going to be polite. They made it clear that they wanted to prove what a dysfunctional, bad family we were.

It was a terrible new experience. In all the other trials, no one had been so cruel or so conniving as to try to go after our family as a means to subvert the jury's sympathy. It appeared that the defense team wanted to make it seem like Nick's murder hadn't been such a tragedy after all, because Nick didn't love us. And when they referred to his age, rather than saying he was fifteen, they kept making the point that he was *almost sixteen*, as if that made it less tragic. Sixteen—why, he was practically ready to retire!

Jeff was first on the witness stand, giving the jury a little background about Nick and Ben and our family dynamic. He explained that he tried to keep the two boys separate because of Ben's troubled history, and he talked about the night before Nick disappeared, when we'd caught him with drugs in his pocket.

Pauline Mahoney, one of the women who'd called 911, was next, and they played her call to the jury. I'd heard it before; it was still difficult to listen to it again. In that moment, everything could have changed. If only . . .

Don't waste your thoughts, I told myself. *Can't change anything about the past now, no matter how hard you wish it.*

Brian Affronti, William Skidmore's friend, was next on the stand. He said that when they'd gotten to the apartment in Santa Barbara, Nick's hands had been duct taped together, so he'd helped Nick smoke pot out of a bong. After Nick was murdered, Affronti said that he received a phone call from Skidmore, warning him to avoid Hollywood. Hollywood had labeled him a "weak link" and told

Skidmore to kill him. Affronti also testified that he had seen the TEC-9 gun at Hollywood's house.

Chas Saulsbury was the next person on the witness stand, and he showed up in shorts and flip-flops. He was the childhood friend whose doorstep Hollywood had shown up on after he'd fled from California. Saulsbury was granted immunity right away when he went to the police, although he had originally lied when he told them that he didn't know why Hollywood was in trouble. He claimed that he'd driven Hollywood to Las Vegas thinking Hollywood was just running from some kind of drug charges—but on cross-examination in this trial, he admitted that he knew about Nick's murder before they ever left his mother's house in Colorado.

The defense team tried to rattle Saulsbury by telling him that if he was caught lying in a capital murder case, he could get life in prison or even the death penalty. The following day, the defense apologized for the threatening remarks and asked Saulsbury if he had been crying. He said no, but defense attorney James Blatt insisted that he had seen Chas Saulsbury cry after court.

Saulsbury testified that Hollywood told him he got the TEC-9 from a worker at an auto body shop and that he asked Ryan Hoyt to use it to kill Nick Markowitz. Hollywood told Saulsbury that, initially, he was "not sure" what to do with Nick but that he'd ordered the shooting after speaking with attorney Stephen Hogg and finding out that kidnapping could carry a life sentence.

The defense hammered Saulsbury about why he hadn't gone to police immediately when he found out what Hollywood had done, and he said, "I was scared. I didn't know what to do. A little boy got killed here."

That's what I was thankful to Chas Saulsbury for—no matter what they asked him or how many ways they hammered at him, he kept bringing it back around to the point—*don't forget that a boy was killed*, he kept reminding them.

The first lighthearted moment in the trial came when the judge could no longer stand watching Saulsbury squirm around in his chair. He asked the bailiff to please bring the witness a chair that didn't swivel.

Chas Saulsbury was openly angry with the defense team. He got into trouble for speaking when there was no direct question posed of him. "Your client came running to me and then ended up in Brazil!" he said at one point. Toward the end of cross-examination, he was flustered and agitated.

On redirect, the prosecutor asked if the defense's rapid-fire questioning had confused him, and Saulsbury said yes. Toward the end of the morning session, had he been willing to say "yes" to anything? Yes, Saulsbury said.

He looked beat up, and prosecutor Josh Lynn was worried that he had crumbled pretty badly. Lynn's impression had been that Saulsbury was a sort of harmless, happy-go-lucky pot-smoking teenager who had turned into a happy-go-lucky pot-smoking adult. He thought Saulsbury had really been tricked into helping Hollywood in the name of friendship and that he had spent the years afterward trying to right his mistakes, but by the end, Lynn wasn't so sure he understood Saulsbury or his true intentions anymore.

There was some to-do about the name of the type of pot he said they smoked: Paranoia. Lynn asked Saulsbury if there were other types of pot he could name. Still looking sullen and totally serious, Saulsbury said, "I don't think we have time for all those names." Giggles around the courtroom ensued.

The judge threatened to make him come back for another day of testimony. He had already been away from home for six days, and he was anxious to return; he had learned that his dog had been poisoned while he was gone.

"She's bleeding internally," he said on the witness stand. "There's been so much bleeding it's coming out of her eyeballs." He said he was going to have to go home and have her put to sleep.

An investigator from defense attorney James Blatt's office had called Chas Saulsbury's wife to ask for their home address on the day Saulsbury arrived in Santa Barbara— and the following day, their dog began showing signs of having ingested rat poison.

"Are you accusing me of poisoning your dog to threaten you?" Blatt asked on cross-examination.

"Yes, I am," Saulsbury replied.

"How could you say that?" Blatt asked, throwing his arms open dramatically.

The prosecution objected, and the judge put an end to that line of questioning . . . but of course it left the question in my mind. Was it really just coincidence that on the day Chas Saulsbury began testifying at Hollywood's murder trial, his dog had been poisoned?

Saulsbury wasn't the only one who had strange stories to tell about the defense team. Michael Mehas, who was a researcher for the film *Alpha Dog*, said that his initial refusal to cooperate with the defense to make statements about what sorts of evidence District Attorney Ron Zonen shared with him "resulted in several threatening phone calls" to his home.

———

Stephen Hogg was also granted immunity for his testimony. Of course, he denied having suggested that Hollywood "dig a deep hole" and have Nick killed, but he did admit that, in the midst of the kidnapping, Hollywood had showed up on his doorstep. Hogg told Hollywood that he and his friends could get life in prison if they hurt Nick or asked for ransom. He said that he had wanted to "impress upon [Hollywood] that his friends could be in some dire trouble."

And how did Hollywood react?

"He didn't react at all when I said that," he testified.

That's not what got Hollywood upset, Hogg said. It was

when Hogg suggested that he should go to police that Hollywood freaked out.

Hogg claimed that he told him, "The first person that gets on the train gets the shortest ride," meaning that if Hollywood went to the authorities first to tell them about the kidnapping, they would be lenient with him. But Hollywood vehemently insisted that he was not going to police. He smoked three cigarettes, paced around the table, then left.

"I didn't run after him. I regret that, but I didn't."

Because of Hogg's immunity deal, he wouldn't face any consequences for his inactions; he got to just move on with his life. *Oops, a boy got killed and I could have prevented it. Oh well.*

———

Where Chas Saulsbury had acted hostile toward the defense, Hollywood's former and possibly still current girlfriend, Michelle Lasher, was hostile toward the prosecution. She sauntered up to the witness stand as if she were modeling on a catwalk. During her testimony, she kept flipping her hair and bending over and bouncing her breasts, presumably for Hollywood's enjoyment. She was irrational and dramatic and cartoonish, with Valley Girl inflections.

Lasher wanted everyone to know that the prosecution was "traumatizing" her. She frequently burst into tears on the stand while describing how she was still in love with Hollywood and how a detective had upset her by saying that the murder was Hollywood's fault and that "they were just going to shoot him when they saw him."

She also wanted the jury to know that she'd overheard a conversation between Hollywood and Ryan Hoyt after the murder, and that Hollywood had asked Hoyt if he was crazy and then got very upset.

"That was around the time that the blood vessel in his eye burst," she said.

But, Lasher claimed, Hollywood had never told her about any kidnapping or murder. "He was panicked when he came to see me in Palm Springs," she said, but she hadn't pushed him to find out why.

Out came a hotel registration card. It was the registration that Lasher had filled out when she and Hollywood stayed in Colorado. Interestingly, it had a false name, false address, and a false vehicle make and color. But she said that had nothing to do with being on the run from authorities.

"I never give my information," she said. "That's something I've been taught since I was very little."

Prosecutor Hans Almgren questioned her, and Lasher kept saying that she didn't know or didn't remember things—"It was nine years ago," she said. But she refused to read her transcripts to refresh her memory. That's not what she wanted to talk about. All she wanted to talk about was how the prosecution and the detectives and the police officers had all made her very upset.

"I'm very afraid right now!" she said at one point. The judge asked her to stay silent while no question was pending, but she ignored him.

"You are attacking me!" she said.

The judge ended court early that day.

When the defense team cross-examined her, they knew just where to start.

"Are you aware that your boyfriend or ex-boyfriend, the man that you love, is facing the death penalty?"

With that, she dropped her head and sobbed into her hands. When Michelle Lasher cried, she didn't just let a few tears fall; she puffed her cheeks out and clawed at her eyes, pulling out tissue after tissue. The judge asked if she wanted a minute to compose herself, but she held up a tissue with her hand and said bravely, "No, no, no. I'm fine." Then she whipped out her powder puff and powdered her nose. On the witness stand.

I wondered if she had gotten the memo that there were to be no cameras in the courtroom, because it sure appeared to me like she was auditioning for a movie—or at least a soap opera. Was she hoping for a role in *Alpha Dog II*?

It was such a double standard, really—the way the defense was purposely playing into Lasher's hysterics, while at the same time they had made sure to have the judge tell our family that we were not allowed to show any emotion or we'd be thrown out of the courtroom. At one point, the bailiff even told Leah that she was using too many facial expressions.

To make Hollywood appear more likable, the defense asked Michelle Lasher questions designed to make him sound like an upstanding family guy. She said that he celebrated Christian holidays with his own family and Jewish holidays with hers, and that "He was just more mature than the other boys in high school."

The judge cut off the defense before they could go on with these very touching questions; they were irrelevant to the matter at hand, he said.

Lasher went into more detail about Ryan Hoyt: "He was a liar, he would sleep on everyone's couches, he was always messing everything up. If Jesse gave him a car, he would leave it on the side of the road."

Then she said that Ron Zonen and Senior Deputy District Attorney Hans Almgren were "threatening to charge me with murder for someone I've never met." She claimed that they'd said, "Either perjure yourself or we're going to charge you with murder."

But it turned out that Lasher had never even met Ron Zonen, who was no longer prosecuting the case. She backtracked on that one, saying that he hadn't threatened her *directly*, but he had threatened her through lawyers.

At one point while Almgren was questioning her, Blatt objected. "There's no reason to point at the witness," he said.

"That's not a legal objection," the judge answered, causing giggles in the courtroom, an amusing diversion. I wasn't sure how much more I could stand of seeing Michelle Lasher talk about how *her* life had been affected by these lousy people who were trying to apprehend a murderer. She didn't know Nick and didn't care about Nick, neither in life nor in death. It didn't seem to occur to her that his life had been in any way significant, only that it was affecting her negatively, so she could no longer freely run around with her outlaw boyfriend.

I'm sure that part of her "trauma" came from the fact that Hollywood had moved on and had a baby with his next girlfriend, whom he actually called his wife. I waited and wondered if that would ever come up.

———

Graham Pressley was the next person to testify, and we all knew that his testimony could be the most important in the trial. After all, he had actually been there right up until Nick was taken to Lizard Mouth to his death. Because no one was going to call Ryan Hoyt to the stand—he was an unreliable witness, and his own case was on appeal— and it was still questionable whether Jesse Rugge would be called, Pressley was likely the only one able to offer first-person testimony about how the murder really happened.

Like just about all of the others, Pressley had initially lied to the authorities about his own involvement in the crime. It wasn't until he took a polygraph that he came clean about what had happened.

On the stand, he re-created the timeline of events for the jury, explaining what Nick had been going through and how people were reacting. He came off as completely calm and levelheaded. Mature, even.

When he explained that Ryan Hoyt had arrived at the Lemon Tree Inn carrying a duffel bag with the TEC-9 gun in it, the prosecutor asked why Pressley hadn't warned Nick.

"Because I was more concerned with myself at that point," he admitted. Several times, he referred to his decisions that day as "selfish." His concern for his own safety came first, and it had clouded his judgment. All he'd wanted to do was to follow whatever orders Hoyt gave him and stay out of the way so he wouldn't become their victim, too.

Why did he stay in the car when he heard the gunshots?

"I wasn't at a place where I could think rationally," he said.

The defense must have expected to eat Graham Pressley alive. They tried . . . but they failed. Pressley remained remarkably calm, even when the defense lawyers yelled at him and tried to get him to crack, and that seemed to get under *their* skin.

I understood that defense attorneys were a different breed of people, but these two clowns—Kessel and Blatt—were the worst kind I'd ever encountered. I couldn't find any shred of decency in either of them.

Kessel kept trying to get Pressley to answer questions in the way he wanted—with simple one-word responses, but Pressley often elaborated a bit. When Kessel asked if he had gotten into the car voluntarily or involuntarily, Pressley didn't choose either word—he said he acted out of fear. When Kessel asked if he'd intended to hurt Nick, Pressley said no, but that "being afraid to do something is not a defense for murder."

"Can you just answer the question?" Kessel yelled.

"You are badgering the witness," the judge said.

One of the new tactics the defense used was to call our relationship into question. Pressley had said that my confidence in him motivated him to come clean about some prior testimony. But Kessel wanted to make that ugly.

Wasn't the real motivator that I had struck a deal with him that I'd ask for his early release from prison if he would falsely testify against Hollywood?

No, Pressley said.

Then Kessel asked if he had made a deal with prosecutors to cooperate, but the judge stopped the defense attorney and admonished him for asking "an improper question."

Still, Kessel tried again. He wanted to know if my presence in the courtroom made Pressley feel compelled to lie. He said no.

After his testimony ended, I learned from his mother that Pressley had received death threats.

———————

On Pressley's fourth day on the stand, the defense planned to play a one-hour tape of his polygraph test. Since I had heard it already maybe six times before in other trials, I decided that this would be a good time for me to take a break. I really didn't need to hear it a seventh time.

So I let my friends know that I was going to just separate for a little while, and I sat outside. A woman in a green sweater walked past me. I closed my eyes and tried to feel the sun on my face. Then I heard her shuffling back toward me, so I opened my eyes.

"I'm waiting to get into the courtroom," she said. "They said it was full and I have to wait until someone comes out in order to go inside. Are you waiting also?"

"No, I have a seat," I said.

I don't remember how the discussion started, but she told me that she was depressed because her own son, a pilot, had died in Hawaii. We got to talking, and I said, "I lost a son also. The trial that you're trying to get into? I'm Nick's mom."

She almost fainted.

It was no mistake, my being out there just as she was out there. We talked about signs—about how I felt that praying mantises were a sign of Nick, and how she felt that broken glass was a sign of her son. I asked her if she acknowledged these signs and thanked her son out loud for trying to communicate with her. I told her I imagined that it must be frustrating being on the other side, wondering if the person is "getting" the way you're trying to communicate.

She told me that she didn't want to talk to anyone who hadn't lost a child anymore; she found it impossible to relate. I understood that. Even more specifically, I had trouble relating to people who hadn't lost a child to murder—and even more specifically than that, I was continually searching for parents who had lost their *only* child to murder. Sometimes we all need to feel like we've found others like us.

In that place, at that moment, she was soaking in my words and looking for healing. We both were.

As we talked, I realized something: I really was getting through this. Taking it "one day at a time" was too much. I was taking it about ten minutes at a time. Sometimes one minute at a time. My goal was to just get through that minute and not look ahead.

I went back to the hotel and slept early each night. Most of the time, I was in bed by about 7:00 p.m., just completely emotionally exhausted. It took a lot of effort to be that detached! At one point, Leah had looked right into my eyes and said, "I just wanted to make sure you're still in there."

There was only so much I could handle, I knew, so I tried to withdraw from reality as best I could whenever it got tough. Because of the gag order, I was not allowed to talk about the trial with anyone, and that was tough, too, because sometimes I just wanted to decompress with a friend who would understand. After we left the courtroom each day, I wanted to talk about the defense's shady tactics, and the difficulty of listening to the details, over and over, about how my son had been bound and gagged and eventually executed with a machine gun while standing in his grave.

"What can it hurt? She won't tell," I would think, spotting a homeless woman who looked friendly.

But the best I could do to keep friends and family updated was to point them to whatever was in the news. Each day, my webmaster for Nick's website would put up the latest article that had appeared about the previous day's court session, and anyone who cared could read through the articles, sorted by date, to keep up on what was happening.

Casey Sheehan, Kelly Carpenter, and Natasha Adams had all told their versions of what they had seen, and then it was Ben's turn. I didn't know if I was ready to hear Ben's testimony. It seemed that every time Ben spoke, I found out another little something I hadn't known before and never really wanted to find out.

The defense had tried to block Ben from appearing as a witness because they said he wasn't credible, but the judge denied their request. As it turned out, he was one of the most credible people to appear in front of the court.

Ben didn't try to whitewash anything; he admitted to the court that he had been a drug dealer and a fighter, that he'd threatened Hollywood, that he'd done things out of self-interest when he saw possible dollar signs. And he described that after he'd accrued the $1,200 debt to Hollywood, he was trying to straighten his life out, and he was engaged to be married and working a real job.

Every couple of questions, the defense would object to something, seemingly just to interrupt the process with things that appeared to have absolutely no bearing on what a jury would decide. For example, the prosecutor asked if Ben seemed to have "mutual interests or have things in common" with Hollywood, and Blatt objected and wanted him to break it up into two separate questions. So the prosecutor had to ask, "Did you have mutual interests?" (Yes.) "Did you have things in common?" (Yes.)

Because of this, all of the testimonies went extremely slowly. Every minute or so, the proceedings were interrupted so the defense could object, and the judge would have to rule on whether the objection would be sustained or overruled, and there was frequently a little discussion about it. People in the courtroom were rolling their eyes and groaning every time the defense called out, "Objection."

And sometimes they just called things out for no good reason at all. While the prosecutor was explaining that Ben had changed after Nick's murder and became the kind of person who was looking for a confrontation, Blatt called out, "Vague. Let it in. We want it in."

The prosecutor said, "You know, I don't need these comments during—"

"Yeah. No comments. Do you have an objection?" asked the judge.

"No."

All pretense of politeness between the prosecution and the defense had gone out the window long ago. Kessel has a loud voice, and he chattered throughout the trial in a voice loud enough for everyone to hear, frequently speaking negatively about Josh Lynn, and the judge had to remind him to keep his voice down.

The nitpicking over words soon led to this exchange:

The prosecutor asked Ben, "Would you have characterized yourself in those days as a tough guy? As a—"

"Objection. Vague. As a tough guy," Blatt said. "What is a tough guy?"

"I'm asking him," said the prosecutor.

"Well, overruled. I'll permit it," said the judge.

"Tough guy, Your Honor?"

"Yes, Mr. Blatt. Overruled."

"Yes, Your Honor."

"You can cross-examine him. Go ahead. You can answer the question."

"At the time, yes," Ben said.

"What do you mean by that?" the prosecutor asked.

"I was definitely, to be frank, I was a fucking dickhead. I mean, I was—I walked around with a chip on my shoulder, and if you looked at me sideways I'd kick your ass. I was just . . ."

"Do you understand the term now?" the judge asked the defense.

"I think so. Thank you. This witness said it better," said Blatt.

The prosecutor also asked if Ben had ever seen Jack Hollywood supply his son with marijuana to sell, and Ben said yes—but the defense objected to that as well, saying it was irrelevant.

Ben then described what happened when he got out of prison for armed robbery. Despite that he was on parole and was not supposed to be drinking, he'd gone out to a bar about a week after his release and happened to run into Casey Sheehan, the boy whose car Hollywood had borrowed to send Ryan Hoyt off to kill Nick. Ben threw Sheehan up against a friend's truck and tried to get him to tell the truth about what Hollywood had told him when he'd asked to borrow the car. Had Sheehan known that his car was going to be used in Nick's murder?

"At some point did you explain those events to me, the confrontation with Mr. Sheehan?" the prosecutor asked Ben.

"I'm sorry, I didn't hear the question," said Blatt.

"Oh, it has to do with explaining the confrontation with Mr. Sheehan," the judge said.

Ben started to answer, but Blatt interrupted again. "Excuse me, Your Honor. The question is vague and ambiguous."

"Well, if he didn't hear it, I don't see how he could make that objection," said the prosecutor.

It was exhausting, really. By that point the trial had already been going on for a month.

The newspaper articles were frustrating as well. Some of them seemed accurate, and others made me wonder if the reporters just enjoyed stirring up more drama. Ben certainly aggravated the defense because he gave them nothing to work with; they wanted to pry out of him what a jerk he was, but Ben was open about all that before they even got started—so there was nothing for them to "catch him" about. About all they could do was try to nitpick him to death over dates; he could no longer remember exactly what month he had become friends with Hollywood, for example, or when they'd picked up the useless Ecstasy pills, or what month he'd seen the TEC-9 at Hollywood's house.

It seemed like the defense had completely run out of questions and they were just stalling for time to think of some new ones when they had this crazy exchange:

"You called yourself Bugsy, right?" Blatt asked.

"Yes," said Ben.

"And Bugsy is after the infamous Jewish gangster Bugsy Siegel, correct?"

"Yes."

"That's what you—and by the way, have people told you you look like him?"

"No."

"He was a very handsome man. It was meant as a compliment."

"Thank you."

"All right."

The judge interrupted: "No more questions along those lines."

"All right," said Blatt. "Going back to the glorious '40s. All right. But you put a—did you put a tattoo of a Bugs Bunny on your arm to represent Bugsy?"

"Yes, I did."

"And you wanted to emulate Bugsy Siegel, didn't you?"

"No. No."

"Well, did you know anything about him?"

"Yes."

"You knew he was a glamorous figure, correct?"

"Yes."

"And he was Jewish?"

"Yes."

"And came to Hollywood in the '40s?"

"Relevance, Your Honor," Josh Lynn interrupted.

"Sustained," said the judge.

"All right. And he was tough, wasn't he?"

"Yes."

"So, when he—had a girlfriend named Flamingo, right, a nickname?"

"I'm going to say 'Relevancy,' Your Honor," Josh Lynn said.

"Sustained," said the judge. And on and on it went.

The defense tried everything they could to gain the jury's sympathy, like, "You knew that [Hollywood's brother] had heart disease, right?"

"I had no idea he had heart disease," said Ben. What

difference did that make? Ben had never done anything to Hollywood's brother. Was the defense getting brothers confused? *Hollywood was the one who murdered Ben's brother, remember?*

Yet some of the articles made it sound like the defense really took Ben apart.

Leah was so upset about the way that the trial was being written about that she wrote a letter to one of the papers with her corrections, asking if the reporter had been sitting in the same courtroom as she had.

The papers were also split about who was "winning" the trial. Many said that the defense was earning their keep and complained about a lackluster job from the prosecution, while others said the opposite—that the defense was using tactics meant to confuse the jury and that reporters had such a hard time following what they were saying that they sometimes just stopped taking notes. Online, people had heated debates about whether they thought Hollywood would be convicted or acquitted.

None of that concern even entered my brain—I knew the jury was going to convict Jesse James Hollywood. I had confidence in that from the very beginning, from the moment he was caught. It was only a matter of time. Others around me were nervous, including Jeff; he was afraid that I would not be able to handle it if the jury came back with a "not guilty" verdict. Perhaps he was right, but I didn't even consider the possibility. I had too much on my plate as it was; worrying about future catastrophes would have been an unnecessary burden.

Ben's testimony was very emotional at times. He spoke about his regrets and how he knew that his little brother, Nick, had looked up to him. He cried when he saw a picture of the gun. At least this time they hadn't brought in the actual gun, which they had done in previous trials. Ben opened up in ways I had never seen before, and for the first time, I felt like he was one hundred percent there for his brother.

After he was through testifying, Ben came over to me outside the courthouse and we just hugged and cried together for a long time. Although he had apologized by letter before, now he said the words to me in person, and I felt a wall coming down between us. It was a beautiful feeling that I hoped would last.

———————

Next to testify were the four people who'd been at Richard Hoeflinger's house the night Nick was bound and gagged there. They testified that they were all afraid of Hollywood, and that he had a gun, and had told at least one of them to keep his "fucking mouth shut."

Then came one of the hikers who found Nick's body, and a forensic detective who described the condition of his body in its grave at Lizard's Mouth. A forensic pathologist also talked about the autopsy. I tried not to hear any of it. Thinking about his body rotting in the summer heat was still very hard for me to block out. I didn't even like very hot days because it made me think about Nick's body out there, burning up in the sun.

Paul Kimes, an investigator with the district attorney's office, then took the stand to clarify what had happened with Michelle Lasher and her claims that the district attorney's office had been threatening her. He was there when the supposed "threat" had occurred, and he said that what was actually going on that day was that Hans Almgren had been signing her immunity papers—the opposite of a threat, really. He gave her the immunity papers to sign. She'd marched in the room angrily, refused to read the papers, didn't listen to what he said to her, then signed and threw the papers and the pen at him and walked out.

———————

When it was the defense's turn to call their witnesses, they wanted to turn it into a red-carpet event. They wanted to call filmmaker Nick Cassavetes and Justin Timberlake, ostensibly because Cassavetes and Timberlake had had access to the district attorney's notes, but the judge didn't see how that was relevant to the trial so he disallowed it.

He did, however, allow them to call Jerry Hollywood, Jesse's seventy-year-old second cousin, who had never been questioned about any of the events before. I don't know why no one had ever interviewed Jerry—there's a record that Jesse called him just before Nick was murdered. But he said he never came forward and told police about that phone call because no one ever asked him. We had never heard a word about him before that day either. There was really just one reason the defense wanted him there: Jerry Hollywood had told the defense's investigator that Jesse said Nick was going home.

But the prosecutor didn't believe it. The elderly man didn't come across sharp enough to have recollection of the exact words that had been used nine years prior, and it was very fishy that he had never before come forward to mention something that was in his cousin's favor. Wasn't it true, Josh Lynn wanted to know, that it was the investigator who'd put those words into his mouth? That it wasn't really Jerry's memory, but the investigator's story he was telling?

"Most of the statements he [the investigator] said were correct," Jerry agreed. "It's just that they weren't quite my words."

Then, on June 22, 2009, the judge called out, "Next witness," and the defense said . . .

"Jesse James Hollywood."

Oh my God.

The room was silent. No one had known that this was coming. It was very rare for an accused murderer to take the stand in his own defense, and apparently, even Hollywood's own lawyers disagreed about it, one wanting him to and the other opposed to the idea. In the end, it had been left up to him, and Hollywood had decided to testify.

My heart raced. Finally, I would get to see this man face-to-face, hear the words out of his own mouth. It was both horrible and yet satisfying at once.

Hollywood buttoned his black suit jacket and walked up to the stand to swear on the Bible, looking ghostly pale, a stark contrast from the tanned complexion he'd had upon his arrest. For the first time, I heard his voice. The only other time I'd ever heard him speak was in a video where he was acting like a gangster a few months before Nick's murder. This was his real voice, and it was small, almost feminine. This short guy with the wimpy voice had become the leader of the pack? It was unimaginable without the drug-dealing father and the guns.

Why is he taking the stand? I thought. And the only explanation I could come up with was that his lawyers must have told him he was toast, and he'd better get up there and save himself. That they had done all they could.

On the stand, Hollywood used few words, answering most of his lawyer's questions with "Yes, sir" or "No, sir." When asked to describe himself, he said he had "full-blown OCD" (obsessive-compulsive disorder) and that he was a health nut who was always dieting and working out. They did a bit of bragging about his organizational skills and his excellent credit score (which surely should cancel out a kidnapping and murder, no?).

Hollywood spoke about baseball, saying that it had been "pretty much my life" until a shoulder and back injury had forced him to stop playing. And he spoke about his drug dealing, saying that he began selling drugs as a teenager in Colorado but claiming that his father hadn't been the source. While growing up, he always suspected that his dad was into "illicit activities," but they didn't talk about it directly until he was older, when he learned that his dad was selling large quantities of low- to mid-grade marijuana— more than one hundred pounds at a time. While his dad made sales across the country, Jesse concentrated on selling high-grade pot in the San Fernando Valley region, which earned him about ten thousand dollars a month when business was going well.

OK, I thought. *He's telling the truth.* I hadn't expected him to, but it gave me just the smallest bit of hope that he'd continue telling the truth about the things that really mattered.

On his second day of testimony, Hollywood began talking about the kidnapping . . . except that he didn't call it a kidnapping. He called it a "taking." The "taking of Nick."

"I pinned him up against a tree and I said, 'Where's your brother? Where's your brother?'" he testified. Then, after William Skidmore got in a few punches, the two of them "ushered" Nick into the van.

He said it was an impulsive and irrational decision he'd made because he'd been so mad about his broken windows. But he said that he hadn't intended to hurt Nick and didn't think that anyone else would, either.

As Hollywood spoke, he was sweating so profusely that he had to keep wiping his brow, but he didn't seem to want to touch his face. He kept wiping it with the back of his hand or his sleeve. I wondered if that was an OCD thing or if it was because someone had told him that touching your face was a sign of lying.

Once he got into talking about Nick, Hollywood's answers appeared well rehearsed and repetitive. It was as if he were trying to work in certain key phrases over and over: primarily, "I regret that" and "I feel terrible about that."

"I just feel terrible about everything that happened. I feel terrible for the Markowitz family. I feel terrible for all the families involved. I feel terrible that people would think I would do something like that."

It got to the point where Josh Lynn would say, "I appreciate that, but now . . ." and try to get him to actually answer a question instead of just talking about his supposed remorse. Of course, Hollywood had probably been told to show remorse for the jury's sake, but where had that remorse been for the past nine years?

The prosecutor asked how much force Hollywood had to use to pin Nick against a tree. Hollywood said that it had taken quite a bit of strength because "Nick is taller than me."

"Nick *was* taller than you. He *was* taller than you, Mr. Hollywood," said Josh Lynn. He also made fun of

join me in the courtroom because there was no chance he would be called back to testify—but he didn't last long.

The prosecution showed pictures of Nick in his grave. The last photo was of Jeff's ring on Nick's bloated finger, and Jeff cried. I rubbed his back and tried to shield him from view.

Ohh, hold it together, Jeff, I thought. *Hang in there or they're going to kick you out.*

And indeed, the defense did complain. They suggested that Jeff was putting on a show for the jury with his tears, because, after all, we had seen pictures like that several times already and should be used to them by now.

Exactly how many times were you supposed to look at pictures of your son's decomposing body before it became no big deal?

So the next morning, the judge addressed the jury.

"Yesterday, apparently, in the audience there was some audible crying or displays of emotion at some point in the proceedings. I didn't notice it, but it has been brought to my attention . . . I'm going to admonish you that that is not to be considered at all during the course of this trial. During your deliberations sympathy has no role."

Then he turned to the audience and said, "I've admonished the audience; I'll admonish them again: no displays of emotion. Any display of emotion will result in removal from the courtroom."

But not long after that, defense attorney Kessel was talking about how it had been some time since Nick's death. A few years, he said.

"Nine years!" Jeff blurted out.

That was it. The judge admonished Jeff and called for the bailiffs to escort him out of the courtroom.

Jeff didn't come back to the courtroom until he was called back to speak. It was a relief for him, really—he felt he needed to be at work to keep the business afloat, whereas I felt I needed to be in that courtroom every day.

The closing arguments went on for hours and hours over

the course of two days, and finally, the jury was sent off to deliberate.

After six weeks of talk, talk, talk, now suddenly there was . . . nothing. There was nothing else I could do or see. Now we just had to wait. It could be hours, days, or weeks before the jury reached a verdict, and all we could do was wait by the phone for someone to alert us that the verdict was in.

It took the jury four days. I rushed off to the courtroom, fielding a few last-minute calls on my cell phone to wish us luck. Jeff was to meet me there.

Because no one knew which day we'd get the call, Jeff had been taking his "court clothes" to work with him each day. In a hurry, he threw on the shirt and slacks from the dry cleaning bag he had brought, and then realized . . . it was my blouse he was wearing.

"Someone's got to get me a shirt!" he said on the phone. Luckily, his cousin's husband was in the area and was able to bring a shirt to the courthouse. Once Jeff arrived, people were running around trying to find him to hand him the shirt, and the sheriff grabbed him and brought him into a van where he could change. With no time to spare, Jeff emerged from the van and walked into the courtroom . . . with his fly unzipped.

The foreman read the verdict.

On the charge of first-degree murder:

Guilty.

On the "special circumstance" of murder using an assault pistol or machine gun, which would make Hollywood eligible for the death penalty:

Guilty.

The rest of the world faded away. Justice had been served.

CHAPTER 18

SON RISE, SON SET

Ben had been late to court to hear the verdict, so he walked in while they were reading the kidnapping charges. They found Hollywood not guilty of aggravated kidnapping but guilty of simple kidnapping. That's all Ben heard, and he was not seated next to us, so we couldn't reassure him. He was very concerned: had Hollywood just gotten away with murder? Eventually, we were able to ease his mind.

We all hugged, both in and out of the courtroom, while the media snapped their cameras and expected us to say cheerful things. I couldn't talk about how I felt. All I knew was that it was a relief to be done; it was a relief that the verdict was the right one. Aside from that, I couldn't offer the words they wanted to hear about "closure" or happiness.

Next came the penalty phase, where our family members would answer questions from the prosecutor and the defense could cross-examine us. I tried to explain to the jury that if they saw that my reactions were sometimes blank or not what they would expect, it was because I had been forced to disconnect from reality for a very long time in order to survive.

When the defense cross-examined Jeff, they asked him when Nick's birthday was. I shouldn't have been surprised, but it still managed to freshly horrify me that they would be so cruel. They were attempting to catch Jeff off guard, so that they could make it seem like he was exaggerating his closeness with his murdered son. Did they really think Jeff would forget Nick's birthday?

The penalty phase should have been the easiest part of the trial—the main decision of guilt or innocence had already been decided, and now it was just a matter of deciding which of two sentences was most appropriate. But several things came out during this stage that complicated the proceedings and almost derailed them.

After court one day, a stranger with a ponytail approached us to offer his sympathy, then walked over to Jack Hollywood and began talking to him. We thought that was odd, for this man to go from one family to the other. It turned out that the man was the husband of one of the jurors—juror number three—and he told Jack that his wife had been unable to sleep since the verdict was announced. She was very upset about something that had happened during the course of deliberations.

This became a break for the defense in two ways: first, the juror wasn't supposed to talk about the case to anyone, including her husband. And second, what exactly was she troubled about? Of course, the defense team hoped to dig up some dirt to help their client get off the hook, so they asked the judge to question her.

The juror said that she had *not* talked about the case to her husband, but that he could see that she was obviously upset about something. She had written the judge a letter earlier but had not given it to him. When questioned, she cried and said this trial was the worst thing that had ever happened in her life and that there were "ugly things" going on in the jury box.

What were these ugly things?

The only example she gave was that, after Casey Sheehan said he was an electrician, juror number 5 had said,

"Maybe Jesse can get Casey to do one last electrical job for him" and made a buzzing sound to imitate an electric chair. "I thought that was terrible," juror 3 said.

"OK. And certainly in poor taste. I would agree with you," said the judge.

And juror 5 had also made a comment about a "surprise witness" on the day Jerry Hollywood testified, saying something like, "I wonder if it's a cousin." When it turned out that it was a cousin, juror 3 decided that juror 5 must have been reading outside material about the case. She didn't think it could have been just a guess. She really, really did not like juror 5, who she claimed didn't want to hear anything "redeeming" about Jesse James Hollywood. I wondered what the redeeming things might be.

But did juror 3 think that the deliberations were fair?

"I do think they were fair. They were extremely difficult. Our foreperson was determined that in order to do our job we had to come back unanimously. He was not willing to accept I guess what you call a hung jury."

As soon as the juror left the room, the defense team wanted to have juror 5 removed.

"How can my client have a fair trial with juror 5? How can he even have a chance? How can you allow her to remain on this jury?" Kessel asked the judge. "But more importantly, Your Honor, how can you let juror 5 remain without even asking her . . . and I don't even think you have to query her because I bet she won't be truthful about her insight. But I think juror 3 was very credible. She was very honest. You can see from her emotion she's been troubled by this."

Josh Lynn said he took issue with Kessel calling juror 5 a liar before even speaking with her, and the judge said juror 3 was "emotional."

"There's nothing I've heard from juror 3 that is so strongly suggestive of misconduct that would rise to the level of setting aside the verdict that we're going to interrupt these proceedings."

So the penalty phase continued, even with the knowledge

that the defense team was surely going to file for a new trial afterward. And with the knowledge that juror 3 would almost certainly not agree to the death penalty.

The following day, a new controversy arose. It turned out that after the jury had turned in their guilty verdict, and it was in a sealed envelope locked in a room, some of the jurors asked the bailiff to see the TEC-9 gun. The foreman called it "morbid curiosity."

The bailiff showed it to them. Then the foreman started asking some questions about it—why the grip was hollow, for instance. Then he asked, "So a gun like this would be illegal, right?" and the bailiff said, "It would now."

Then the bailiff realized that this kind of discussion wasn't proper—he was not allowed to speak to sitting jurors about any aspects of the case, including about the evidence. So he went to the judge and "told on himself."

The judge and the defense team questioned the bailiff under oath.

"Did you seek any advice from the Court or your supervisors with respect to their request to see evidence?" asked Kessel.

"No," he said. "Because they had access to all the other evidence."

"Well, the gun was not accessible to them as the other exhibits were, correct?"

"It was locked, but I was under the impression—understanding that they could see it whenever they asked."

So despite this having all occurred after the jury had already turned in a sealed verdict, here was another nit for the defense team to pick. I hated that they had any loose threads to pull on; all it meant was that this case was going to drag on much longer than anyone realized. Even after the media went home and forgot about us, this case would haunt my life until the verdict was final and Jesse James Hollywood had run out of appeals. That could literally take a lifetime. But for now, I reminded myself to just focus on that day. We had to get through sentencing.

The district attorney's office warned us that the death

penalty would be unlikely, so I had already come to terms that life in prison would be the probable outcome. And it was—or at least, that was the jury's recommendation. The judge still had to approve the jury's recommendation, and that would take weeks, at minimum, though I don't know why.

When the media asked me what we thought about the sentencing, I told them that I didn't think it served anyone to have someone else's son die. I was satisfied with the jury's decision, and so was Jeff.

————

Of course, Hollywood was not satisfied.

His team searched for every possible reason they could to throw out the whole trial and start from scratch with a new jury. Even before the trial was complete, they had already once asked for a mistrial based on Graham Pressley's testimony, because the judge had allowed Pressley's "impressions" to enter the record. Now that it was over, they did their best to prolong our misery—the defense team asked for and received extra time to prepare their motion to file for a new trial. So weeks turned into months, and we remained in the dark about exactly what it was that was holding up the process.

We knew the defense team was going to question some of the jurors. In October 2009, they requested and received some jurors' contact information. At that hearing, the defense also approached the bench to complain that the court reporter had sent me a letter that had been posted on the Internet. I have no recollection of any such letter, and the prosecution never saw it, but the court reporter was removed based on their complaint. That made me feel terrible. The only contact I remember having with the court reporter was when I wrote to her to request copies of transcripts, which I paid for and she sent to me.

At the end of that hearing, Hollywood began tapping loudly on his table and talking in an aggravated and angry fashion, interrupting his attorneys and the judge. He was complaining about something a juror had said, though the record didn't make it clear what he was talking about. Then he said to the judge, "They're still saying to the media I ordered the killing, that's what—"

"Mr. Hollywood, we're going to exclude you from the courtroom if you continue to speak out," the judge said.

"Take me back to the jail then."

So they did.

The results of the jury questioning were supposed to be presented in November 2009, but instead, we drove three hours just to hear the defense team say that they needed more time (again). The judge again granted it. I turned and saw Ryan Hoyt's mother sitting just a few seats away from me in the row just behind me.

I don't know why she showed up on that day; I hadn't seen her at any court procedure in years, since her son's trial. She still had the same bugged-out eyes and wiry hair, the same look of a woman who's been emotionally unstable for a long time. She was heavier now, but aside from that, she looked the same.

Again, in January 2010, the judge granted the defense more time to come up with a motion for a new trial, even though the district attorney's office had pled for an end to all this on our behalf.

I received a card from Christina Pressley letting me know that she was thinking about me and telling me about the pain in her own life. Her family had not pulled through the tragedy very well, and she was doing her best to find something in her life that mattered.

"I wish I could bring Nick back," she wrote. "I wish all of the pain would just stop, but it doesn't, does it? It just pops up whenever it feels like it, grabs you by the neck, and won't let go. I am sure it is much more difficult for you when it comes. I often think about how life used to be, before Nick died, before everything, when our families were together and happy. . . . The best thing I know how to do is to keep going. I'm helping kids get sober. I'm helping meth-addicted kids, too. I feel like it's for Nick. In fact, whenever I help another one, I say it out loud while alone in my car: 'For Nick.'"

Her letter ended with "I love you." I could feel the depth of Christina's heart, and I wished that any of the other families had shown just one-tenth of her compassion. It would have meant so much. But her friendship is important to me, and it made me feel so good to know that there was someone out there, like me, dedicated to making a difference in Nick's honor.

While I waited for the next court date, I worked on my "Victim's Impact Statement," the last one I would ever have to write. It would be the first time I would face Hollywood and his family directly and get to say the things I had wanted to for almost ten years. For days, I wrote and rewrote, asking friends for feedback and trying to get it just right. Jeff wrote one, too—shorter than mine, more to the point and poignant. And so did Leah. Hers was focused on Nick's life, not on Hollywood.

On February 5, 2010, we headed back to court again, not knowing whether or not this would be the day that Jesse James Hollywood would finally be sentenced and we could put an end to this long nightmare. The defense had submitted their motion for a new trial, which included about eight different points about why they thought it was warranted.

The judge dissected those points one by one. Among the most important were the claims by juror 3, who thought that some of the other jurors might have been reading outside material about the case—but what it came down to was that she was only guessing. None of the other jurors had actually said anything about reading material about the case. And as for juror 5, who made the comment about the "one last electrical job" for Hollywood, she was also questioned, and the judge didn't believe that she had been unfair in her deliberations. He thought that she just made an inappropriate comment in the context of a pressure-cooker climate where emotions were high and jurors had no way to vent.

The judge acknowledged that there were some moments

of misconduct throughout the trial, but that none of it rose to the level of throwing out the whole trial. "This is a human endeavor. We are not robots. There are going to be mistakes," he said.

There would be no new trial granted.

We squeezed each other's hands in relief.

I clutched my impact statement, knowing this would be the time to get up and read it. Instead, just as we were about to start, the defense objected. As always. Kessel said we'd already had our chance to speak during the penalty phase—which was half true; we had been allowed to answer questions that were asked of us, but we were not allowed to speak freely.

But the heartbreaking part was that the judge agreed with his objection. Prosecutor Josh Lynn said he had never had a case in all his years where the judge didn't allow the family to read their impact statements. The judge said it wouldn't serve any purpose to the court, considering the sentence was already decided and this was basically a formality. We wondered if the judge just didn't want to incite any more conflict because Hollywood's family was there and might be angered by things we had to say.

Ben was so upset by the ruling that he walked out of the courtroom. I stuck around to hear the sentencing but was deeply disappointed. It had meant a lot to me to be able to speak.

The judge said that he was upholding the jury's recommendation for sentencing: life in prison without the possibility of parole. Thank God for that. It was finally over.

We did an interview outside of the courtroom, as did Jack Hollywood and Laurie, whose last name was now Haynes. We said we were thankful to the jury; Hollywood's mother, Laurie, said she was confident her son would win on appeal. With a detective standing by Jeff's side, Jack Hollywood walked over and shook Jeff's hand.

"I'm just really sorry," he said.

Jeff had no idea how to respond. He said it felt like when ball players lined up to shake hands and say "Good game" after it's over. Like Jack Hollywood was conceding that we had won this "game." I didn't see it happen, and as usual, no one from the Hollywood family approached me. I don't know why I held out any hope, but for so long, I kept thinking that one of them would turn out to be decent enough to say to me, "I'm sorry for what happened to your son."

Then we headed home to celebrate and unwind. When stories began popping up online about the verdict, I decided to make use of that impact statement after all: I pasted it in the "comments" section of every article I could find that had that feature, along with putting it in my Facebook notes.

In part, it read:

My son, Nicholas Samuel Markowitz, is dead because of Jesse James Hollywood. Jesse had him murdered to cover up his own crimes and stay out of prison. And worse, he had someone else do the dirty work, and then took off to let him take the consequences. Little did I know that as I was paging my missing 15-year-old son, he was on his way to his execution. . . .

The first six and a half years after hearing of my son's murder, I wanted to die, and almost succeeded several times. I would mix alcohol and pills to the point where I had to have my stomach pumped. Thirteen times, I ended up in the hospital because of suicide attempts and depression. I hung on solely because I wanted to make sure there would be justice for Nick. He deserved this, and so much more. It was the least I could do, but I didn't realize it would take so long.

For five years, while Jesse was one of America's Most Wanted, I drove with "Wanted" poster billboards on my car. When I was not looking for Jesse Hollywood, I went to every trial and parole hearing for the other selfish cowards involved. I traveled as far as Canada. I believe that Hollywood may have taken the ferry that I was on in Canada shortly before me.

I left thousands of "Wanted" posters and key chains everywhere I went, and it didn't frighten me to think we might bump into each other one day. I knew I was not capable of committing murder for revenge as he had done. I also knew I would not lower myself to the embarrassing level of immaturity and callousness that his family had. . . .

My son, Nicholas Samuel Markowitz, would have been 25 on September 19, 2009. These past nine years have been filled with thoughts of who he'd be today. Would he be in the film industry, a psychiatrist, or still working with his dad? My heart still skips when I see a teenager with a backpack and grocery stores still have me cry over his favorite foods. I wonder, of his size 14 shoes and height of six feet, when would he have stopped growing? And it tears at my heart to wonder what he would have named his babies.

What it comes down to for me is that my son was murdered, for no good reason, because this man didn't feel like dealing with any consequences. My son was tricked into thinking he was safe and would be going home. Instead, he was marched up a mountain and shot. Later, Hollywood was out partying with his friends as usual. As soon as my son's body was found, Hollywood skipped the country. While I was in a mental hospital struggling to find a reason to live, this man was living it up on the beach in Rio. . . .

When it comes to justice, it should not enter into the equation how much money you have, or the attorney you hire to make a wrong into a confusing right. . . .

I am very thankful that the jury in this case was able to see through the nasty tactics meant to confuse them and allow Hollywood to get away with murder. It was not until this trial that I witnessed such heartless attacks directed to the victim and his family.

I now ask for an appropriate sentence to put an end to this very long quest for justice. My son was stolen from all the people who loved him, and we are irreparably broken. But despite the terrible picture the defense team attempted to paint, we are together. We

are grieving and we are aching, but we are all doing
our best to honor Nick, and we love each other. I wish
Nick could have known his nieces and nephews, and
been the best man at his best friend's wedding. I wish
for things every day that will never come true because
my son was stolen from me.

I hope it is not forgotten that this would never have
happened if it were not for the orders given by Jesse
James Hollywood.

Nine years later I still wake up every morning with
a gut-wrenching emptiness. But I must continue to be
strong and share the story about my stolen son, and
encourage people to think of the consequences before
making a choice.

Nick, I promise you will never be forgotten.

Nick deserves justice and as the voice of my son I
am asking the court to sentence Jesse James Holly-
wood to the maximum extent of the law.

—*Susan Markowitz, Nick's mom*

Most of the responses were supportive, but there were a
few very cruel ones, like someone who called me a "wacko
drama queen" whose fifteen minutes of fame were up. Did
anyone really think I wanted my son to be murdered so I
could be on the news?

———————

I awoke excited on the morning that I was scheduled to
speak to the group Action, the same support group I'd
joined in 2006 after one of my hospital stays. "I'm Nick's
mom," I told the audience before me—mostly troubled
teens and their parents. The organizer had asked me to
come speak, and I was finally ready to do it.

Nervous but honored that they wanted to hear what I had to
say, I told them, "I hope that somehow, somewhere in asking
me questions, you grasp hold of something worthwhile."

My talk was about choices and consequences—about

how all the decisions we make as parents and as teens have consequences that we may not foresee. I told them about my own story, and Nick's. Then I told them that no question was off-limits and they could ask me anything they wanted.

I told them the lessons I had learned about putting children first when there are problems between parents or stepparents. I urged the parents to pay attention and be present for their teens, guiding and disciplining them even when they don't like it, because the investment in keeping a connection with your child has rewards that will last a lifetime. And I told them about how some unbelievably stupid choices led to my son's murder.

I looked around the room, and it seemed no one was even breathing. They were listening so intently, so sympathetically, and I knew that I was reaching them. The tears spoke silently on several cheeks.

I'm reaching them, Nick.

My life wasn't over. There was a strange calm there now, where all the years of fighting for justice had been displaced. Jeff and I had made it. Ben and Leah had made it. All of us, one way or another, had found our way back into the world. We step forward, one step at a time, building bridges where there weren't any before. We teach and share and remember and cry and love.

And we do it for Nick.

EPILOGUE

The whole legal process took just about ten years . . . and I am so thankful for that.

If there had been just one killer and one trial and all of it had been over soon after Nick's execution, I know I would have killed myself. But the way that this dragged on year after year turned out to be a blessing in disguise; it meant that I had to keep hanging on and on, telling myself that I couldn't kill myself until it was all finished.

Even this book made that list of chores to do before I left this earth; I figured that I had to write down Nick's story so that he would not be forgotten and so my memories wouldn't die with me. Most days, I just wanted to hurry up and get it all finished—I wanted to get the book done, but I couldn't, because Jesse James Hollywood hadn't been caught yet, or hadn't been convicted yet, and there was no ending to the story.

And then, suddenly, there was.

We finally got him. Every one of Nick's killers and accomplices were finally either in prison or had served their time. William Skidmore and Graham Pressley were both out in the world again, getting their second chances (unfortunately, both of them were soon cited on separate charges of driving under the influence). The book was just about finished. But . . . I didn't want to die anymore.

I used to feel such guilt for having fun after Nick's death. If I had a good day, it would be tempered with thoughts that I *shouldn't* have a good day. But finally, I have allowed myself to live, to embrace the life I have left. It's not the same life I would have had, and I will never "get over" Nick's death—you don't ever "get over" a loss like that— but it is still a life worth living.

I think back to the dream I had where Nick told me that I was doing so well, and I believe him. I am doing well.

In 2010, Jeff and I were honored with Citizen of Courage awards from the Santa Barbara County district attorney's office. Our victim's advocate, Joan, nominated us with a beautiful letter describing our tireless fight and the odds we overcame in our quest for justice for Nick. In reading it, I thought, *We really have come a long way. Am I all the way over here now? Have I made it to the other side of grief?*

The award was so meaningful to me, both because it made me feel proud that we were recognized in this way by people we respected so much, and because it represented a new step forward for us.

My life now seems brimming with possibilities and hope. I know I want to do good in this world in Nick's honor, and I am just taking the first baby steps in that direction. I've begun attending Toastmasters meetings and learning how to speak in front of groups so I can carry the messages I've shared here with people in person. I have been asked to speak before, but I wasn't ready. Now I am.

Until you make it through, you cannot know how strong you are. I've found a strength in my spirit that is bottomless and undefeatable. There are still days when I cry, or when I feel wiped out by the aches of missing my son, but I am not letting that stop me. I have things to do. Big things.

I have to believe someday I will see my son again, in

heaven. He'll stand tall over me, his widow's peak grown back in and a smile on his beautiful face, and he'll be surrounded by stacks of books. He'll wrap his arms around me and tell me he's proud of me. And I will tell him that the greatest thing I've ever been in life is Nick's mom.

This is one of my favorite memories of Nick's writing, and I'd like to share it with you. He wrote it when he was eight years old.

Tigers, Teeth and Tails
By Nick Markowitz

There is a jungle
with a tiger
so big
so big
so big
They're my favorite.

He had eyes
so dark
so dark
so dark
They're my favorite.

He had claws
so sharp
so sharp
so sharp
They're my favorite.

His stripes
so black
so cool
so bad
They're my favorite.

He had friends
the leopard
the jaguar
the ocelots
They're my favorite friends.

They all live
in the forest
in the dark
green forest
It's their favorite.

The bugs
that live
in the forest
with them
Bite.

In the forest
where I have
never been
sounds scary
so scary
Oh, so scary!

They tell me
it's not
for kids
no kids
allowed.

So
I think
I'll stay
right here
where it's
safe
with my
Nintendo.

ACKNOWLEDGMENTS

FROM SUSAN MARKOWITZ:

Nick, thank you for all the beautiful memories. I will cherish them in my heart and share them with the world to honor you. I am so grateful to have had you in my life. You are worth living through this emptiness I now wake up to every morning. Baby, this is for you, all for you.

Jeff, my husband and Nick's dad, thank you for your love and your belief that I had what it took to survive this. You are what every woman wants in a man, where two souls become one. Your patience helped me to not make a fatal quick-response decision. You gave me room and the time to help me find my own way. Today I am more known as "Nick's Mom" than the Susan you married more than twenty-five years ago. I will forever be so thankful for our Nick that I would do it all over again. For the rest of our days, know I love you with all my heart.

Ben, thank you for turning your life around, and being a good husband and father. Thank you for humbling yourself, sometimes above the call of duty regarding your feelings about Nick's death. Know that without your turnaround,

I would be so lost and confused. You have my heart and compassion always.

Leah, I know it was difficult for you to make it to Santa Barbara for each of the trials and motions with two children to take care of. I want you to know it was so comforting having you with me. We did it together, just as it was meant to be and will continue to be. Thank you for your ability to understand or at least tolerate my need to separate myself from some of the family gatherings during this unbelievably long journey.

Mom and Dad (Sam and Barbara Markowitz), from Nick's birth I always felt he had two sets of parents; he was "our boy" together in heart and soul. I am so grateful for the two of you. It is because of you that this family has stayed together. Your love and support in many areas of our ups and downs has seen us through the roughest times in our lives. I love you with all my heart.

Robyn, you are unbelievable! I don't recall a day when you were not there either holding a seat or my hand. I have been blessed to get to know my husband's cousin and her family. You and Kirk have touched my heart with your tender support. I am proud to know you. I know you are reminded daily of Nicholas, seeing your sons grow and pass the age that he was taken. You know you are blessed and don't waste a moment, and it shows.

Mom and Dad (Buster and Arleen Benner): Mom, I knew from the beginning you would have attended every single trial and their lingering motions and hearings if you hadn't had a heart attack during the very first trial, in Colorado. Thank you for taking care of yourself while I was busy all these past years. It means everything to still have you now that this is behind us. I am sure Dad is looking down on all of us with a "Whew!" Thank you both for giving me an upbringing with morals, love, and stability.

My sister Brenda, thank you for being there for me in more ways than I can count. But one I will mention is thanks for literally helping me get out of my closet. My brother Buster and his wife, Bobbie, thank you for the

endless hours it took to start the website NicholasMarkowitz
.com. It has brought such comfort in seeing the worldwide
responses, knowing Nick will never be forgotten. My baby
brother Ed, without a doubt I knew if I needed to smile
and disconnect (and the times were numerous), you were
there.

I had no idea how vital making new friends would be to
eventually let me see and feel again. Sheri, thank you for
making that call that led to me finally leaving my house
again. Nadine, I thank you for "Helping Me Dance." Our
connection is sad, each of us victims of crime. But together,
we will make a positive impact in our lifetime. You're the
best!

Marlene, everyone's favorite mom, with our creative
minds we connected immediately, and I love it. Thank you
for taking on the task of making Nick's clothes into a quilt.
Thank you for your smile, friendship, and support.

Victoria, Vivian, and Gwen, thank you for the countless hours spent on the phone listening to my rambling and
for the unconditional friendship. It's wonderful that we can
pick up where we left off, knowing I wouldn't hear "Why
haven't you called me?" I am so blessed to have you in my
life. I love you.

Susan Chapman and Barry Browne, thank you for the
inspiration and time spent in the beginning trying to make
little sticky notes turn into a readable page.

I have also had three therapists who saved my life time
and again and made it easier for me to cope. Thank you to
Dr. Schulte, Dr. Rutland, and Dr. Fulton for all you've done
to help me through.

One person who started out as a stranger ended up with
a big piece of my heart. The sincerity in her support never
wavered. I will always treasure the flowers, cards, and
personal gifts she gave. I began to look for her, knowing
she was there, and there were times I didn't have time to
say hello or good-bye. She was always, always there with
a smile in her eyes. Thank you, Jennifer Stafford, for your
compassion. You will never be forgotten.

Wachsman Stanley Photography graciously allowed us to use a photo they took at Nick's bar mitzvah on this book's cover, and I appreciate that very much.

My wonderful agent, Sharlene Martin, you believed in me and in this story from the start, and you have the energy and dedication of twelve other agents combined. Thank you for all your help through this process.

My equally wonderful editor, Shannon Jamieson Vazquez, thank you for caring and for giving this book a great home. You listened to our input and you kept us involved in the process, and that has been a blessing. I hope we will make you very proud with the end result.

My biggest thanks go to Jenna Glatzer. You are the one responsible for throwing me a lifeline. For years I struggled to find something worth hanging on to besides another court procedure. Honoring my son by telling this story in the hopes of helping others is the connection to life for me. Without your dedication and believing in it as I do, this story would just become old news. I thank you with all my heart for the countless hours on the phone or computer conversing with the many people needed to make this book memorable for generations. It is because of you that Nick will live in the hearts of others. I imagine him at the age of fifteen telling you that "You're the bomb."

For almost a decade, our family traveled back and forth to Santa Barbara, where my son was murdered and where his kidnappers and killers stood trial. We were at the mercy of the system.

There were times when law enforcement and the district attorney's office were perceived as unfeeling. We feel it is important to express the complete opposite. Throughout the years of fighting for justice for Nick, we have come to understand with gratitude the intensity of meticulous work by everyone involved.

Nick spoke at his bar mitzvah about the importance of fairness in the justice system, reading from the Torah about biblical laws that are to be handed down through the generations. He stated that fair trials must include testimony from both sides and no bribery. He said he knew right from wrong and would live by those laws. We are proud that those who worked for justice for Nick understood these principles, too.

It is with praise and love that we acknowledge:

SANTA BARBARA OFFICE OF THE DISTRICT ATTORNEY

Ron Zonen, Senior Deputy District Attorney: You are a highly educated attorney who always spoke to us in terms that we could understand. Your dedication was clear, as you selflessly fought for justice for Nick every step of the way. We knew you would not leave us hanging; you knew the facts of this case like the back of your hand, and possessed the perfect balance of energy and determination. Thank you for always doing what was right, being mindful, and showing us compassion. You have the biggest heart, and helped us make it through this.

Joshua Lynn, Senior Deputy District Attorney: We didn't know what to expect when we were introduced to a new attorney for the final trial, but you eased our fears right away. We felt confident and knew that you would fight hard for Nick. Thank you for caring so much about our son, and for your calm, professional demeanor.

Joan Fairfield, Victim/Witness Assistant: You are the most amazing woman we have met. You are first class and professional, with compassion that is untouchable. You held my hand every step of the way. It was not by accident that we were connected.

Our deepest thanks also to Paul Kimes, Christie Stanley, Greg Wilkins, and Jane Grand.

SANTA BARBARA SHERIFF'S DEPARTMENT

To Commander Bruce Correll, Sergeant Ken Reinstadler, Detective Steve Johnson, Detective Mike West,

Detective Jerry Cornell, Detective Lorrinda Lepore, Gang Unit Detective Steven Gonzales, Narcotics Detective Mark Valencia, Probation Officer Maria Bongiovanni, Lieutenant Sonny LeGault, Lieutenant Andrew Standley, Lieutenant Jeff Klapakis, Undersheriff Kenneth Shemwell, Sheriff Jim Anderson, and the numerous others who worked on this case:

We would be lost without you. Thank you for the untold hours you put in, even when it looked grim. None of you did it for the glory. Thank you for showing up, years later, to hold our hands at the final trial. Thank you for "getting personal" even when you're trained not to get personal. It meant everything to us to know you were all there, being strong in this quest for justice when we felt our weakest.

THE FBI

To Special Agent Louis Perez, Special Agent Kevin Kelly, Special Agent Dave Cloney, and Assistant Special Agent Patrick A. Patterson: thank you for all you did to ensure that we'd have the ending we so desperately needed. Your dedication was outstanding.

Our endless thanks, also, to the Santa Barbara Regional Narcotics Enforcement Team (SBRNET); the FBI offices in Los Angeles, Seattle, Chicago, and especially the FBI Legal Attaché in Brazil; the Brazilian Interpol agency; the Royal Canadian Mounted Police; the Chicago Police Department; the Seattle Police Department; the Colorado Police Department; the Cook County district attorney's office, in Chicago; court reporters Sharon Reinhold and Sandra Flynn; and deputy probation officer Judith Parker.

We would like to express our gratitude to the community of Santa Barbara for "adopting" us during the roughest days of our lives, and to everyone who wrote us letters, added memorials to Nick, visited Nick's grave, kept up with Nick's story through newspapers and our website, and offered us support through the years. Knowing there were so many people around the world who cared and who hadn't forgotten Nick kept us going. I'm sorry I have not been able to write back individually to everyone who's written to us, but please know that your words have meant a great deal to me.

FROM JENNA GLATZER:

I thank Jeff Markowitz, Ryan Orenstein, Ben Markowitz, Leah Markowitz-Goyanes, and the many people who made suggestions and offered feedback. Big thanks to our agent, Sharlene Martin; and our editor, Shannon Jamieson Vazquez, for caring about this story and for being so good at your jobs. It's a pleasure to work with people who are as dedicated as both of you are.

I thank my family for their support and love, and my daughter, Sarina, for being the most loving and fun little girl in the universe. You're everything to me. I also thank my friends Keith Potter, Dave and Debbie Sobel, Paul and Faye Catanzarite, Kristin Paye Baker, Stefanie Smith, Samantha Ozarin, Frank Baron, and Charlie Stuart for their general awesomeness. Finally, I thank Susan Markowitz for her wonderful friendship. I love you, and you're one of my heroes.

Hollywood's euphemisms for kidnapping, at one point referring to it as "the event that caused Nick to be ushered into the van." Even the jury couldn't help but grin at that one.

At another point, the prosecutor approached the witness stand with an envelope. He pulled Jeff's ring out of the envelope and showed it to Hollywood.

"Do you recognize this ring?" he asked.

"No," Hollywood said.

"You're telling me you don't recognize this ring?"

"No."

He let that answer just hang there in the air for a few seconds before moving on. It was the ring that Hollywood had taken off Nick's finger, then had been pressured by Rugge to give back. It was the only piece of jewelry Nick had been wearing when he died. And there it was in an evidence envelope right before us.

We could have it back after the trial was finished, I was pretty sure. Would Jeff want it back? I thought he might. He would probably give it back to Ben, to pass along to his own son.

Hollywood took the stand for several days. One morning before the jury was called in, the attorneys met with the judge to complain about each other. Blatt said he was "concerned" that the district attorney was editorializing and commenting too much with sarcasm, which "destroys the decorum and dignity of this case." On the other hand, Josh Lynn told the judge that Kessel had "loudly called me a dickhead" on three separate occasions, and he could call in a witness who had heard it, too.

So much for decorum and dignity.

That was the same day I just fell apart. I'm not sure why it was then; it wasn't during Hollywood's testimony but during a lull in the day's events when the jury was waiting for something, and I just burst out crying and had to excuse myself. No displays of emotion were allowed in the courtroom, so my friend Nadine accompanied me outside, where I could sob freely. A million thoughts had been going through my head, not the least of which was an unexpected sympathy. Sometimes, while Hollywood spoke, I actually felt bad for him. He looked so guilty and scared, and for the first time, I thought, "That's someone else's son up there."

Then he would open his mouth and another lie would fall out, and my sympathy would disappear. Hollywood's mother, Laurie, had gone up to Jeff before court on the first day, put her hand to her heart, and said, "I am so sorry." The same woman who'd flipped me off. And although I saw her in that courtroom every day, she never saw fit to say a word to me. Why did I care that this was her son?

Now that Hollywood himself was testifying, the media had packed the courtroom for the first time since opening statements. Which made it harder for me to escape unnoticed. I was overwhelmed and just wanted to disappear for a while. I was tired of this circus and just wanted it all to be over.

In talking about the TEC-9, Hollywood said Ben was the one who'd given it to someone to have it modified into an automatic weapon. Then Hollywood said that that he, Ryan Hoyt, and Ben had all gone to a firing range to shoot it but that an employee told them they could get jail time just for having it modified that way. At that point, Hollywood said, he gave it to Hoyt to store in his grandmother's house, which is why Hoyt had had it when he murdered Nick.

Ben had forgotten that he had testified earlier that part of that was true—at some point, the gun was being stored at Ryan Hoyt's grandmother's house. But it still belonged to Hollywood, and it didn't make a whole lot of sense that Hoyt would have chosen to use it to murder someone he'd never met if Hollywood had actually just told him to go drive Nick home, as he claimed.

When at last we reached the closing arguments, I felt like a boxer in the ninth round. Finally, Jeff was allowed to